A Reluctant Film Critic

Gerald Peary

Sticking Place Books
New York

www.stickingplacebooks.com

ISBN 979-8-89976-039-6

CONTENTS

A Reluctant Film Critic is the story in many guises of a person who loved movies from boyhood, but never thought seriously of being a film critic until offered a job in his thirties reviewing for a Boston newspaper. Yet soon after settling in doing weekly columns, he started wondering seriously if this is how he wanted to live his life.

I've never tired of seeing good movies, never not wanted to attend a film festival. I took great joy in interviewing film actors and directors. But for forty-five years I've been writing film criticism with one foot in, one foot wanting to flee the critic profession. I've done lots of other things, from curating to teaching to making documentaries. And yet as hesitant as I am to write reviews, I keep doing them, damn it. I'm 80 now and still doing them.

I want to acknowledge my brother Danny Peary for our shared devotion to cinema from childhood; Russell Campbell, a mentor who published me early in *The Velvet Light Trap* in Madison, Wisconsin; Joseph McBride for half a century of cinema conversations and shared John Ford love; the late Karyn Kay, who led me to feminism and to us both interviewing Dorothy Arzner; Patrick McGilligan, who took a crazy chance and hired me for my first critic job; Amy Geller, my super-talented wonderful wife and documentary partner; and Bill Marx, my wise editor at *The Arts Fuse*, who was the perfect person to conduct with me a career interview.

Finally, thanks to my valiant editor, Paul Cronin, who—I'm very flattered!—commissioned this book by and about me. And to my pal Gus Freedman, who managed to take a cover photograph of me which I genuinely like.

A Boy Genius in the Old South

Preface

Look elsewhere for a saga of childhood trauma. My parents were peculiar people, no question of that, but they were invariably kind to me. My mother was especially doting and, for a time, put me on an awkward pedestal. When my first-grade teacher declared me, at age 6, a "genius," my mother believed it. I was, my mother bragged, the smartest child by far where we lived, in the town of Philippi in the mountains of rural West Virginia. Perhaps so. Whatever, by age 11 in 7th grade in the big city of Columbia, South Carolina, I got my comeuppance. Not so brainy after all.

This is the story of my life from early childhood in Appalachia and the Deep South to my graduating high school and moving north. My memoir is related in "snapshot" paragraphs because that's the way I recall my earliest years. My narrative is offered chronologically. Nothing is consciously embellished. Stories are not stretched. They stop where my recollection stops. Dialogue is what I think people actually said.

Undeniably, this is the tale of an outsider several times over. We were the only Jewish family in many many miles when we resided in West Virginia, and among the only Jews without money in our years in Columbia, South Carolina. My parents were immigrants with European accents and foreign sensibilities at a time, the 1940s and 1950s, when multiculturalism was not the American way. When we lived in segregated South Carolina, my father taught at black colleges, considered in the white world a shameful thing to do.

And instead of acquiring roots, we moved and we moved, many times when I was very little, and I was in different schools in 4th, 5th, 6th and 7th grades. Summers were especially disruptive, as we traveled to many places for my father's work. In all this upheaval, I went from being the "genius" star of my class to someone estranged from educational institutions and with terrible grades.

But a nightmare life? I don't think so. I had several years in high school where I was angry, perhaps ugly, and acted out. Otherwise, though my family had little money, there's little Dickensian misery. Let's start with the obvious: except for the geographic isolation, it wasn't bad at all being the only Jews in Philippi, West Virginia. The locals, mostly evangelical Christians, were genuinely nice to my family.

Have I repressed the worst? I don't think so. Some of my memories are indeed odd. But many of the anecdotes are slight and ordinary, perhaps most remarkable in that I actually recall them. Few people, I believe, can call up so many childhood things.

For the most part, I am far more bemused by what I remember than upset by it. As an outlier, what was my secret for survival? From the earliest age, I was consoled by books, and equally by movies. I *always* read, I *always* went to the cinema. If I had several friends, that sufficed. I, a private intellectual, was biding my time to meet the right people. My kind of people. It happened finally in my last year of high school: teenage beatniks with a love of Ferlinghetti and Kerouac. A positive ending for my memoir!

But before all that, my parents…

My Father

Joseph Pisarevsky was born in White Russia, in Vitebsk, in 1914. A single child. His patrilineal line included influential rabbis, and there was wealth never to be experienced by later generations of my family. The household name was not Jewish. "Pisarevsky" came from a family forebear who served as the Jewish community's "pisar," a transcriber of official documents from Yiddish to Russian and vice-versa.

My great-grandfather owned a huge estate in Vitebsk, surrounded by a brick wall. There were seventeen children born, though only four—Sonia, Manya, Samuel, David—lived to adulthood, and David was murdered by the Nazis. Several generations of the family would scatter through Europe, running away from the Bolsheviks and, a second time, from Hitler. They continued to New York, to Beverly Hills, to Sydney, Australia. Quite a few Pisarevskys converted to Christianity. My grandfather, Samuel, retained his Judaism.

According to family lore, Samuel in Vitebsk became the first art patron of his Jewish friend, a poor boy whose painting showed great promise. Marc Chagall. Not only were he and Chagall very close, but their wives-to-be, Ida Karmi, my grandmother, and Bella Rosenfeld (Chagall), were roommates at Moscow State University. In the late Czarist era, Jews were rarely allowed to attend universities, and it was virtually impossible for women. And yet, there were Ida and Bella as students. Even more: when in 1916 Marc and Bella had their only child, Ida, she was named after my grandmother.

My grandfather was, I was told by my parents, the lieutenant governor of White Russia in 1917, during the brief post-Czar, Kerensky presidency. He was a Socialist Revolutionary, both radical and rich. With the ascendancy of Lenin, he fled westward with his family—my grandmother, Ida, and Joseph, 3, my father—first to Amsterdam and then to France. The Pisarevskys settled in comfortably with the elite Russian-Jewish émigré crowd that included the exiled Kerensky, the now-famous Chagall, and world chess champion Alexander Alekhine. Paris in the 1920s wasn't only Gertrude Stein, Fitzgerald, and Hemingway. It was artsy intellectual Jews.

My grandparents purchased an apartment in Paris with an elevator. They had a country home in Montgeron. Still, my grandmother Ida was greatly troubled. It was explained to me that—so rare for Jews!—there was alcoholism in her Russian lineage. Liquor ran in their blood through generations, and the negative weight, like in a fatalist Émile Zola novel, was passed on to her. Though she didn't drink, that was a major reason for her unfortunate temperament. More family lore: when my grandmother was a philosophy student at university, she went mad trying to understand Immanuel Kant. Afterward, she was quarrelsome, vain, and loopy.

In Amsterdam and then Paris, Ida tried to establish herself as a painter among the Jewish art colony. Certainly that was quite a task for a woman. I have inherited several of her oils: she's good, not great, her works much influenced by post-Impressionist French artists. In contrast, there was my father Joseph, painting also. He was an amazingly precocious artist as a young boy, an original. I have some of his visionary work. Tragically, he quit drawing and coloring at age 14 because his mother was so envious of his talents, and jealous that other artists were impressed.

My father was a poor little rich boy, an only child mostly neglected by his self-absorbed parents. He loved animals and had as a pet a raccoon, which sat high on his shoulder. He would often give away his lunch to fellow students, those with little money. In high school, Joseph won a national contest for translating Latin and, as a prize, was given a trip to the French colony of Algeria. His companion for the voyage was his mother, and they rode camels together in the Sahara. After studying at the Sorbonne, Joseph, at age 21, got his Ph.D. in biology from the University of Nancy, with a monumental dissertation on water buffaloes. The same year, 1935, he was awarded two medals, which I have inherited, from the Académie d'Agriculture de France, for the excellence of his scientific research.

When our father was about 60, my brother, Danny, and I coaxed him to translate his dissertation into English, naively believing we might locate a publisher. However, the language of the book was stilted and old-fashioned and the research—we should have realized this—needed major updating from 1935. We went to work but hurt our dad's feelings when we wanted to modernize his writing and his thinking. He balked at virtually all our changes, so, sadly, we gave up. There would never be public recognition that he in his time was the world's expert on the water buffalo.

I vaguely recall mention from my father of girlfriends while he studied in France. Joseph is quite dapper at 5'5" in early photographs, with a kind, round face and dimples. Still, it's hard to imagine that there were women in his life before my mother. Are some people asexual? My brother and I never once heard him express an erotic thought, even about an actress or singer. There was no hidden *Penthouse* or stowed-away porn. It was science, science, science for Joseph.

When in Sydney, Australia, I met a first cousin of my father, Felix Parry, and he told me a revelatory story of taking my father in France in the 1930s to a brothel. Felix partook. My father sat in the lobby patiently waiting for Felix to finish his business.

Joseph arrived in America in 1939, ahead of the Nazis entering Paris. He'd been a distinguished young scientist in France. One would hope there was a prestigious job waiting for this Jewish refugee escaping Hitler. At the New School, perhaps, or even Harvard? Somehow, Joseph with his lauded Ph.D. ended up in Wyoming toiling on a horse ranch. Then he was in Sarasota, Florida, as an unlicensed animal doctor at Ringling Brothers' winter headquarters. It was there that he attempted to persuade Karl Wallenda, scion of the Flying Wallendas trapeze artists, to invest in a healthy product for the USA. Wallenda wasn't interested. "Certainly it's popular in Europe," he said, "but Americans will never want to eat yogurt."

Though very wary of driving, my father got a license c. 1941 when employed in Florida for the circus. One weekend, Joseph drove cautiously from Sarasota into the Everglades to observe wildlife. He had a crash on a back road with another extremely slow-moving vehicle. Nobody was injured. But the other driver, totally shaken, exited his car, put his hands across his eyes, and ran down the road screaming. My guilty father swore off driving for the next 15 years.

My father's parents divorced in Paris and neither remarried. They lived apart but stayed connected. After my father came to America, he needed to get his Jewish parents here also, away from France under the Occupation. I wish I knew how he accomplished it for his mother. His father, Samuel, went to Lisbon to escape but was in despair on how to leave there. He spent several months in detention before being released. One day he was walking in a park and saw a French ex-girlfriend on a bench in the arms of a Fascist military man. According to family lore, that Portuguese Fascist helped my grandfather embark for New York.

Joseph Pisarevsky listened carefully to the advice of a border guard when he entered the US: "Your name is too long. Nobody will remember it." But he waited until a few years after, as part of his naturalization ceremony, to shorten his last name with letters contained in his original lengthier one. On June 30, 1943, at the U.S. District Court in Washington, Joseph Ygor Pissarewsky (the spelling on the naturalization document) became Joseph Ygor Peary.

I was once contacted at my home by a relative of the esteemed explorer Robert Peary. "Are you a member of our family?" he asked hopefully, querying my lineage. I gave him disappointing news. "I'm extremely sorry," I answered. "I'm a Russian-Jewish Peary and really a Pissarewsky."

My Mother

Larissa Chaitan was born in Odessa in 1917, and, in the winter of 1919, her family fled White Russia and the Bolshevik Revolution. Somewhere in the journey westward, they crossed a frozen lake, resulting in my mother, 3, suffering from frostbite. Forever after, she sighed in the slightest chill, "Oh, it's so cold!" After a year in Berlin, the Chaitan family chose to relocate to Bucharest, to join a Jewish community that included many Odessans. Embedded among Russian speakers, my mother's parents, never felt a requirement to learn the Romanian language.

Larissa's businessman father, Jacob, was tough, patriarchal, withholding. He made it a wretched home for his three daughters. My very shy mother hardly spoke and, in reaction, I believe, never ever stopped talking as an adult. Her equally subdued younger sister, Tania, remained always a reticent person.

Cultured Jewish visitors stopped at the Chaitan home, including, regularly, Yiddish theater troupes on tour. They had to deal with the family's nasty Chihuahua, Fufu, who bit and terrorized every outsider. Among guests was the famous violinist, Efrem Zimbalist, who fell in love with my grandmother, Miriam, and begged her to run away with him. Adoring her daughters, she rebuffed his sexy offer of illicit romance.

In 1930s Bucharest, Larissa's older sister, Paula, was the chanciest of three daughters, the only one who could swim and who fervently danced the Charleston. She also wed early, to a paranoid guy who felt that his new family despised him. One day, my grandmother, Miriam, said to him, "Idyom," meaning "Come" in Russian. He was sure his mother-in-law had called him "Idyot," and, so insulted, he literally walked out on Paula. Later in Romania, she would marry again and stay married to Abe, a successful lawyer.

My quiet, subdued mother was educated early by nuns, and then attended a music conservatory and studied piano. A story she loved to tell: she was strolling on a city street and noticed passing by the royal coach of Romania's monarch, King Carol II. The driver of the coach was ordered to stop and back up so the rakish monarch could check out beautiful, buxom Larissa. He looked hard, she said, but did not call out to her.

Wikipedia describes King Carol as possessing a "hedonist" personality.

In 1940, Larissa walked into the American embassy in Bucharest for a curious look. When a man stopped her and demanded, "What are you doing in here?" she blurted out, only half true, "I want a visa to go to America." How am I, Gerald Peary, walking the earth in the USA? Because the embassy employee found my mother attractive, so he granted her impossible wish. She got a coveted passport and exit visa. The next I know of her story was my mother crossing Europe in a train, her eyes low to the ground as she was sharing a second-class car with rowdy Nazi soldiers. They didn't catch on that the dark-haired woman in their midst was a Jewess, and on her way to embark for the nirvana of New York.

Larissa never returned to Romania, and had not the slightest sentimentality about the country where she grew up. When my parents took several bus tours through Europe, Bucharest was not among the cities visited. In 1989, I informed her one day of the fall in Romania of the dictator, Ceauşescu. "Who cares?" my mother responded. "It's just anti-Semites killing each other."

Here is a remarkable true-life saga: all of my mother's Jewish relatives who remained in Bucharest—her parents, her two sisters and their husbands—lived through the War and without being sent to a concentration camp. My uncle, Sylviu, Tania's husband, had a day job as unpaid help for the Nazis in a city park. At night, he would go home to his wife and mom.

It was the Romanian Queen Mother, the British-born Marie of Edinburgh, who was a genuine friend of the Jews, who almost singlehandedly stopped Hitler from a mass deportation. Most Jews, though not my family, still were murdered, and within Romania's borders, by the Iron Guard paramilitary and the local police. In New York in the 1960s, Sylviu told me the harrowing tale of his family hiding in their Bucharest apartment while emboldened Romanians ran amuck through their building killing Jews residing there. Did he dare tiptoe to the kitchen when his frightened mother kept crying out, "I need a glass of water"?

When Larissa arrived in America, all she had in hand were the names of her Russian relatives and the knowledge that they lived in New York City. No telephone numbers, and she didn't know about boroughs. Thank god her relatives knew to meet her and actually recognized her. Soon she was living in the Bronx with her mother's sister, Marusya, and Marusya's husband, Israel, garment workers. At 23, she shared a bedroom with Harold, her 17-year-old first cousin. Their colorful address: Mosholu Parkway near Jerome Avenue. It was a blue-collar neighborhood where Israel could play pinochle in the park with his Jewish cohorts.

I'm fairly certain that the year my mother settled in New York was 1941 because she later talked of seeing people weeping in the subways about the death of Lou Gehrig and not knowing who that was. Though she never learned a thing about baseball, America's Pastime, she Americanized her name from Larissa to Laura.

In 1942, my mother's cousin, Harold, enrolled at City College, the welcoming home of upwardly mobile Jewish young men. As Laura was female, it was time for her to go to work. Coming from Bucharest, she spoke Russian and Romanian and French. She was learning English in night school. Her first job was a demanding but quite top-end one, and she was hired certainly in part for her good looks. She became a hostess at the flagship restaurant of the fancy chain, Longchamps. It was the dining destination in New York of Hollywood film stars. Laura's favorite movie-actor customer was the gentlemanly Raymond Massey, renowned for starring in the 1940 bio-pic, *Abe Lincoln in Illinois.* She also regularly seated Henry Fonda, his socialite wife, Frances Seymour Brokaw, and their little children, Jane and Peter. My mother told me that she could feel the tension with this unhappy couple. A few years later, Brokaw committed suicide when Fonda demanded a divorce.

The monumental day was December 25, 1942. My mother attended a Christmas party at the home of a wild-haired Jewish intellectual named Gourevitch, who had authored in Russian a mammoth "encyclopedia of peace." Gourevitch's 17-year-old son had a mad crush on Laura, a prime reason why she was invited. However, Laura was far more interested in meeting there a young Russian-born biologist now in the American army. Some at the party described him as a "genius." Which of them was bold enough to initiate a conversation? At the end of the night, courtly Joseph Pisarevsky (afterward Peary) walked Laura Chaitan across Central Park to a subway stop for her ride back to the Bronx. Was there a good-night kiss? They agreed to see each other again, and Joseph wrote her romantic letters from where he was stationed. In January 1944, there would be a marriage. Less than ten months later, a child was born. Me.

I believe I've discovered the identity of the teenager whose adoration of my mother assured her attendance at that Christmas celebration. Thank you, Victor Gourevitch (1925–2020), for making it possible for Joseph and Laura to meet. He was Professor of Philosophy at Wesleyan University for 30 years, an eminent scholar of Jean-Jacques Rousseau and father of New Yorker *staff writer, Philip Gourevitch.*

A military baby

My father had enlisted in the American army determined to stop the Nazis. He brought his New York fiancée to where he was stationed, in the Deep South of Jackson, Mississippi. Joseph and Laura Peary were married there in Hinds County Court on January 3, 1944, by someone named Meyer Lovitt. That's a Jewish name, yet it says on the marriage certificate that he was a "minister." Was he in actuality a rabbi? On October 30, I was born in a Jackson army hospital. My parents chose for my godparents an elderly Christian couple who rented them an apartment off the base, Mr. and Mrs. Smith. For the first time in her life, my mother was in charge of cooking. She wasn't very skilled, but that was all right for my undemanding father.

My grandfather, Samuel Pisarevsky, kept a diary in Russian and, after retiring it for many years, started it up again in excitement over the birth of his grandson. The diary was inherited by my father, who translated it in longhand into English.

Diary of December 29, 1944. "Your grandpa Samuel today, in Jackson, Mississippi, #8 Oakhaven Court, Clinton Blvd., is looking at tiny you, his two-month-old adorable grandson. I've come down here by train from New York. I have met you for the first time and have fallen in love. You are the first member of the Pisarevsky family to be born on non-Russian soil. I feel confident that you will know the Russian language your parents, grandparents, and great-grandparents spoke and will also appreciate and love the culture, literature, music, of Russia."

Dear Papasha (what we called grandfather Samuel): I never learned more than a few words of Russian, nor any other language than English. In that way, I grew up as a typical American. I know little of Russian classic music but, if this is any concoliation, I have read classic Russian novelists—Tolstoy, Dostoevsky, Turgenev—and Chekhov is my favorite playwright. I have traveled twice to Russia, and once was president of the international critics jury at the Moscow Film Festival.

By rank, my father was a Technical Sergeant, and he was attached in Jackson to the army medical ward, which apparently included wounded German captives. Was what my mother told me true?

She said I was such a charming baby that German prisoners cheerily changed my diapers. I was ministered to by young Hitlerians! Six months after my birth, a photo in the army newspaper showed infant me clasped in the arms of my beaming, uniformed father. The caption: "Celebrating the death of Adolf Hitler." I am embedded in history. *Der Führer* was a suicide in his bunker on April 30, 1945, the day of my first half-birthday. With me, Judaism lived on.

My father was reassigned in summer 1945 to serve in the Pacific. I can imagine my parents' anguish, my mother's hysteria. Dutifully, my father rode a military transit across America to embark for the Far East. But as the train rolled westward, A-bombs fell in August on Hiroshima and Nagasaki. In California, the overseas order was rescinded with the impending Japanese surrender. My father returned happily to Mississippi, but was also anxious about how he could provide for a family of three. I don't know if my father was still in the army when we abruptly moved from Mississippi. On New Year's 1946, my grandfather addressed me in his diary from where we next lived, Columbia, South Carolina: "By and large, you are a quiet, well-behaved, sweet little boy without any tantrums, far less nervous than your father at your age."

I have no idea why we resided briefly in Highlands, North Carolina, where my mother recalled "No Jews Allowed" signs in windows. Then we were in Mountain Lake, Virginia, and I had a brush with death at age 2. I was sitting with my parents in a below-the-street cafeteria called The Cave. My first actual memory? I see vividly in my mind me drinking down a bottle of turpentine on our table thinking it was chocolate milk. Miraculously, there was a physician at the next table, who held me upside down by my legs until I regurgitated it all.

I have been so fortunate. I can't explain how a medical doctor just happened to be there to save my life at age 2. At age 19, I drove through a stop sign onto a highway and was hit by a speeding car on the passenger side. Everything inside my auto was upended and destroyed except me in the driver's seat. At age 34, I choked on a wad of bread in a restaurant and a busboy rescued me with the Heimlich maneuver.

We moved for a short time north, staying in the Bronx flat of my mother's garment-worker relatives. As my parents were broke, they entered a photograph of me in a contest sponsored by Gimbels Department Store. The picture, cleverly posed in a studio, took second place. Not first? My parents believed me to be the most beautiful child in New York. Still, they were awarded $10, considerable for 1946, and this photo of me talking animatedly into a play telephone was blown up huge for Gimbels' window. The whole family would subway down from the Bronx and stand tall on the sidewalk. My mother's aunt, Marusya, told a gloating mother in Central Park, "Your child is ugly next to Gerry." At 2½, for my relatives I was the crown prince of New York.

My father, always very slow and meticulous, typed out carefully argued job letters. One worked, and he was hired in the fall of 1946 to teach in North Carolina at Pembroke State College for Cherokee Indians. How unusual it was in the 1940s South for a white professor to take a teaching job at a school for Native Americans. A native girl my age, Helen, is the first friend I am aware of having. I remember her with earmuffs and a coat with fur on the wrists. My father was a professor at Pembroke for one school year. Why he left I don't know.

My father wrote a December 1947 letter to his father which I still possess: "Gerry... already knows all the letters of the alphabet," he said, and I crayoned to my grandfather, "I LOVE YOY." But then the shock: Joe hit me on the bum for using these same crayons on the walls of our rented North Carolina apartment. I was so angry. Little Gerry had been drawing on these walls for many weeks, and I'd never before been stopped by either parent for my nascent artistry.

It would be 16 years before my dad hit me again, slapping my face. He thought me uncaring and disrespectful because, while John F. Kennedy's 1963 funeral processional passed by on our TV, I sat there reading a book.

Diary of my grandfather, January 4, 1947. "We've met the New Year together and celebrated together the 3rd wedding anniversary of your parents ... We drank some wine to toast everyone's happiness and health, and we even let you taste a drop or two. After that, laughing merrily, you repeatedly tried—and finally succeeded—to blow out the candles." At age 2, I was crazy about strawberries but was cut off from them after I broke out in hives. At age 3, I became the monarch of fussy eaters, subsisting for many months on shaved carrots with raisins. For lunch and dinner, I would eat nothing else. Do I remember right that my skin started turning a jaundiced yellow?

My mother adored my androgynous looks, and sobbed when she couldn't hold out any longer for my first haircut at 3. I was far less attached to my radiant blonde locks and grumbled to my parents: "I might as well wear a dress, because people keep thinking I'm a girl." The hair got cut, and what grew back stayed shorter, turned darker, eventually went to brown. Little Lord Fauntleroy looked now quite ordinary. My mother retained one thick, rich blonde curl, and scotch-taped it for immortality into a coffee-table album called The Baby Book.

My first remembrance of a movie is indelible. It was seeing a live-action *Goldilocks and the Three Bears*, with a jubilant climax of the characters, people and animals, bashing each other with pillows, and with feathers flying everywhere. There were real bears dressed in nightgowns and Goldilocks was played oddly by an adult woman.

Philippi

No American university of stature was sufficiently impressed by my father's Ph.D. from France or his dissertation demonstrating that he was the world expert on water buffaloes. None offered to hire him. He and my mother and little Gerry kept bouncing around the South. While taking courses at Virginia Tech, VIP, in Blacksburg, Virginia, Joe—he'd stopped calling himself Joseph—received, in Fall 1947, an offer of a full-time job. It wasn't Harvard. He was asked to teach biology and head the science department at Alderson-Broaddus College, a faith-based Baptist institution located in the hills above Philippi, West Virginia. What was renowned about Philippi, population 3,000 or so? The Battle of Philippi in 1861. Its pre-Civil War covered bridge.

My grandfather's diary, January 3, 1948. "Could it be, my darling grand-sonny, that you are fated in your life to travel about as much as your father and grandfather? I do hope, however, that here in Philippi... your parents have found, at least for the next 2–3 years, a suitable domicile in which to build a happy and more stable nest." My father, a stay-at-home introvert, hardly cared where he lived. Philippi would be fine. My mother was gloomy about being in West Virginia, so isolated once again, and so far from her Jewish relatives in the Bronx.

My grandfather's diary, also on January 3, 1948. "I am appending a clipping from a local paper concerning your father's invitation to be a professor at Alderson-Broaddus College. They failed to mention that he is a veteran of WWII, that he holds a doctorate from France, and was awarded three medals for his dissertation... The blurb is full of mistakes: the town of Blacksburg, where you lived before coming here, is called Blacksville, and you are described as being Professor and Mrs. Peary's three-year-old-daughter."

We lived, from 1947 to 1953, on Faculty Row at Alderson-Broaddus, on a mountaintop above Philippi. There were five identical no-frill stucco houses painted different colors, and we resided in the yellow house, second from the left. One next-door neighbor in a green house was a professor, Bill Sellers, with a hotheaded daughter, Ann. The Hickses were on the other side. Next to the Hickses was the athletic director and basketball coach, his moody, probably unhappy wife, and his lanky, nervous son.

In the last house was a chemistry professor. He had a wife, Shirley, and an uninteresting son, Clark. Shirley, very upset, reported to my mother my bad manners. At age 5, I noticed her extended belly and inquired, "Are you pregnant?" She *was* pregnant. Why shouldn't I ask?

In my room. With the lights off at age 5, a frightening place to be when it was time for sleep. There were wicked people conspiring in my closet. I screamed out, my mother scurried in and switched on the light. She showed me: "It's your clothes on hangers." She shut the closet, and opened the door to my room to the rest of the house. There was a light on in the hall, which made my room less dark. Still, I was traumatized. Finally, mom and dad had a plan. Joe climbed a ladder in the bedroom and stuck little stars and a moon on the ceiling, paper cutouts which glowed in the dark. After that, soothed by the luminous night sky, I dozed off in peace.

Not too long after settling in Philippi, my parents started to plan for a second child. "Gerry wants a younger brother," my mother would say, and I really did. Danny was born August 8, 1949, and, as my father was at the hospital, I spent my first night ever away from home. I stayed with a Hungarian student of my father's and ate something strange and spicy for dinner: beef goulash.

Relatives

The light flashed on in the middle of the night, in December 1949, and a middle-aged woman with a large waist and the thickest coke-bottle glasses peered down, staring inches from my face. Her eyes teared up, she covered my face with kisses, she talked in an incomprehensible language. It was my grandmother, my mother's mother. Behind her stood my grandfather. Jacob and Miriam Chaitan. The language they spoke was Russian. My grandparents had arrived in New York from Romania, and almost immediately took several trains to get to us in Philippi. This was the first time my father had met his in-laws, and my mother hadn't seen her parents since she'd left Bucharest in 1940–41. Everyone was excited and shy at the same time. But the Chaitans quickly became fond of my sweet father. And a second huge treat for my grandmother: my baby brother, Danny.

Diary of my grandfather Sam, January 1, 1950. "Gerry's age is 5 years, 2 months. There have occurred two happy events. 1. Your little brother... a charming, smiling, wonderful baby — you do love him immensely. He'll become your best playmate and true friend. 2. A week ago came to America... your Mom's parents, the Chaitans — and, Lord willing, their arrival will bring happiness to your entire family. Your parents, your two grandfathers and grandmother celebrated the advent of New Year 1950 and, in keeping with our old custom, sang 'Happy Birthday to You.'"

Assimilation was the USA's ideology in the 1950s, and my parents seemed to accept that they should try their best to be Americans. They conversed with each other in English in public and even at home. So what a culture shock for me when my parents talked Russian with my mother's parents. Oh, how alien were the hills of West Virginia for the Chaitans, after living in Bucharest, surviving Hitler. One afternoon when my parents were away, there was a knock on the front door. My terrified grandmother stripped Danny of his clothes and had him parade naked as she opened the door. She was certain it was Nazis, and somehow they might take pity seeing a toddler nude before them.

Our Babushka never got over her fears. Twenty years after, she would retreat into a closet and sit on the floor whenever there was a severe storm, putting her fingers into her ears to hide the sounds of thunder. Was that a trauma from bombings over Romania in the war?

The Chaitans got an apartment in Manhattan at 311 West 95th Street. The building was where my mother's aunt and uncle, Marusya and Israel, had moved from the Bronx. My mother's cousins lived there also, Danil and Molly and their daughter, Luba. This address would be our destination for yearly journeys to New York. I would go upstairs from my grandparents on the 5th floor to visit my aunt and uncle on the 6th. They doted on me, fed me chicken soup, and encouraged me to read about medieval knights in their opulently illustrated volumes of *The Wonder Book*. The "super" was a guy with suspenders named Louis. I didn't understand why he lived in the basement since I assumed he owned the building.

Growing Up

A letter I sent in pencil to my grandfather, Sam, in NYC at Christmas, 1950: "I am Six years old. I am in school. I have a little brother, Dannis, he is 16 months old. I am going to be a cowboy like Gene Autry when I grow up. Gerald Peary." Using crayons, I wrote very short stories. One was about a fairy who fell into a glass of orange juice.

My brother's birth certificate erroneously listed him as Dannis Peary, when our parents wanted him to be Dennis. Whoever was charged with hospital records in West Virginia must have been confused by our mother's accent. Also, Joe and Laura inadvertently gave him a girlie-man middle name by calling him "Fayette," after a female relative of my father's in Europe.

It took Danny till adulthood to accept both names. He learned to like being "Dannis," and even embraced it. In college, he made satiric use of his peculiar middle name, creating a French film critic faux persona, François Fayette, whom he "quoted" in movie blurbs on self-designed film posters.

When we traveled by rail, I would push on the seat in front of us as we left the station, tricking my little brother to believe that it was my superman strength moving the train. My clearest recollection of Danny is him dashing about Faculty Row with his friend, Suzy, the tiny daughter of the college president. She had straight blonde hair and bangs and an upturned nose and was very protective of him. Danny was sent off proudly with a wrapped gift to Suzy's fourth birthday party, but soon he was pounding on our back door, sobbing, "They took my present away from me!"

Recently, I located Suzy via social media, seeing that she's still living in West Virginia. I told Danny but he showed no interest in contacting her after 65 years.

I am often asked when I became a movie fan. My answer is, "Always, always." There were two theaters in downtown Philippi, and, ages 4–8, I attended them often. The more fun one specialized in rural comedies, like those starring Judy Canova and Ma and Pa Kettle and, better, double features of "B" Westerns. For even more pleasure, there was an endless play of Coming Attractions and always a chapter of an action-packed serial. However, West Virginia could be behind the times. I recall the 1939 *Jesse James* and the 1940 *The Return of Frank James* playing in a Philippi theater in the early 1950s as first-run features.

My brother also has been a movie lover since early childhood. In 1952, we saw Abbott and Costello starring in *Jack and the Beanstalk*, and, home afterward, Danny giggled hysterically whenever I pronounced the name of the character played by Bud Abbott: "Mr. Dinklepuss!" A few years on, my brother and I showed our loyalty by zealously purchasing Chunky candy bars, which Lou Costello peddled on TV.

At 6, I was greatly disturbed by a film which, when I grew up, I asked everyone informed about movies to help me track down. There was a typhoid epidemic, and an obviously feverish woman, maybe played by Joan Crawford, drank from a public fountain. Then an innocent little girl skipped up and gulped down the tainted water. Frightening!

69 years later, I found the movie! It's The Killer That Stalked New York *(1950), and the actress isn't Joan Crawford, she's Evelyn Keyes. The fatal disease is smallpox, and it's a little boy, not a girl, who drinks the lethal water. The "B" thriller film was inspired by New York's 1947 smallpox epidemic, where the first mass vaccination in history saved literally millions of lives.*

One winter, my parents pushed through a harsh West Virginia snowstorm to take me to a campus screening of *The Count of Monte Cristo*. I had been anticipating for weeks a fabulous evening of swordplay, swashbuckling, escapes from subterranean castle dungeons. But we'd misread the advertisements. The lights went down, the film projected in 16mm was not the Dumas classic at all. There were no stabbings or bloodshed, no weaponry or period costumes. Suitable for a Christian evangelical college, the movie chosen was a family-oriented ice skating escapade with Sonja Henie: *The Countess of Monte Cristo*.

Snapshots of my parents: with any impending precipitation, Laura and Joe both with raincoats and umbrellas. "You never know" was their motto. Laura with bad ankles—she repeatedly sprained them—stumbling around in high heels carrying a large pocketbook with a clasp. Her kissing your cheek, leaving an annoying smudge of red lipstick. Joe in sweaters, even in summer. Him always rubbing his hands together for warmth as if still in White Russia.

The relationship I had with my mother was later quite fractious, but she always said that I was a "wonderful child." I think that was mostly true, that I was a good kid growing up in West Virginia. Though I was spoiled: I never cleaned my room or made my bed. And I recall one moment when I was cocky and bad. At age 7, I slapped the face of Clark, 4, the neighbor boy. His mother, Shirley, chased me around their yard, screaming, "Pick on someone your own size!" I didn't mind what she said, laughing all the way, because she was squat and fat and couldn't catch me.

My favorite songs when little were "How Much Is That Doggie in the Window?" and "Buttons and Bows." I learned them off the radio, not from our parents. My brother and I marvel at this: we never once, as children or adults, heard our mother sing anything. Not one note! The only music from them was our father booming out strands of opera arias in the loudest voice. In our teen years, Danny and I goaded him to sing out at the dinner table to irritate our mother. She would throw her hands over her ears and beg her oblivious husband to stop, "PLEASE! PLEASE!!"

I was an obsessive thumb-sucker, my thumb jammed behind my two front teeth and pushing hard on them, so much that those teeth ultimately stuck out. Kids rewarded me with a nickname: "Bugs!" A compensation was that, when I was in junior high school, I got to miss parts of many school days by going to the orthodontist for my braces.

By age 6, I was reading newspaper comics, especially *Blondie*. I never tired of traveling salesmen with useless gadgets trying to lodge a foot into Dagwood's door. Dagwood reminded me of my father because of the soft pajamas and because he was too meek to demand a raise from his intemperate boss. Also like Dagwood, my overworked dad squeezed in short naps on the couch, turning his back on his playing children.

For lunch, I commanded my mother to make me "Dagwood sandwiches" like those devoured in the comic strip: bologna, salami, ham, bacon, lettuce, tomatoes, mustard, mayonnaise piled high within three or even four slices of white bread. I watched to make sure she did them just right. They had to be too big for my jaws and held in place with a wooden toothpick.

What a holy terror lived next door to me on Faculty Row: Ann Sellers, one year older than me. She was spoiled, getting hot dogs with mustard every day for lunch. Ann went wild screaming at me when I took a turn at her coloring book, because my clumsy crayoning wandered outside the lines of the characters. When I mishandled her electric scissors and sliced into one of her cutout paper dolls, she tossed me out of her house. As I licked my 6-year-old wounds, my mother tried to calm me: "Ann is a very nervous girl."

My family didn't own a camera, so there are only a handful of pictures of our time in Philippi. One surviving photograph is of little Gerry in an open-collar shirt and blazer at a wedding where I am part of the bridal party. I'm holding the wedding ring on a tiny pillow and seem quite dazed. The bride, my mother remembered, was studying nursing at Alderson-Broaddus College, and the groom, a chemistry major, was my father's student. He was from a family of Baptist ministers. My mother said. "The bride came to our house to measure a suit for you, but you were so shy and embarrassed that you wouldn't let her. So your uncle, Israel, in the garment industry in New York, made a suit and sent it to you. Your first wedding."

I have never met anyone with fewer photographs of their child-hood. Danny and I have maybe ten in all, and most of these are bent, curled, the images poorly framed, and would be tossed away if only we had some good ones.

In Philippi, I was proudest of my dad when he carried me on his shoulders for field trips with his biology class around the woody Alderson-Broaddus campus. I would yank leaves off the trees and pridefully announce what kind—oak, elm, maple—showing off to his students. But there was an incident with my father of profound disillusionment. Our collie, Laddie, whom I dearly loved, would bark all night in our backyard, keeping the little girl next door awake. Her father, Bill Hicks, arranged with a farm to take Laddie to live there and pushed my father to accept the plan. There was the dreadful day when Laddie on a leash was hoisted onto the back of a pickup truck, and my dad did nothing as I screamed and screamed and the truck drove away with our dear dog. Dear Joseph Peary: you were not the powerful man I wished you to be.

My introverted biologist father was always uncomfortable around people, but adored animals, and they adored him back. In Philippi, we had Laddie, then a kitten, Fluffy, regular pets. But one day, my father came home with two baby alligators, Ollie and Brody, and nonchalantly dropped them into our bathtub. He turned on the taps so they had a congenial environment. They sat in there for several days while my mother argued bitterly, and justifiably, about getting our tub back. Fortunately, there was a fountain at Alderson-Broaddus College where goldfish swam about. Into that water went Ollie and Brody. I don't know what happened to those two fine alligators when the deadly West Virginia winter arrived. Nor to the goldfish.

Only once in our five years living in West Virginia did Joe leave home, taking a train to Washington, D.C. for a two-day science conference. I was anxious and very angry at being abandoned, and treated my dad meanly when he returned bringing gifts. I approved of a miniature glass sow and a chain of piglets. But I screamed out with ingratitude at receiving a foot-long souvenir pencil with WASHINGTON D.C. embossed on the side. "I can't write with such a large pencil!" I snorted and pouted until my father, genuinely wounded, retreated near tears to the bedroom.

Normally, I didn't demand much of my parents, even for birthdays. I accepted that they had little discretionary money. Gifts were modest ones and usually rather impersonal, and that was OK. In the last dozen years of her life, my mother mailed me annually the same birthday gift, a $100 bill stuck into a Hallmark card. As for presents from non-family, even today I'm confused and embarrassed and feel a bit decadent accepting them because of expecting so little, receiving so little, in my childhood.

Joe had no office, so he sat each night at our kitchen table correcting papers from his biology students. Since he taught a grim 22 hours a week, 5 classes, at Alderson-Broaddus College, the assignments were piled up, endless. And as he was deathly slow doing anything, my father couldn't find time to stop work and play with me. That was my whining complaint. I was totally unmoved by his need to support me and my mother and little brother.

Our house on Faculty Row was too close to the neighbors for a loud argument with my mother, Laura, when she bought me sandals, and I howled, "I hate sandals! I won't wear them!" Our small living room was not a place for me to go bouncing a rubber ball off the wall. I knocked an invaluable antique china vase from the mantelpiece onto the floor, shattering it. I tried to console my mother by reminding her that the vase was part of a matching pair. Wasn't it enough that she still had one intact?

There was a small hornet's nest on our unscreened front porch. Should we poke it with a broomstick? We chose to ignore it. The nest got larger, the size of a Chinese lantern. And larger. Our family raced across our porch and into the house, fleeing for safety. Hornets swarmed everywhere: a science-fiction eruption. One day I tried to sneak through and was stung twice. We needed to do something concrete. HELP! What a sight: a fire truck from downtown Philippi sat on our small front lawn and uniformed firemen knocked down the nest with a power hose. My parents and I watched from inside as dazed hornets hit our living room picture window and then crashed dead to the ground all over our porch.

School Days

All 12 grades were jammed into the same brick building in downtown Philippi. If you were from Barbour County, that's where you went to school. At 5½, I was a pygmy in the hallways, walking among towering high school students. When I entered 1st grade (there was neither nursery school nor kindergarten), I'd been reading for a year and a half. I was mystified when the other kids were handed "Dick and Jane" primers and they stumbled over the simplest words: "See Dick run. See Jane run. See Spot run."

My white-haired 1st grade teacher, Mrs. McLeod, was challenged by this precocious little boy who'd been reading books on his own. What to do with him? She moved my desk away from the other kids and gave me my own assignments. The first week of school I alone had homework. A puzzle to unravel: "On the way to St. Ives, I met a man with seven wives, and each wife had seven cats, and each cat had seven kittens. How many were going to St. Ives?" For many hours, I struggled at home at the dining room table adding and adding, as I hadn't learned yet to multiply. I returned to school with my proud answer, a very high number, and the teacher shook her head and chuckled. "Only *one* person, the man, was going to St. Ives." Tricked!

I peaked at age 6, when Mrs. McLeod asked at the end of the school year for my autograph and predicted I'd go to Harvard University and be famous. My mother started deciding I was a "genius," and believed this puffery. In Spring 1951, when I was 6½ and finishing 1st grade, I was given a Stanford Achievement test. My mom copied out the results for my grandfather, Sam, in New York, and informed him that I was at the level of a 9- and 10-year-old in reading, spelling, word meaning. She boasted, "He made such a test that they never had it in a school year." I think this is true: at a meeting of the West Virginia State Board of Education, I became the first student ever in the state permitted to skip a grade. Which would that be? My parents gave me a choice. Because the 3rd-grade teacher was said to be mean, I opted to go to second and skip third.

I started my thespian life auspiciously, starring as Billy Boy in a brief theatrical presentation in 1st grade. I stood on stage in the middle of a semi-circle of my 6-year-old peers, who sang in my direction, "Can you bake a cherry pie, Billy Boy, Billy Boy, can you bake a cherry pie, darling Billy?" My arms crossed proudly, I nodded and nodded. Though I had no spoken lines, the shaking of my head on cue got the message concisely to the audience: "Yes, I can bake a cherry pie."

I was lucky to be cast at age 68 in an independent film feature called Computer Chess. *What great joy being the center of the action in several scenes surrounded by a large cast! I'd like to think I was channeling my Billy Boy.*

In my 1st-grade class, there was a hapless boy who struggled mightily with the alphabet, who every day had green boogers fermenting in his nose. My disgusted teacher would send different students to sniff if he went in his pants. His name, I swear, was Paul Pugh. In 2nd grade, a popular girl was throwing a party and asked everyone but me and the untouchable Paul. I stepped before her and demanded to be invited. "OK, you can come," she patronizingly assented. But I recall the hurt when my mother absolutely forbade me to attend without a formal written invitation. And another humiliation. In 2nd grade, I challenged my teacher on some arcane academic point, and, in retaliation, she asked the class to vote for who was right. Every single child but me raised a hand in support of the teacher. I voted for myself, loathing my sucky classmates.

From what sprang my sense of humor? Jack Benny on the radio and Abbott and Costello movies and, a role model, a kid named Roy Mann in my 1st grade class. He'd walk up to other children and nudge them, "Say, 'I'm hot, I'm cold.'" When they said, 'I'm hot, I'm cold," he'd grab their hands, pump them, and declare, "I'm Roy Mann, glad to meet you!" What a card! By 2nd grade, I was offering up humor myself to my classmates such as, "What's the difference between a fisherman and a bad student?" "One baits the hook, the other hates the book." Ho! Ho! And by 4th grade, the far more worldly joke: "I don't smoke, drink, or swear. Goddamn it, I left my cigarettes at the liquor store."

At age 80, I started doing Open Mic comedy. Blame it on West Virginia.

At 7, I was on a school bus of grades 1-8, off for a field trip. The driver, holding an attendance list, called out our names. When the driver said, "Gerry?" I bellowed out a smart-ass response. To my extraordinary pleasure, those on the bus, even the 8th graders, laughed uproariously at what I said. For the next year, I held a conversation in my head in which I auditioned sarcastic retorts to an imaginary bus driver. So disappointing, there was never another field trip. But my smarmy sensibility had been set in stone.

Weren't all artsy adults once sickly children? I missed probably 150 days of school in 1st and 2nd grade, lots of colds and coughs but also I was knocked silly by the big three: mumps, measles, and chicken pox. Of the last: I've still got an oval scar on the bridge of my nose because I lacked the willpower not to scratch. Worst of all: I was a child deeply exhausted by endless waves of sneezing each summer. Dr. Cora, the sole woman physician at Philippi's Meyer's Clinic, gave me test injections all along my arm and many of those puffed up. I was allergic to practically everything, starting with ragweed and golden rod. For my non-air-conditioned childhood, I often lay on a couch struck down by dreadful hay fever, my eyes tearing, clutching a handkerchief for the next "Achoo!"

My report card from first through 4th grades was top-of-the-line, all "S" for satisfactory with an even better "S+" often sprinkled in. There was one glaring exception, a "U" for Unsatisfactory in 2nd grade Health. It resulted from a conspiracy between the teacher and my parents to break me of the intolerable habit of biting my fingernails. Their strategy failed, and, undeterred by the bad grade, I kept chomping away. Putting terrible-tasting stuff on my fingernails was another failure. I gagged a bit but kept on biting.

Biting my fingernails: it's never stopped, it never gets old.

Catty-corner from my school was a penny candy store. I was in there as often as I had change in my pockets. My favorite for two cents was red licorice. If I was lucky enough for a nickel, that went for an Oh Henry! chocolate bar or Wrigley's Spearmint Gum. If I got Life Savers, I offered my friends the undesirable lime and pineapple and kept for myself the luscious orange and red ones. Most wonderful of all at that candy store were Lips! They were inedible, yet what enjoyment strutting about with my mouth covered with the red-dyed paraffin.

I had a favorite song in music class: "She'll be coming 'round the mountain when she comes." We also sang spirited songs of the armed forces: "Anchors Aweigh" (Navy), "The Caissons Go Rolling Along" (Army) and, by far the most rousing, "The Halls of Montezuma" (Marines). I was a little patriot and militarist. I had the briefest moment of learning an instrument, taught in 4th grade the fingering on a cheap plastic flute.

All 12 grades were to participate in this special entertainment in the school gymnasium, and we in the 4th grade would perform the old chestnut, the Mexican Hat Dance. For some surreal reason, we would be dressed as bumblebees, with stingers coming out of our foreheads. Our mothers were sent patterns to make our orange tops, and Laura did her best. But why, I wondered, the puffy sleeves? I learned that miserable day when I came onto the gym floor to perform. Hopping foot to foot, I realized that my mother had inadvertently outfitted me in the girl's top! I was dancing around with a girl my mirror image. The shame, the shame, as these were not gender-fluid times in rural West Virginia.

My first original pun as a 7-year-old was agonized over, a riff on two popular 1950s candy bars. I declared, for the amusement of my classmates in the schoolyard, "Almond enJoying a Peter Paul Mounds." (Almond Joy)

Outside of School

How little my parents knew of American ways when they named their first-born Gerald. I must have been seven when I balked at such a sissy identity and declared myself Jerry. That's who I remained for decades. But increasingly bothered that Jerry was really short for Jerome, I became, still am, Gerry for Gerald. A second complication persisted: my parents never reflected for a second that I would be—ugh!—Jerry Peary. Later, Gerry Peary. Don't anyone call me that grotesque rhyming name.

I have spent a lifetime introducing myself, awkwardly, by only my first name. I once interviewed the King Kong *actress, Fay Wray, and we commiserated over our travails having rhyming names.*

At age 7, this Jewish lad walked out on his front porch on Easter Sunday to behold a magnificent sight. The yard next door was alive with painted Easter eggs, all of them vaguely hidden but easy to see in the green grass. With glee, I raced off my porch and gathered six or seven eggs in my clutches. A treasure, and all for me! But then a neighbor lady ran out of her home and screeched: "Put those down! Those are for the little kids, not you!" So that's why they were so effortless to find! I put the eggs back on the lawn and retreated to my house, bawling, bawling.

We weren't sung to as children. Were we read to? I can't remember, though we were encouraged to bring books home from the library. Sports? Neither parent knew a thing about them. Both were lost relating to popular culture.

Joe and Laura didn't change much when they resided later in urban environments. I remember asking them in 1965 to name any of the four Beatles, and our mom and dad looking to each other desperately for an answer.

Some early literary memories. 7-year-old me circling every "I" in the first-person *The Adventures of Robinson Crusoe* until, twenty pages in, I gave up my inexplicable project. My grandfather, Sam, shipping from Paris a book about a dog named Jerry. A nice gesture, but he forgot I didn't read French. My water buffalo expert father gifting me with what he knew about, a novel, China-set, called *The Water-Buffalo Children*. I checked out from the school library a chilling eco-fantasy which exploded into a

Manichean war between good and bad garden crops. I still can't comprehend why my beloved cucumbers were placed among the villainous vegetables.

There were no McDonald's yet in West Virginia, and I don't think I ate a hamburger until age 10 or so. We were hot dog people. We always had Cokes, never Pepsis. We had oval Ritz crackers not the square Saltines. Every trip to the grocery, our mother returned with a six-pack of Hershey Bars with almonds. Danny and I would run our fingers over the wrapping paper trying to detect how many nuts were inside. The scheme: grab the chocolate bars with the most nuts for yourself, leave your brother with the almond-deprived leftovers.

Who even had heard the word "cholesterol"? We had bacon and eggs sunny side up regularly for breakfast, sometimes frozen sausage links, and meat every night for dinner: Southern fried chicken, pork chops, or, our father's favorite, lamb chops. Our green vegetables were iceberg lettuce and spinach once in a while. Danny demanded the latter because of Popeye's recommendation. Our meals ended with a 1950s flourish: on a good night, with strawberry shortcake (frozen berries, store-bought sponge cake) or banana cream pie with vanilla wafers! On a normal night, canned fruit cocktail with a sprinkling of maraschino cherries. No one had heard of the carcinogenic, Red Dye 40.

Our mother despised lamb, wouldn't eat it, and my brother and I heard her tell people literally a thousand times about her detestation of it. She was still saying, "Do you know I hate lamb?" when she passed at 91.

Aren't people dumb? A faculty colleague of my dad, Dr. Ludwig, a plump, hoarse German, performed a magic trick of making a nickel disappear between his fingers. I acted duly amazed, the nickel reappeared, and, for my feigned astonishment, it was given to me. Once, Dr. Ludwig held in his palm a thick nickel and a thin dime and asked me to choose. Obviously, I grabbed the dime. Duh!

I visited NYC and the 2nd grade class of my cousin Luba. The teacher poured water in a tall thin vessel and then more in a small squat one and asked the class, "Which has more water?" The NY sophisticates sat silent, puzzled. This West Virginia rube raised his hand and shouted out, "They have the same amount of water!" What was up with those Manhattanite 7-year-olds? Dumb, dumb, dumb.

My grandfather Sam brought me in New York to 42nd Street. I remember turning the corner from 7th Avenue and gasping at the half-dozen or so movie theaters jammed into one block. "Pick what you want to see," my grandfather said. After anxious deliberating, I made a wild guess as to the most appealing: an evening of Mighty Mouse cartoons. But I was red-eyed for being gypped. Who knew that these were *musical* cartoons? Corny and girlish, animated operetta! Oh, the cinema I might have picked: a shoot-'em-up Western, a Danny Kaye or Jerry Lewis, a Francis the Talking Mule.

My uncle Israel took me to Madison Square Garden for the Ringling Brothers Circus. There was a march around the perimeter of cheery Walt Disney characters, Goofy and Donald and Snow White, etc., all waving to the kids in the crowd. We were sitting up high in the cheap seats, but close enough for me to get agitated when I saw Mickey Mouse. I became determined that I wanted to buy him. I kept insisting and insisting, even though I had no pocket money. At the end of the circus day, my uncle had no choice but to walk me downstairs, find a credible employee, and have that person tell me to my face that, "No, Mickey is not for sale."

Even though Jewish, I bought into Santa Claus, until I was in NYC over the Christmas holidays. There was Santa Claus at Macy's and then there was Santa at Gimbels. How could Santa be both places at the same time? At Gimbels, I caught sight of the string holding up Santa's beard. I returned to West Virginia a Santa disavower, and told my 7-year-old classmates and friends that Santa was a big fake. A shocked neighbor parent overheard, and cautioned me to shut my fat mouth, to let the little kids believe what they believed. I complied, but a contrarian was brewing!

And a skeptic. The double-bill of "B" Westerns in downtown Philippi was always accompanied by a serial. I would leave the theater traumatized because the hero of the serial, falling off a building while wrestling a blackguard with dynamite in his belt, was surely killed in the mid-air explosion. But when I went the following week for the next chapter of the serial, there was a recap of the end of last week's chapter. Lo and behold, a shot was INSERTED in which our hero grabs a flagpole on the way down and is safe and sound when the dynamite goes off. At age 7, I knew: a SHAM!

There was only one barbershop in Philippi, West Virginia, therefore always full, often with a two-hour wait for a haircut. I didn't mind because of the large stack of comic books held for the mostly adult customers. It was there that I first discovered

Archie comics. It was where, feeling slightly wicked, I devoured ghoulish EC horrors like *Tales from the Crypt*. What possibly could improve on cobwebbed characters with green rotted faces rising from their graves?

A distaste for superheroes was evident in my comic book and comics page aesthetic. I preferred underachieving lazy guys—Dagwood on his couch, Popeye's Wimpy caring only about eating hamburgers—to square-jawed musclemen. Instead of *Superman* comics I purchased *Superboy*, relating far better to a teenage hero. A comic book I bought monthly was *Blackhawk*, about a cadre of uniformed manly men—Andre from France, Olaf from Norway, Blackhawk from the USA—battling the Germans in World War II. But my preferred *Blackhawk* character was the least valorous, and indubitably the most racially stereotyped one. It was the pig-tailed, buck-toothed, diminutive sidekick Chop-Chop, a good-natured Chinese, who seemed as interested in fighting a war as did cowardly Falstaff.

How did he know we were there, the only Jewish family within countless miles? In 1951, a rabbi appeared one day at our Philippi home, the first I'd ever seen. Was he a proselytizing Hasid? He spoke gently to my parents for several hours about the beauties of Judaism and offered them Haggadahs for the next Passover. He also gave me a stupendous present: a Torah-themed coloring book. My favorite picture by far was of Joseph and his coat of many colors, though I was limited in my art. Our family couldn't afford to buy for me the jumbo 64-color Crayola box. I was held to the starter box with the 8 basics: blue, green, yellow, red, etc. The lasting effects of being poor: I never know what fuchsia is, or maroon, or magenta, or mauve, or chartreuse.

There was so much Christianity around us that I felt its pressure. At 8, I begged my parents to let me go to the local Baptist church. Warily, they gave me permission. For several months, I attended Sunday school. There was a day when the teacher related a story about Jesus and some craven Jews and I felt all the kids staring at me. Once, I attended an adult service and, unthinking, went for the host and stuffed it into my mouth. In a second, I grasped that it was not for children and gagged as I tried to swallow it quickly. But nobody commented on my heretical behavior, and, all in all, those West Virginian evangelicals were very decent to me.

Danny remembers Patti Page singing "How Much Is That Doggie in the Window" on the first television set we ever saw, in a shop window in Philippi. Nobody we knew in West Virginia actually owned one. The total media of the Peary family was a radio we plugged into a wall and a telephone on a party line with several of our neighbors.

I have no recollection of my parents listening to radio programs, just me. I was a weekly fan of *Johnny Dollar*, a hard-boiled detective show, and *Gene Autry's Melody Ranch*. And *Amos 'n' Andy*, of course. Jack Benny made me laugh with his *The Lucky Strike Program*. At 7, I obsessed about mimicking the alpha cry at the end of each broadcast of *Tarzan*, after he'd saved Jane from the jaws of an African beast. I practiced and practiced and perfected it. There was a ravine in the woods near the college. I would swing across it on a vine, my shirt flying up showing my belly button. Mid-air, I'd do the mighty Tarzan shriek. I would land hard on my feet, thumping my chest. King of the Jungle!

I got my tonsils out at 7. A crude ether mask held over my face, I gasped for oxygen, sure I was dying as the anesthetic knocked me into sleep. However, there was a prize awaiting me for going through this anguish. I awoke in the hospital to my dad and mother presenting me with a bagful of comic books, and surprisingly excellent ones. How did they know which to get me? Give Joe and Laura credit for coming through, and for more. It was West Virginia's fiercest winter in years. When it was time to discharge me from the hospital, a taxi could only take us to the edge of Alderson-Broaddus College. I remember well my father carrying me home in a blanket to Faculty Row, as both parents pushed valiantly for a mile or more through three feet of snow.

My slight knowledge of the rich was the nearby estate of Alderson-Broaddus's president. Unlike our four-room stucco house, President S. and his family occupied a 19th-century brick castle with a football-field lawn. That seemed reasonable for the college's chief executive. But one day I was invited to the 8th birthday party of a classmate. I became aware of being in a lovely Philippi neighborhood and in a beautiful house with property, and learning that some people had wealth and we did not. My class-mate brought his child guests for a tour of his spacious bedroom. And there it was: hundreds of comic books, all in pristine shape, in the neatest piles and all shelved. I could never afford those, or have space for them. I trembled with jealousy.

Our home on Faculty Row was small and basic but with one extra. We had a basement. The steps were too steep for my mother, so my father and I escaped there, an early 1950s man/boy cave. My father worked on eccentric inventions: a piece of shaped metal that you turned clockwise in your hand and moved the laundry along on the line; a thick, scratchy paper made of some vegetable which, when perfected, could replace wood pulp. Meanwhile, I drew with crayon what had delighted me at the post office: wanted posters. I invented names for my criminals, who I equipped with mustaches and beards, and below the drawings I listed the offenses of which they were allegedly guilty: armed robbery, kidnapping, murder. These pictures were scotch-taped on the basement wall. Little Gerry's art gallery.

In West Virginia, our mother put aside the Eastern European and Jewish-style cuisine from her Romanian adolescence. She provided Danny and me with regular 1950s American meals, exactly what her sons wanted. But Laura thoughtfully put home-cooked meat in my sandwiches for school, and also she'd pack a little box of Sun Maid raisins. When I could, I swapped with my classmates the nutritious lunch for more overtly tasty ones with processed meats and pimiento cheese.

My mother asked out of the blue one day, "Gerry, if you had to decide whether to go with your mom or your dad, you'd choose me, wouldn't you?" At age 7, I was too stunned to answer, so I just breathed very hard. What an inappropriate question! And here's a strange thing about mom: she almost never put pen to anything except signing her name. Our father was charged with correspondence, and he wrote in an over-polite English and in the most florid style. As we learned later, what Laura did with proficiency and joy was talk on the telephone. There was nobody in Philippi to really chat with. In the early 1950s, to have telephoned long distance to her relatives in NYC was to spend a small fortune.

This is my most sustained and detailed remembrance of a day from my West Virginia childhood. It began with a screaming hissy fit. I, age 8, refused to go out in public in what my mother insisted I wear, a tank-top undershirt. I held my arms folded in front of my chest in embarrassment. My memory of that day then jumps to a classroom at Alderson-Broaddus, where I sat by while Laura took a beginner's art course. I became captivated by an oil painting on an easel in which a multi-storied building was sliced in half so you could see everything inside. The building was on fire, which I liked, and firemen were on ladders putting it out. I wanted badly to be a firefighter when I grew up.

A college student joined me in looking at the intricate painting, and she and I focused on a marital party on the ground floor oblivious to the flames. "See the little people!" we said, and giggled together. That young lady was from Huntington, West Virginia, and we were pen pals after that for several years. Meanwhile, the art teacher, Miss Skinner, with pink-framed eyeglasses and her hair in a bun, boiled several potatoes in a pot for her lunch. She ate one, and gave me the other, with the advice that I heeded: "Don't forget to eat the potato skin. That's where you'll find all the nutrients."

That was the only time in my childhood that I was lectured by anyone about what constituted healthy eating. Though my parents never ate fast food in their lives, my mother could never understand those issues of a proper diet which came to obsess my generation. She would proudly show me a package that she bought which said, "All natural," and assume I'd be impressed.

In downtown Philippi, I saw two men in a hotel restaurant spooning up bowls of beef stew. It was all new to me, never having eaten anywhere but home. My mother shopped, my mother cooked. We were so very frugal, and my Jewish mother ascribed forever to the "you never know what they put in their food" antipathy to restaurants.

I was weaned on the most sexist, ageist, and ever-popular card game: Old Maid, in which someone gets stuck with the unwanted card of a bespectacled, unmarried, ancient biddy. I graduated at age 8 to playing Authors. The deck I inherited was an early edition, since every writer pictured flourished in the 19th century. Curiously, Herman Melville did not make the cut. The women writers represented were Louisa May Alcott, Harriet Beecher Stowe, and George Eliot. Not a Brontë or Jane Austen. And certainly no one of color. I didn't notice the inequities. Instead, I looked at the titles of books on the Authors cards and vowed to read them all.

Seventy years later, time is running out on James Fenimore Cooper and Sir Walter Scott. And Uncle Tom's Cabin*.*

My first rub with death occurred at age 8, when I attended a high school football game. The word passed speedily around the stadium that, at halftime, the father of one of the players had died of a heart attack behind the grandstand. During the second half, I kept staring at the dead man's son, who, maybe 15, sat stoically on the bench of his team. He would try to watch the game for a bit, then he would look down at the ground. When he removed his football helmet, I could see his broken face.

I have done my best all my life to avoid death up close. I don't want a last look at the deceased. I have never been to an open-casket wake. I made it into my fifties before having a dead person in my sight. A player on my basketball pickup team keeled over on the parquet floor, turned blue, and succumbed from a heart attack.

In all-white Philippi, my backwards ideas of race came from books and the media: kindly Uncle Remus in Walt Disney's *Song of the South*; trickster Little Black Sambo coaxing tigers to race around a palm tree until reduced to pancake butter; and the malaprop-driven *Amos 'n' Andy* on radio, though I never imagined the hilarious characters were voiced by white men. And then one day in the Philippi forest, I saw real people of color for the first time: two young men running by on a pathway in a sweat, frazzled and anxious, as if being pursued. Who or what were they? "They are geechee," someone informed me. Only much later did I learn of African-Americans using that self-description, who resided in the Lowcountry region of South Carolina and Georgia. But what were those guys doing so far from home, in the alien West Virginia woods?

My father had two heroes, Albert Schweitzer and the black agriculturalist, George Washington Carver. Joe's stellar moment: desegregating Philippi by inviting an African-American veterinarian, William Waddell, to practice his profession in our all-white mountain town. Dr. Waddell was the first black person I ever met, and also his radiant daughter, Kay, and they had dinner at our house. How urbane they were! How sophisticated! In 1984, our parents were afforded a trip to Hawaii from an insurance settlement after a moving car smashed our pedestrian mother's wrist. They visited the veterinarian and his wife in Honolulu. Dr. Waddell gave our parents a copy of his 1978 memoir, *People Are The Funniest Animals*. Sadly, my dad is not acknowledged within, but Dr. Waddell did sign the book: "Best wishes to a great American family."

Through Facebook, I traced down Kay Wadell, who still lives in Honolulu, was a professor at the University of Hawaii, and is the distinguished poet Kathryn Waddell Takara. She wrote, "So glad you found me. I recently reread my dad's book and remembered Philippi."

What a great moment when the Olsons moved next door to us on Faculty Row. They had arrived from Minnesota after Olaf Olson was hired at Alderson-Broaddus to teach history. Evangelical Lutherans, they were warm and intelligent and became best friends of my Jewish parents. Olaf was slightly balding with glasses, his wife, Margaret, as I remember her, looked like Liv Ullmann. Their son, Stanley, my age and good-natured, was quickly a pal. We played King of the Mountain, throwing each other down a hill at one end of Faculty Row. He was hard-fisted Roy Rogers to my gentler Gene Autry when we impersonated cowboys.

I think he is the same Stanley Olson whom, several years ago, I tried to "Friend" on Facebook to no avail.

My polymorphous childhood sexuality ran riot on Faculty Row. Stanley and I would hide behind an observatory building, drop our pants to our shoes, and jump up and down, rakishly holding the cheeks of our behinds. Nobody could see our piggly-wiggly nakedness. We called these our "butt acts," and Stanley shamed me by blabbing to Rex, the coach's 13-year-old son, about what naughtiness we did. And then there were my misadventures with a girl in a basement while her little brother, Carl, rode around a pole on his tricycle. Every time he disappeared behind the pole, I would put my pointer finger there. Our dalliance was one time only, perhaps why her name eludes me.

Patty, 8, oldest daughter of the president of Alderson-Broaddus, was a prize. Whose girlfriend would she be? Stanley and I walked a log in competition, Stanley fell off, so Patty was mine. But the free-spirited girl went for Stanley anyway, becoming in our cowboy games Dale Evans to his Roy Rogers. Her skittish mongrel dog, Cedric, substituted for steady Bullet, Rogers's German shepherd. One day, Patty cheated on Stanley by taking me to the side of her castle home and allowing me to watch her pee. The excitement was stopped abruptly by the appearance of her imperious father, a devout Baptist. President S. grabbed Patty by her wrist and dragged her away, admonishing both of us, "Act like ladies and gentlemen."

It spooks me today recalling my folly at age 8. Alone in the West Virginia forest below my home, I climbed on tiny branches to the very top of a fir tree, maybe fifty feet in the air, and then down again. I could easily have tumbled to my death.

My regular climb was into the limbs of a trusty oak tree several hundred yards behind our house. That's where the kids at my 8th birthday gathered and played, until my mother yelled out the back door, "Come inside and open presents!" The other children immediately raced toward my house. But something compelled me to stay behind, some surge of power in having a delayed entry. So I remained alone in the oak tree counting the minutes. After a time, I hopped down and walked slowly toward my home, then inside to the room where everyone awaited me. Seeing the pile of gifts, I abandoned my deliberateness. I pounced on the presents, ripped through the wrapping paper, ignored reading the cards. I held up my new riches for all the kids to see: a dump truck, an erector set, a pair of handcuffs with a secret lock and key.

As our family had little money, the magic set I received from my parents was on the low end of what you could purchase. Inside a thin cardboard box were, among a dozen items, a marked deck of cards, several magnets and trick coins, a wooden magic wand, and a little instruction pamphlet about how to do the wizardry. I soon outgrew these pedestrian beginner tricks and turned my attention to homemade magic concoctions. I would sneak into the bathroom with a kitchen glass and create a brew out of cough syrup, my mother's pungent perfumes, bubbly shampoo, and whatever else was liquid in the medicine cabinet. Though it all eventually went down the toilet, this elixir was worthy necromancy for a potential Harry Houdini.

My biggest talent as a chef is an ability to create sauces out of random items sitting in my refrigerator and cupboards. I love mixing various things together, changing colors and consistency, and I trace this enjoyment back to my bathroom concoctions.

I listened avidly on radio to "Here's LIVE from Clarksburg: Cherokee Sue!" I was comforted by her Kitty Wells-style country singing, yodeling, guitar picking, and down-home chitchat. One day, I was taken to Clarksburg, a neighboring town, and brought to the radio station. It was my chance to talk to my favorite radio star. I was pointed to Cherokee Sue in the hallway: a woman with a bony nose, rouged cheeks, and a cowgirl hat. I was gravely disappointed. I thought I would be meeting a flesh-and-blood Indian. I shook my head about speaking to her. Her real name, I would later find out, was Hattie Graham. She collaborated with her husband, "Little John" Graham, on sentimental songs like "Mother's Old Checkered Apron."

Philippi is very small and not a place that many famous people come from. There was an NFL football player named Scott Mayle and, top of the heap, Ted Cassidy, who would appear regularly on *The Addams Family*. But Danny and I were ecstatic as youngsters to learn, via a 1953 baseball card, that a player named Jim Fridley hailed from our Philippi. He had three undistinguished years in the major leagues, except for the day that he went 6 for 6. And he was involved in the largest trade in major league history, 17 players shuttled in 1955 between the Orioles and the Yankees.

My brother, a baseball historian, actually talked to Fridley. Danny e-mailed me: "I interviewed him in Florida. I don't remember much: he wore multi-colored shorts, he insisted for no reason that I NOT record our conversation. It was as if he met people from Philippi every day, because he had no reaction when I told him that we shared a birthplace. And though I said I left when I was three, he responded, "You remember that river there? Well, I'd hit the ball over it." Jim Fridley, Philippi celebrity.

One year, the whole town of Philippi transformed into a county fair, and I had one of the best times of my young life. On the courthouse lawn, I watched local men fighting to catch hold of a squealing greased pig and, after that, barefooted male contestants trying to shoo themselves up a greased telephone pole. I ate cotton candy and fresh corn plucked from a vat of boiling water, and also a hot dog or two. There was a Shriner's Parade down Main Street with waving locals dressed as red-nosed clowns.

The enjoyment went into the evening, with the Five and Dime lit up after business hours. The basement became an emporium for children's games. I handed over nickels so, among multi-colored confetti and *papier-mâché* streamers, I could throw darts and try to pop a balloon. On another day in the same Five and Dime sub-level, I had a traumatic experience. I tripped and banged my knee and was instantly circled by customers and salespeople, all demanding, "Son, should we call a doctor?" I was mortified being such a public spectacle, and claustrophobic being shuttered in by stranger adults.

This Philippi moment came back to me when, in adolescence, I read Ray Bradbury's terrifying short story, "The Crowd." Therein, clusters of adults would surround persons who had fallen to the ground and methodically execute them.

Every year, we'd make the grueling train trip from West Virginia to visit our New York relatives. We'd embark on the Baltimore & Ohio at Grafton, West Virginia, and ride and ride, ending at Washington, D.C. around 10pm. We'd have a two-hour wait, and change trains at midnight to crawl up the East Coast to Manhattan. As we couldn't afford a Pullman, we sat up the whole way. We got stuck in smoking cars, where I got brutal headaches. One trip, our mother begged a group of drunken men to put away their cigars for her poor son's health. They laughed at her plea. Still, there are fond train memories, of when our parents overrode their tight budgets and allowed us a meal in the linen table-clothed dining car. Once I ordered a BLT on white toast with the proper toothpick holding it in place. Another time, on New Year's Day, we were treated by the railroad to free cups of creamy eggnog.

As we waited for a train in Grafton, an elderly gentleman came up and offered me a candy bar. I said, "Thank you," and grabbed for it. When the man walked away, my shaken mother pulled the gift chocolate from my hand and threw it on the tracks. "It could very well be poison!" she said. I would have taken a chance on that candy bar. I was so angry at my hysterical parent.

Of our long train rides to see relatives, the longest, made just once, was to Boston, for the marriage of my mother's cousin, Harold, with whom she'd shared a room in the Bronx. We stayed several exciting nights at the Statler, the only occasion ever through my college years that my parents splurged this way. A grand hotel! I was the ring boy for Harold's marriage to Patty, a Boston girl, and at the wedding reception at a private home, it was the first time in my life that I watched a TV program. A Western. The second viewing was at the New York apartment of my cousin, Luba, downstairs from my maternal grandparents. I saw an episode of *Howdy Doody* and another of *Captain Video and his Video Rangers*.

About 65 and 70 years after serving at their wedding, I attended the funerals of both Harold and Patty. I have no idea of the where-abouts of cousin Luba, who would be in her late seventies.

Around this time, my New York second cousins, Dickie and Donnie, twin doctors, also moved to Boston. I think it was Dickie who was the first in my family to marry outside of our faith. Oy, what a mistake! I overheard our mother telling our father what a terrible thing had happened. The Christian bride, an airline hostess, turned on Dickie, demanding a divorce, and calling him, "JEW! JEW!"

Likewise, I have no knowledge of what happened to Dickie and Donnie.

Once in New York, our father took me and Danny to visit his mother, Ida, or "Dussya." She kept us on the stairwell for a while before allowing us into her apartment. There were no kisses and hugs and she was cool to her son, Joe. Being vain about her looks, Dussya pretended on occasions that my father was her younger brother. She didn't want people to think she was old enough to have an adult son. And she definitely was not thrilled that she was a grandmother of two. Were we upset about her behavior toward us? We had been duly warned by both of our parents that she was mean to all.

In 4th grade in Philippi, there was a portable library in the back of the classroom and I read my way happily through many of the Old Mother West Wind novels of Thornton Burgess, featuring Reddy Fox, Old Mr. Toad, and Peter the Rabbit. In spring 1953, my 4th grade year over, we abruptly left West Virginia behind. We said goodbye to where Danny was born, and where we'd lived since 1948 as Philippi's only Jews. This was quite touching: the Baptist church where I'd attended services said a heartfelt group prayer for the Peary family's future, led by the evangelical minister.

Is there any thought of Philippi which I have not squeezed dry? My brother, Danny, asked me recently if I knew about semi-pro ball there, and I had a flash of a recovered memory, something I hadn't thought of since early childhood. The day that I went to a very bizarre charity event: a game by locals of donkey baseball! Except for the pitcher and batter, everyone on the field sat on a donkey. As soon as the batter hit, he hopped a donkey and ran the bases. What merriment! And so much the essence of rural West Virginia, something I'd never encounter again in a lifetime.

Neither Danny nor I have ever returned to West Virginia. At sentimental moments, I've fantasized about going back to Philippi and making a documentary about this little town, especially in the Trump era. Would I, a Northern left-liberal, be treated in as decent a way as that once upon a time when I lived there?

Summers

Joe's salary was paltry teaching biology at Alderson-Broaddus. Needing additional income for our family, he tried each summer for a job doing science research elsewhere than West Virginia. And so we landed in 1948 at a marine biology station at the tip of Louisiana, on isolated Grand Isle. I was old enough, 3½, to become excited that this locale is where the pirate Jean Lafitte was said to have buried his treasures. It was also where I got a terrible shock to my system. I was walking one day on the beach with my father when we encountered a mammoth sea turtle dead on its back in the sand. We stood there in awe, and both of us distressed. What was there possibly to say?

I was walking behind my father through a Grand Isle swamp and saw something peeking its head out of the muck. I leaned toward it and pointed my finger. "What's that?" My dad turned white, and yanked me back from the edge. A water moccasin! Some trained biologists returned to the spot and captured it. It was defanged, its venom drained, I believe, and was shipped by my father to Philippi as a gift to Jenny P., who lived several houses away on Faculty Row. She was the wife of the athletic coach but also the only artsy-looking person I'd ever seen in West Virginia, with large hoop earrings, gypsy blouses, and eye shadow. "Jenny likes snakes," was my dad's explanation for this unusual present.

During our Louisiana summer, our family of three was invited by a sea captain aboard his ship, and that included a lavish dinner. It was the rarest of times that we ate anywhere but at home. The meal was a special treat for my father who, growing up in France, had loved seafood, something he never tasted in West Virginia. It was bouillabaisse in a deep red sauce and with heaping portions of Gulf shrimp. While my parents and the captain ate in the ship's hold and conversed, I snuck away and up on the deck. Braving danger, I trod along a narrow pathway on the side of the boat above the water, and peered down into a small oval window. It was the kitchen of the ship and this is what I saw: a golden yellow uncut lemon meringue pie. A shimmering dream image, a child's introduction to Surrealism!

All of his life in America, my father had book manuscripts, inventions, and science discoveries which he was unsuccessful getting others to buy into. And so it was in 1948 that my mother and I sat in a car in swampy, moss-covered rural Louisiana waiting for my father. Somebody had driven us to the mansion of Avery

McIlhenny, president of the Tabasco Company and a self-taught naturalist. My father went inside to make a pitch requesting financial backing for something biological and ecological. As usual, the worthy project came to naught.

For several years, 1949–1950, because of my mother's pregnancy and the birth of Danny, we remained full-time in West Virginia. In 1951, we were traveling again for my father's work. He brought his family, including baby Danny, to Long Island so he could do marine biology research at the Cold Spring Harbor Laboratory. This summer was the most idyllic of my childhood. My dad and I got to swim every day in the Long Island Sound. Israeli scientists in shorts and sandals sang and danced around a campfire at night in a delightful emulation of a kibbutz.

Inspired by all this science about us, a friend and I pledged to take a nature walk every morning and study facets of our environment. Our eco-voyages lasted for three or four days. There was a teenager in Cold Spring Harbor named Phil who played tennis in white shorts and was very kind to me. I probably got a "kid crush" on genial Phil. A local boy and a girl offered to allow me in their secret club for those 7 and older. This 6½-year-old was honored until they informed me of the initiation rites. In a huff, I refused to comply. I would not strip off all my clothes so they could peek at my privates.

In the summer of 1952, my family rented a flat in Cambridge, Massachusetts, so my father could take biology classes at Harvard. I was then 7½ and most excited about the public library. It had a thousand more children's volumes than at my school in Philippi. I got a library card and was soon walking through the city with high stacks of books, as you were allowed to take home ten at a time. At the end of the summer, I won a certificate for checking out more books than any other child in Cambridge. And I read them too! My favorites were about dinosaurs and time machines. But that library was the place also for an act of disobedience. I and a boy my age snuck to the back side of the building and tiptoed along a narrow ledge. The challenge was not to fall to the concrete below and be killed.

In our time in Cambridge, I became cognizant of Danny as a vibrant human being, as he turned three that August. Wearing coveralls or a sailor suit, my barefooted little brother compulsively did somersaults on our living room floor. He was prodded on by our parents telling him, "Make a trick! Make a trick!" One day, Danny did his "trick" with a lollipop in his mouth, jumping between pieces of furniture. When he hit the ground, the lollipop pushed back in his throat and excised his tonsils. He was rushed to the hospital, where the doctors proclaimed that a medical miracle had happened. His tonsils had been sliced off surgically. Danny could be taken home.

I have a sharp memory of going to the Brattle Theater with my father for a Technicolor comedy adventure starring ventriloquist Paul Winchell and his hilarious dummy, Jerry Mahoney. But according to sources I have consulted, no movie starring this delightful duo ever was made. How is that possible? I couldn't have confused this with a TV program since we had no television. A second movie memory also doesn't jell with the facts. Our family took a subway into Boston and I remember with clarity looking out the window at the Charles stop and seeing a billboard advertising what I thirsted to see, Alfred Hitchcock's *Strangers on A Train*. But that was a 1951 film, and this was already the summer of 1952.

When my father and I emerged into the afternoon sun one day at the Brattle, I carried with me an overflowing bag of popcorn. As we walked, popcorn fell to the ground and pigeons swooped down to pick at the kernels. When we turned onto Brattle Street, I purposefully dropped popcorn pieces in a trail behind me, and more and more birds came to eat. I was mesmerized: an army of pigeons eager for food from my hand. Such power for a 7-year-old boy! I loved those pigeons! Could they come home with us? And then we reached Harvard Square. As we crossed into traffic, my father said that those pigeons had to stay behind. Trying not to sob, I turned to my bird friends and waved a melodramatic goodbye.

Living since 1978 in Cambridge, I take no notice of pigeons but I've been hundreds of times to the dear and ancient Brattle. My first wife nixed my idea of us getting married there.

Our father had several Russian relatives in New York. His great aunts were the sisters, Jenya and Manya, who seemed ancient to Danny and me, deep in their sixties. Jenya was the nice one, though everyone agreed she looked like a monkey. Max, a scientist who did primate research with my father, met Jenya and said, perplexed, "You seem so familiar. Why?" Manya, the mean one, had long white hair looped in braids on the top of her head. She owned a boarding house in Far Rockaway, Long Island, where we stayed (did we pay?) in the summer of 1953. It was a lonely vacation because, if children came to play with us, the witchy Manya would chase them from her lawn.

Our family of four lived upstairs in a studio apartment in temperamental Manya's rooming house. Escape for us was the Far Rockaway beach and the first boardwalk of my life. There was an antique machine where, for a nickel, you could peer inside and watch flipbook, one-minute movies; and there was the best arcade game in the world, Skee-Ball. I loved pulling the lever and hearing the clunky sound of the wooden balls coming down the chute. I slowly learned the secret of how to be an 8-year-old Skee-ball maestro. Don't toss the balls straight into the hoops but spin them off the side walls.

I have had many astonishing reading experiences: *The Hound of the Baskervilles*, *The Martian Chronicles*, an all-nighter of *In Cold Blood* from start to finish. But nothing compares with, that summer in Far Rockaway, my fear-and-trembling discovery of the Hardy Boys. The first book of the serial I read was *The Secret Panel*, followed instantly, in a sweat, by *The Missing Chums*. Oh, I loved you, Frank and Joe, and your stalwart dad, Fenton the detective, and your supportive housewife mom Laura, and your eccentric aunt Gertrude. As usual for movies and books, my deepest affection was for the clumsy, funny sidekick. So Chet Morton, the Hardy's chubby friend, was my true favorite. How dreadful in *The Missing Chums* that Chet and Biff disappeared for a while off the face of the earth! But the Hardy Boys, whiz teen detectives, came to the rescue.

In 1953, I embraced Topps baseball cards in a big way, five in a pack with a dry slab of bubble gum. I coveted every single card. And that brings me to one of the most shameful moments of my life. I was 9, and this was during our Far Rockaway summer. There was a nice 5-year-old kid whom Danny and I played with: Sammy, with dark curly hair. Well, one day Sammy went to the beach and drowned. I remember lying on my bed afterward, face down on my pillow, horrified at his death and yet, conscious-stricken, wondering if I dared ask Sammy's parents if I could inherit his baseball cards.

Columbia

My childhood in West Virginia ended with the move of the Peary family in September 1953 to Columbia, South Carolina. It was a city familiar to my parents because of a stay there in 1945, when our father was, I think, in the army at Fort Jackson. This time he came as a biology professor. He'd resigned from teaching at all-white Alderson-Brauddus to accept a dual appointment in the science departments at adjoining historically black colleges in Columbia, Benedict College and Allen University. In those days, they were called "Negro" institutions. My brother Danny was 4, I was turning 9, and this was a new world. For one thing, the city of Columbia had a population over 100,000, 25 times larger than Philippi.

It didn't take long to register that things were different here, as our family was transported from hillbilly West Virginia to the urban Deep South. The State House capitol building had spread across its grounds commemorative statues of Confederate soldiers in battle. And a high-flying Confederate flag. The capitol was also the place to buy from a cart a Southern treat, peanuts in their shells boiled in salt water and placed in a brown paper bag. They were a remnant from Confederacy days: "goober peas."

At my segregated school, I was lectured in the 5th grade that it wasn't the Civil War but the War Between the States. I was taught Southern ways. My first day at school, a teacher asked me a question, I answered "Yes," and, before my new classmates, she sharply corrected me: "Here we say, 'Yes, ma'am.'" I soon learned to sing "Dixie" — "I wish I was in the land of cotton" — and a song which, at age 9, I actually liked belting out: "If you're from Alabama, Tennessee, or Caroline, anywhere below the Mason Dixon Line, then you're from Dixie, I said from Dixie, and I'm from Dixie too!"

Though my father taught full-time at two colleges, his combined salary was meager. We moved into a small rented apartment in a low-income housing development called Wales Garden. We still had no television set but the middle-aged woman across the hall did. Peeking in her open door, I saw her captivated watching a show starring an oddly-acting pianist named Liberace. What was up with him? Wales Garden had among its renters a local television celebrity, a friendly family man under a straw hat who often stood outside socializing with excited kids. He had an afternoon show, *Bar-Q Ranch*, in which he'd introduce "B" Western movies. I sure remember his colorful name, "Cactus" Quave.

Danny and I we were both baseball-crazy, and delighted that our new city hosted a Single A "Sally League" farm team of Cincinnati called the Columbia Reds. Many Cincinnati Reds began careers there, including, in 1955, one proud African-American, the future Hall-of-Famer Frank Robinson. Across the street from where we resided was the home of a kid named Ricky. His divorced mom, all dolled up with eyeliner, lipstick, and fancy stockings, was seen stepping into autos with Columbia Reds ballplayers behind the wheel. People gossiped about her, insinuations beyond my understanding.

There was a bit of a lawn between the buildings at Wales Garden Apartments and that's where the boys played baseball. One day, a freak accident: a swung bat broke in two, and the heavy half went flying through the air and smashed into the head of Jackie, a 10-year-old girl who'd been part of our game. Who imagined that my mother, Laura, also standing by, knew first-aid techniques? She placed her fingers on Jackie's temple in the right compress spots to stop the bleeding until a medical crew arrived.

In 2010, a 50th anniversary party in Columbia of my high school graduating class. I talked with Jackie, and, yes, she remembered with gratitude what my mother had done 57 years earlier. I saw her again at the 60th anniversary, and she introduced me to a classmate as "This is the man whose mother saved my life."

The only food-related story I remember from my father was that he ate chocolate bars wrapped in baguettes as a boy in Paris. Otherwise, he was as uninterested in dining as he was in anything that was not science-related. Not once through the years did he express a wish to go to a restaurant. If Danny and I were tired of what was on our plates, we'd pass it to our father who, unthinking, swallowed it down. That's why Danny at about age 7 proudly announced to our neighbors, "My daddy is a garbage can!"

We finally ate out! And what a grand experience. Our family ventured into downtown Columbia for an evening at Caldwell's Cafeteria. We got food on our trays and then carried them into the restaurant basement, where a Chaplin silent short and Warner Brothers cartoons—Bugs Bunny, Daffy Duck, Porky Pig—were projected on a screen. Danny and I would have gone gladly every week to this special activity for children. But as our family had little money for such extravagances, we went twice in all for Caldwell's great movie night.

The best things were the pomegranates and pecans dropping from trees as I walked to school. I wasn't fond of the actual academic day. My 5th grade teacher, Miss Monarch, was quite pretty at 23 or 24, surely a sorority girl when attending the University of South Carolina. She sensed that I, one of the smart students, wasn't inspired by her conventional pedagogy. She tried to win me over. She took me aside to confide that she knew lots of football players from the USC Gamecocks and could get me their autographs. Ungracious me, I rejected her offer: "Miss Monarch, I don't care about college football. I am a major league baseball fan!"

"What is a spider?" I asked my classmates, standing in front of them. "An insect," several shouted out. I shook my head. "Any other guesses?" Silence. I gave the answer: "A spider is an ANIMAL!" and then launched into my book report. Praise from Miss Monarch about my unusual way of starting, of grabbing everyone's attention instead of just telling the book's plot. For one day, I liked my vapid teacher.

A kid in my 5th grade class punched me hard in the stomach for no reason. I retain his name and an image of what he looked like: Tommy Bone. I also remember he was a Mormon. I think I had a friend with rimless glasses named Billy Brooks. I'm sure of the existence of Gus and Carl. They were from an orphanage and came to school barefoot. That they had neither socks nor shoes, nobody—teachers, administrators, or other students—said anything about it. Gus and Carl were not the best students but they were athletes, especially bony, compact Carl. He could sail a kickball deep into the outfield with his bare foot. Meanwhile, I who excelled in classwork failed in sports. I was the first one picked for spelling bees but the last boy for kickball, chosen reluctantly after even some of the girls. One day, an easy fly ball popped out of my baseball glove and, like Charlie Brown, I wept sour tears, ground down by my ineptitude.

At age 9 I got my first job, toiling after school as an assistant paperboy. An entrepreneurial 11-year-old asked for my help distributing the afternoon *Columbia Record*. The work was intimidating at first, mastering the proper folding of newspapers—like learning to tie shoes. And then it was knowing which houses on which streets got the papers, and tossing the papers so they landed on people's porches. Once a month, it was time to collect money for our deliveries, home by home. For that task, the older boy didn't trust me. I stood back while he rang doorbells and chatted with the customers. However, I did my part serviceably for several months, collecting each week fifteen cents for my labors.

Philadelphia

About six months after moving from West Virginia to South Carolina, our family was made to relocate again when my father impulsively took a non-teaching science research job in Philadelphia. It was April 1954, and Danny and I suddenly lived for the first time in the North. I was in 5th grade in Upper Darby Township, a Philadelphia suburb. I must have been a novelty when I suddenly popped up late in the school year. To my wonder, other 5th graders were eager to be my friend. One boy put an arm around my back and another boy pushed the first boy's hand away so he could hug me. How weird and wonderful! I had been resigned to estrangement always as the too-smart intellectual kid. For the first time in my life, I was "popular."

Each day, our bald teacher, Mr. Adams, would have us watch the Army-McCarthy hearings on a TV monitor. At 9 years old, I had no conception of politics. My parents were Democrats and had voted for Adlai Stevenson in 1952, that's all I knew. I have no idea if Mr. Adams was anti-Communist and pro-Joe McCarthy or giving us a liberal civics lesson. At some time, I became aware that my parents were disgusted by the omnipresence of Roy Cohn in the proceedings. Cohn was bad for the Jews.

In moving from Columbia to Upper Darby, we went from one housing complex to another, though we now had a small park across the street that had an actual baseball diamond. A mile away was a resplendent park, with tall, elegant trees and planted flower banks, which you reached via a stairwell from a narrow opening on the street. I had taken rural West Virginia for granted, so this was the first time I thought consciously about the beauties of nature. Upper Darby was also the first time I'd ever walked into a bakery. The fragrant aroma of lemon tarts just out of the oven!

In Upper Darby, we got our first television set. At last, in 1954. It was a black-and-white Motorola with rabbit ears, and we had it for many years. I recall that day when we slid it out of a cardboard box, placed it on a stand, put in the electric plug and... VOILA! The first program that popped on was *I Remember Mama*, a Scandinavian family melodrama, and it was the middle of a typically schmaltzy episode. For my brother and me, it seemed unequivocally great. Danny and I sampled lots of shows the first weeks, and we quickly had two we rated above all: *The Adventures of Rin Tin Tin* on Fridays and *Your Hit Parade* prime time on Saturday nights. We loved the freckle-faced little boy, Rusty, adopted by the US Cavalry, siccing his dog on hostile Natives: "Yo, Rinty!" We fell hard for Dorothy Collins and Gisele MacKenzie singing in the straightest way imaginable early rock 'n' roll hits. Our mother also approved of Gisele MacKenzie because she played classic violin.

Our uncle Israel, who lived in the Bronx was a Yankee fan, and he took Danny and me to our first major league games in 1954, to Yankee Stadium. He also brought us to the Polo Grounds, where we witnessed Willie Mays hit an inside-the-park home run. But when we moved to Upper Darby, I turned on the radio and heard the lowly Philadelphia A's beat another team 16–4, and their rookie third baseman, Jim Finigan, got three hits. Instantly, the A's were my team and Finigan was my favorite baseball player. I avidly followed Finigan's career for six seasons and several trades, as he went from an all-star hitting .302 to a so-so journeyman as his eyesight faltered. He returned to his hometown of Quincy, Illinois, and became coach of the Quincy College baseball team before he died of a heart attack at age 53. Poor Jim Finigan. His greatest fan confesses to never having visited his holy grave in Quincy's St. Peter's cemetery.

When our family moved to a Philadelphia suburb, I met at age 9 for the first time in my life... Catholics! Playing baseball at the park across from where I lived were Italian-American kids who attended Catholic school. And they casually mocked each other: "Pauly, you dirty Jew!" I had never encountered anti-Semitism before. I'd like to claim that I stood up for my people, asserting, "Watch it, buddy! I'm Jewish." I didn't say anything. As I continued baseball with the Catholic kids, I passed, I guess, for a little Christian.

In fall, 1954, I looked forward to 6th grade, but with one impediment. Danny was entering the same school in kindergarten, and I was supposed to take him there and back. What an embarrassment being associated with a 5-year-old! My worries were not unfounded. On his first day, my brother flipped out about going to his classroom. He ran to the vacant principal's office and locked himself in. Teachers and then administrators begged him to open the door. Danny refused, until our mother was telephoned to come from home. For days after that, she stood outside his classroom, but my brother never had another fit. Instead, he settled in, finding that he was among the best in his kindergarten class at musical chairs.

Entering the 6th grade, some of my popularity rubbed off from 5th grade. Still, it was a good school year. My teacher, Mrs. Brinkerhoff, could be scolding and hot-tempered but I saw through to her wit, warmth, and intelligence. One day, she grabbed my attention by playing a record of a coloratura diva, perhaps Lily Pons, doing some fancy high soprano shtick. I told my mother about it, and she came to school and conspired with my teacher to get me hooked on classical music. I resisted. My only interest was the pop tunes featured on *Your Hit Parade*. What was grand opera next to "Papa Loves Mambo" and "This Old House"?

In fights, I have a lifetime record of 1-0. At the Upper Darby playground where I played baseball, everyone agreed that this one puny kid was the weakest guy. But who were the second and third weakest? One afternoon, I and the other candidate wrestled on the ground before a crowd of our peers. I pinned the wimp's arms, and he was forced to mutter, "Uncle." He was the second weakest, muscular me was the third weakest.

I discovered the erotic pull of the movies staring at a poster of Jane Russell's considerable chest and also becoming aware of blonde Virginia Mayo. In Upper Darby, my lust flowed over to *Creature from the Black Lagoon*. I identified with the Creature's under-water longing as gorgeous Julia Adams, out for an Esther Williams-style swim in the Amazon, floated over. Voyeuristic hot stuff!

At age 10, I went happily by myself in Upper Darby to movie theaters. I was transfixed by the most peculiar of Westerns, *Johnny Guitar*, especially by the unprecedented woman-on-woman gunfight toward the end. I had a film aesthetic that was nicely eclectic. I appreciated *Seven Brides for Seven Brothers* for the athletic dancing and *Oklahoma!* for the heartfelt melodic songs. My other favorite Westerns were *Hondo* and *Shane*. What was more fun than, in *The Naked Jungle*, having millions of soldier ants devour a portly South American sleeping through his guard? More ants: irradiated giant ones. Nothing was more blood curdling than the little girl, the lone survivor of a giant ant attack, screeching "THEM! THEM!"

I also became conscious for the first time of having an all-time favorite film, and it was a very obscure one. *The Little Kidnappers*, which I saw with my cousin, Luba, in New York. It's about two orphan boy brothers with the same 5-year age spread of age as Danny and me. In a plot somewhat reminiscent of *Heidi*, these laddies, Harry and Davey, come to live with their harsh bearded grandfather. But then *The Little Kidnappers* find its own way: the lonely boys want a dog SO badly and I did too. They steal a baby — the funniest baby! — and secretly adopt it. This charming story won my heart. What a challenge for me to try to imitate Harry and Davey's Scottish brogue.

The first film director I was aware of was Alfred Hitchcock, and, because our mother liked his films, we went as a family to *Dial M for Murder*, *Rear Window*, *To Catch a Thief*, and *The Trouble with Harry*. Good memories. On the other hand, there was that mortifying night when my parents took me to see Marilyn Monroe in *River of No Return*. My father was completely uninterested. He snorted through his nose like a horse, loudly clearing his sinuses every few minutes. I cringed each time. "I hate my dad," I thought, certain that others in the audience wanted to gag him and choke him like I did.

None of these movies I cared for meant anything to my biologist father. But Joe had grown up reading Jules Verne novels in France, so, a good day, he brought my brother and me to *20,000 Leagues Under the Sea*. Danny and I were pleased by the final battle with a giant squid: *Moby Dick* for children! Even more, we were won over by a running gag in which Kirk Douglas kept racing his hand over diminutive Peter Lorre's crew cut accompanied by cartoonish soundtrack music. It was so funny that I imitated it at home, sweeping my hand across Danny's noggin.

Each Mother's Day, our impatient mother was forced to stay under the covers while our non-cooking father tried to fry two eggs and make toast so Danny and I could bring her breakfast in bed. I did something far superior for Mother's Day 1955. A friend at school took me to the home of a gypsy-like woman who made jewelry. I bought for my mother a brooch with what I assumed were real emeralds dotting a Bambi-like little deer. My mother loved that sentimental present. She was deeply touched by my effort to get it for her.

When my mother died at 91, we were unnerved at how few possessions she had. But in a drawer, though some of its plastic jewels had fallen off, there was my deer. I claimed it for myself and it's tucked away in my office. I also feel sentimental about it.

Living in a Philadelphia suburb, I became aware of regional food favorites. I have no recall of trying the obvious selection, a Philly cheese steak, but on several occasions I went to a deli and got a hoagie. That's Philly's rendition of a submarine sandwich but somehow a hundred times better. Is it the German-style cold cuts that make it so great? The cherry peppers? The provolone cheese? My other local enjoyment was a highly processed snack wrapped in plastic with a gooey, sugary paste in the middle: a Tastykake. As the radio voiceover informed us: "Tastykake cakes and pies, official sponsor of the Philadelphia Phillies."

I was a remarkably adept door-to-door salesman, going around my Upper Darby neighborhood peddling tins of peanut brittle. It was a UNICEF drive by my 6th grade class, and I was among the best at knocking on doors, explaining earnestly that "Your money goes to the United Nations International Children's Emergency Fund." One woman in the building where I lived was a repeat buyer, not that she cared about peanut brittle. She was lonely and sad, playing melancholic 78 records over and again. As she told me, her son had been killed in the Korean War and, in 1955, she was still in mourning for him. I hope that I was properly empathetic. Or was I only concerned about racking up another sale?

Before coming to Upper Darby, my favorite newspaper comic always had been *Blondie*. But I made a discovery in the *Philadelphia Tribune* of a cartoon strip without any adults ever and which spoke to my 10-year-old self through its self-consciously articulate child cast. I'm talking about Charlie Brown, Lucy, Linus, and the other denizens of *Peanuts*.

No television show has affected me as profoundly as the original three episodes of the Fess Parker-starring *Davy Crockett*. Not for one second did I find fault as Davy killed Indians, palled with white power militarist Andrew Jackson, was voted into Congress as a rifle-toting nativist, and then died among the zealous Americans at the Alamo trying to grab Texas from the Mexicans. Danny and I shared one coonskin cap and owned a complete set of Davy Crockett cards. One morning, I recited to my 6th grade class a multi-versed interminable poem I wrote about the plight of a young baseball player to the tune of "The Ballad of Davy Crockett."

There was the soft, folksy voice on my answering machine a few years back: "Hi, Gerald, this is Fess Parker returning your phone call." Fess Parker! Calling me from his California vineyard! We never connected for the journalism story I was working on, meaning

I never spoke in person to my boyhood hero. And I was not tech-savvy enough to preserve Fess's voice message forever and ever.

I was annoyed in movies by tiresome love scenes and wanted only to get back to the action. Watching *Shane*, I took no notice of Jean Arthur's crush on Alan Ladd. What mattered was Shane's bravado gun fighting. Watching *Them!*, I was incensed that my favorite character, a noble cop, was killed off by the giant ants while the bland couple in love lived on. In 6th grade, my motto was, "I hate girls!" which I declared openly. However, a friend of mine observed me looking often at a petite blonde violinist in our class. "You're in love with Debbie!" he accused me. How I denied it! But, yes, I had a moony crush—the first of my life. Debbie was fresh-faced, freckled, and so very cute.

When I was 10, for the only time in my life I got seriously religious. In Upper Darby, I began attending a Conservative shul and, for about three intense months, I was there with a yarmulke every single Friday night. I was won over by the Hebrew prayers, the joyous singing, especially of "Ein Keloheinu." I was in ecstasy, giddy with the wonderfulness of Judaism. I went to shul alone; I didn't require my secular parents to be there with me. I also signed up for Hebrew school after the regular school day, the first step toward a Bar Mitzvah. However...

My Hebrew teacher was a mediocre little man with bad breath, and our class was crammed into a windowless room. I didn't take to the other students, and I swiftly decided that learning Hebrew was both too hard and purposeless. So what did I really want to do? Play baseball in the afternoons. With my parents, such decisions were mine, so they didn't object when I exchanged Torah and a future Bar Mitzvah for a baseball glove.

Miami Beach

In Summer 1955, we packed up from Upper Darby for Miami Beach, where our father found summer work doing medical research. We moved into a rooming house a few blocks inland from South Beach. The other tenants were all aged Jewish retirees from the North. Danny and I had never been surrounded by so many old people. For kids, it was depressing and claustrophobic, and with no air conditioning, only one fan running on the floor in our tiny apartment in sweltering Southern Florida.

No sooner had we arrived than our oblivious father took us to South Beach in a rainstorm. That's the memory of my brother, Danny, who at 5 learned to swim that stormy day. Joe loved the beach, and his ritual was to go after work and, with his hands hooked on his belly, float blissfully on his back. Unfortunately, it was our mother who was charged with bringing us day after day to the ocean. From those anxious occasions, being there with our non-swimming, hysteric mom, I explain my lifetime aversion to relaxing at the beach. With her weak ankles, she would trip often in the sand. When I'd go into the water up to my chest, she'd be at the shore pleading with me to get out, or begging the lifeguard to dive in and rescue me from drowning.

For entertainment, we'd watch TV in the hotel lobby among the elderly, where literally everyone in the rooming house packed in for the breathtaking episodes of *The 64,000 Dollar Question*. Successful contestants came back from the week before, and, if they answered the questions correctly, doubled their magical money. And after $8,000: the enormous tension—and the audience identification!—when the contestants dramatically entered an isolation booth to be challenged by the toughest questions of all. Who of us, old or young, thought for a moment that all of this was fake?

There were great Jewish delis in Miami Beach in 1955, but we never went to them. As always with my parents, we ate at home every meal, this time in our rooming house flat. Such arrangement might have been bearable except for our refrigerator, which retained from earlier tenants the stench of rotted food. The odor was embedded in the machinery. Our mother cooked whatever was stored in there; and when we bit into it, Danny and I would shudder and protest, "Ugh! Refrigerator smell!!" Our father, Joe, never noticed anything, he just ate away. Laura would stubbornly insist, "There's no smell." She willed herself to believe it. So for one whole summer, I and my brother held our noses as we ate, choking on our mom's home-cooked, stinky meals.

I had become fascinated watching our beloved uncle, Israel, playing pinochle in the park in the Bronx. In Miami Beach, Danny and I learned its rules observing the elderly from New York who shared our rooming house. "Jewish bridge." A special 48-card deck! We obsessively learned, and mastered, the two-handed version. Danny would continue on, playing double-deck pinochle with a friend and his friend's parents into his teens. I've never tried pinochle again since Florida days. It could not be that challenging a game if a 10-year-old and 5-year-old so quickly became skilled.

My mother and I were felled by hay fever in our rooming house flat. I self-medicated by spending afternoons in an air-conditioned movie palace, often seeing the film that was playing several times in a row. Sometimes, Danny was with me. This was the summer that I discovered *The Land of the Pharaohs*. I fell madly in love with this movie. How great to see the pharaoh bringing captive slaves home to Egypt, and throwing enemies of the state into the mouths of eager alligators. How sublime to see the pharaoh's vixen, cheating wife—Joan Collins with a bare midriff—get the punishment she deserved, being trapped inside a pyramid. Buried alive!

Finally, the excruciating headaches. I lay on the couch holding my pained head, sometimes howling, especially after I'd seen a movie. In Miami Beach, the obvious remedy was found: Gerry was badly nearsighted and required glasses!

Columbia again

So much moving! Did our father know when he took a job in Pennsylvania in spring 1954, that we'd be there just a year? In fall 1955, we were back in South Carolina. Our dad returned to the position he had abandoned going north, teaching biology at the adjoining African-American institutions, Benedict College and Allen University. They must have been relieved having him back. I imagine they had trouble attracting Ph.D.s with the salaries so low.

Our parents both signed up for driving instruction. Joe had not been behind a wheel for fifteen years, Laura never. Our mother quit her lessons after having several anxiety attacks, and that was it for being a driver. Our father managed to get his license, bought a 1950 Chevy, but was terrified behind the wheel. When we were all in the car, our mother would shriek at me and my brother, "DON'T TALK!" Our dad was unable to handle anyone muttering anything as he hyperventilated in the driver's seat.

There were a few white faculty members at Benedict, and several came to our new residence, one side of a duplex. A pale Brit with paler glasses impressed my mother because of his degrees from Oxford. I didn't understand it at all then, but these professors had been blacklisted at other universities, labeled as Communists. Our father, however, was certainly no Marxist, just a well-meaning liberal Democrat. He taught at black colleges because he rejected the idea of racial prejudice. However, no faculty of color visited us.

Everyone, black and white, would have been in grave danger if Afri-can-Americans who were not domestics were sighted at our house. Black female college students looked after Danny on several occa-sions, but the neighbors must have thought they were maids.

Our father rescued his old dean from Alderson-Broaddus College and got him a job teaching at Benedict. Earl Vinny and his wife, Alice Vinny, were transplanted New Englanders, Congrega-tionalists, who served tea in the afternoons when we visited them in Columbia. While my parents and the Vinnys conversed, I perused their bookshelves and borrowed works from a new genre for me: war novels and armed services memoirs. I quickly read through *To Hell and Back*, *A Walk in the Sun*, and a handful of other paper-backs, which I loved for the vivid cast of characters in American uniform and for the robust dialogue with lots of cursing.

Our father did invite to our home a Chinese faculty member, Dr. Yee, and he brought as a gift a wrapped box of coconut candies of various flavors and colors: pink, green, yellow. Danny and I gobbled them up and we both vomited after. I have never eaten another coconut candy in my life, and I shudder whenever offered marzipan. It was our worst culinary experience since we both got deadly sick drinking milkshakes in rural Georgia.

Our year-old Motorola TV was breaking down. The vertical hold wasn't working, often flipping the picture on its side. We spent time every day moving nobs in the back of the set trying to right the picture, also constantly adjusting the wobbly rabbit ears so we got decent reception. But it was all worth it for Saturday nights and our continuing favorite program, *Your Hit Parade*.

How gullible was the 8-year-old boy next door? Danny and I messed with him with an elaborate doppelgänger hoax. We pretended to be evil thugs who looked exactly like us named Boogerton and Blackie. We'd threaten the neighbor boy verbally when we were the bad-guy duo, then we'd approach him in the friendliest manner as Danny and Gerry. But there was a limit to teasing. It was essential to keep the boy on our side so he'd invite us to his house. As our family had no roof antenna, we could not tune in to ABC for *Disneyland*. In Fall 1955, we camped out in his living room for two *Disneyland* prequels, "Davy Crockett's Keel-boat Race" and "Davy Crockett and the River Pirates." By popular demand, Fess Parker's Davy had been exhumed from the grave after a February 1955 TV death in "Davy Crockett at the Alamo."

Did playing the thug Blackie get into my brother's head? I have no better explanation for why, as we sat chatting amiably one day on the pavement, Danny punched me hard, giving me a solid black eye. And what of that poor babysitter who, realizing that Danny was bored with her, came up with a game in which he'd hide a ruler while she left the room and then she would try to find it? Was it the spirit of Blackie that led my brother to throw that ruler out of a window, and to sit there smugly while the babysitter searched and searched every room?

Danny and I took full advantage of our 1950s mother, who did every chore in the house. We never washed a dish, swept a floor, took out the trash, cleaned our room. I never even made my bed. Our mother, a good cook by then, would also make different meals for her two sons, her husband, herself. Only our father liked fish; we all ate lamb except our mother. I got what I wanted: frozen shrimp and mini-pizzas and steak. But Laura also made great fried chicken, chili, spaghetti and meatballs, and, Danny's now favorite, hamburgers. Our father in the kitchen could do literally one thing, mix ketchup and mustard in a pot to throw on hot dogs. We called that "Daddy's sauce."

In 1953, my parents had made friends with the family of a ghostly pale, tight-lipped Baptist minister who, the wife admitted to my mother, never bathed. Their boy, Phillip, collected and hid away *Mad* comic books, and he had a complete set from before *Mad* changed formats to *Mad Magazine*. The preacher father discovered the stash and declared them "immoral," and insisted that his son get rid of them. In 1955, Phillip sold me the first 23 comic books for 10 cents each: $2.30 in all. And here's what I so wisely did: sold them to another kid for 25 cents each, for a $3.45 profit. Brilliant. I don't dare imagine what the whole collection would be worth today intact. *Mad* No.1 alone has sold for up to $40,000.

We didn't have a maid, so the people of color I mostly saw in Columbia were domestics waiting by the road and those made by law to sit at the back of the city bus. The latter inequity certainly disturbed me. But as a kid, I fretted more about myself, about that stressful moment when white folks found out that my father taught at Benedict College and Allen University. What he did for work was deemed lower by far than say, garbage collecting, on a par with being a Communist and/or homosexual.

Starting with Philippi in 4th grade, I survived four different schools in four years. I would be 10½ entering 7th grade in Columbia at my fifth school. Up to that moment, I'd been a fairly confident child, especially about my academic abilities. Coming back to South Carolina from Pennsylvania, I didn't anticipate the travails of junior high school.

7th grade

"Hand Junior High! Hand Junior High! We shall show our loyalty. It shall never die." When we sang about our segregated school, we raised our palms on the word "Hand" in an eerily Hitlerian fashion. In fall 1955, I began attending this most unusual of public middle schools. We students were subjects of what seems now a Social Darwinist experiment. We were channeled into 20 sections, highest to lowest, to see how we'd succeed. But our placing was based on what? Elementary school grades? IQ tests for sure, in those Stanford-Binet days. However it was decided, I was put in the highest, elitist of sections, 7–20. Others didn't do as well, descending and descending to the have-nots of 7–1 and 7–2.

Up to this point, I had been complacent about being at the top of my class. I just knew through elementary school that I was among the intelligentsia. But being in 7–20 altered all that. It was culture shock that many of the kids seemed smarter than I was, some much smarter. They were sharper, quicker, knew all the answers, and I did not. The biggest surprise to this 10½ -year-old was that several of the very brightest were girls. Brainy girls? Never before. Even Debbie, my secret crush in 6th grade, was, though a fine violinist, not up to Gerry for smarts. That had been my expectation of females, fairly intelligent at best, but now what I'd believed was completely discredited. I was particularly struck by one 7–20 girl, who was the shortest in the class, also the most bubbly, open, friendliest. And at least twice as intelligent as I! Dandy Barrett. She was at Hand Junior High for only two semesters, moving away to Texas.

Several years ago I traced Dandy. She has several college degrees, one from Vassar, and a distinguished career in theater in Savannah, Georgia. I explained in my e-mail how she had humbled me by being so much brighter than I was. She didn't seem touched or amused at all. Perhaps she saw me as a possible stalker. But time together on Facebook vastly improved things. Dandy now lives near her relatives in Connecticut and has returned to the theater.

It was serendipitous that my seventh-grade homeroom teacher sat me in the back next to L. He was a very odd bird, and the other kids said that he looked like a camel. We bonded instantly over *Mad Magazine* and science-fiction novels. But there were sides to L that I was unsettled by and too inhibited to query him about. I'd heard through the grapevine that he and a friend went around with BB guns killing neighborhood cats. When he went missing one day, L's father and uncle came looking for him at our house. They were fierce and angry, what some would label "white trash."

After high school, L went into the army and I moved north. One day, he appeared at our Pennsylvania home in his uniform. I got the idea that he'd gone AWOL. He was invited to stay over for the night and I watched as he took off his clothes. From his lower neck down, he was coal black with dirt, not having showered for months. That's the last I ever saw of L. I have heard that he moved at one point to Seattle and started a fantasy bookstore, that he moved again to Oklahoma and died young of cancer.

My homeroom teacher at Hand was a self-consciously wacky woman named Miss Craig, who referred to me, in a teasing manner, as "Smeary Peary." She was also our art instructor, and the first semester was revelatory, a serious introduction to the History of Art, emphasis on the Renaissance. But there was a schizophrenic switch in the curriculum second semester, with Miss Craig now teaching us drawing. I panicked. I could not draw at all. I had not improved an iota since I was 3 years old. My grades in art tumbled. Also, I had a mathematics class, which switched midyear to incomprehensible matters like the workings of the stock market. What did my life have to do with Wall Street? My math grades also dropped off. I fell to the lower half of my brilliant 7–20 class and I never recovered. This child "genius" in elementary school was, in junior high, a sad, mediocre student.

My most heartbreaking moment in West Virginia had been when my beloved collie, Laddie, was taken away for barking all night. My father finally set things right in Columbia. We returned from the pound with a half-collie, half-husky, which had been found by a highway with Ohio tags. I was allowed to name him Laddie after my first dog. I had an 11th birthday party, October 30, 1955, and the guests were half-a-dozen boys from my junior high class. As we played touch football on our front lawn, Laddie, off his leash, dashed away. I went immediately on the chase, trailing my new pet for several miles into strange neighborhoods. Miraculously, I grabbed him and brought him home by the collar. A happy ending, definitely, because we had Laddie for many years. But I do feel sorry for the other kids. It was a sour party for them, I would guess, standing about minus a birthday-boy host.

Becoming 11 at Hand, I was too immature to do anything but gawk at the comely popular girls. There was blonde, regular-gal Rita and also well-bred, wealthy Pam, our Betty and Veronica. Michael—handsome, a great student, the best athlete in the class—seemed to float between them. He casually claimed each at different times as his girlfriend. Michael was one of three Jewish students in our 7–20 class; also Susan, who, all the boys noticed, was prematurely bosomy. At some point, she had Michael's eye also. I was jealous of superior Michael. In two years, I witnessed him do only one stupid thing. Someone on the schoolyard tossed a shot put and Michael reached down to cuff it like a softball. The heavy metal rolled painfully over his extended hand. OUCH! I gossiped with my friends about the incident, smirking that "Even Michael is not perfect."

In spring 1956, it was our 7th-grade talent show! Three girls hobbled on stage in heels and white gloves and carrying suitcases and sang, in unison, "Sentimental Journey." They took second place. At my segregated school, the winner was a chubby girl in a polka-dotted Raggedy Ann outfit and blackface doing a "comic" routine as a ditsy "colored" woman. There was a tie for third place, between my diminutive classmate, Dandy, belting out "The Birth of the Blues," and yours truly. The jury rewarded me for a recitation of a very slight, humorous poem called "Jonathan Bing." In saying the words of Bing, I based my goofy voice on that of the marionette, Mortimer Snerd. I was very pleased with my award. Only once after that was I called from the audience to get a prize: at a raffle in high school, I won a pencil sharpener.

Now the minimum age is 17, but South Carolina in the 1950s allowed you behind the wheel at 14. It's absurd, but I took a mandatory driver's education class in junior high. I am trying to recall my teachers at Hand after 65 years. My math instructor, a sharp-tongued, sarcastic sort, was Mrs. Caldwell, whose tight-curled, blue-tinted hair was a style in the 1930s of Hollywood actresses portraying wealthy matrons. Our social studies teacher was young, cute, button-nosed Miss Langford. Almost all of my grades were mediocre except social studies. I responded to Miss Langford's humor, so I did my work to get an A. My only other A was in music. I was a fair singer, but the teacher, Miss Sweringen, rewarded me for being one of four boys willing to be recruited into her girl-heavy junior high choir.

Some of the boys in my seventh-grade class came up with a perverse prank. They composed a mash note supposedly from me and placed it on the desk of the girl they thought the most homely. Poor freckled B, she was quiet and shy and awkward on the baby-fat side. I found a return note on my desk from B proclaiming her love. I was mortified. But instead of going after the boy pranksters, I attacked the girl victim. I sat behind B and stabbed her several times in the back with a mechanical pencil. B didn't turn to look at me. She knew that I didn't love her, and that she'd been cruelly used. Gerry, you vile little bastard. B, I am so so sorry.

It's unlike me to try something to make myself popular. What was my rationale for taking after-school dancing lessons when I was in 7th grade? There I was, the only boy in the class swinging the girls around, learning over four weeks to do "the shag," South Carolina's version of the jitterbug. Our song to dance to, played many times, was Bill Haley and the Comets' "The ABC Boogie": "Learn your ABCs with rhythm and ease!" And where did I apply my new skills? Nowhere. If there was a social gathering, I stood shyly on the perimeter. Instead of dancing, I nervously gobbled whatever party favors were available. Snacks instead of girls.

Judaism

As mentioned, I'd gone through three months of religious ecstasy at a Conservative synagogue in Upper Darby, Pennsylvania. Back to earth at 11 in Columbia, I was OK with my family joining the Reform temple, the Tree of Life, and very OK that we barely attended Friday night services. Instead, I went to Jewish Sunday school, a class of five. There were three girls and the boy who became my best friend, David Dreifus. Neither of us were pious in any way, and neither was especially fond of Rabbi G. There was that Sunday morning when the Rabbi, passing by our class, walked in and slapped David on the face for yawning!

Nominally a believer at age 11, I was already acting like a heretic. A favorite trick was to bring a Bible containing both the New and Old Testament to my Jewish Sunday school class. The teacher would say, "Gerry, read aloud on page 57," and I would open to the New Testament's page 57 and intone, "Jesus spoke to his congregants…." What a belly laugh! Each December, we were asked to exchange Hanukkah presents with another Sunday school student. David and I always chose each other, and then loudly, ostentatiously passed a 50-cent piece back and forth, palm to palm. "Happy Hanukkah, David." He got the coin. "Happy Hanukkah, Gerry." I got my 50 cents back.

I have few memories of our Reform temple, but here's a random one. A kid we'd never seen showed up one week and the word spread that he was on day leave from a local mental hospital. Everyone felt instantly sorry for him, and showered him with applause when he stood wearing a yarmulke in front of the congregation and sang a heart-wrenching rendition of "Oh! My Pa-Pa!" "He's a young Eddie Fisher," that's what the congregants said of him. After the performance, he went back to the mental hospital and was never seen again at the Tree of Life temple.

I made friends with M, the rabbi's son, who was short and very nerdy, with the clammiest hands. We would pump his moist palm and laugh, and he would good-naturedly laugh too.

I thought he'd choose a non-religious life. But he visited me in Boston in the 1980s and he'd become an Orthodox rabbi and Hebraic scholar in Israel, and was married with seven kids! Also, this once awkward, modest boy had become a boor, lecturing me with condescending authority. That's the last I've seen of M, though give him his due. I see on the Internet that he's a retired professor at Ben Gurion University and an author of a set of acclaimed books on women in Judaism.

Playwright Tony Kushner, whose childhood was in Louisiana, insulted his Southern father by calling him "a business Jew." That phrase really strikes home when I think back to my growing up in South Carolina. It was indeed a tight-knit, conservative enclave of "business Jews," interlocked lawyers and doctors and shop owners with family trees sometimes rooted in the 19th-century South. Being non-South Carolinians meant we didn't fit in, and especially with my non-materialist father teaching at black colleges. Worse, we were Jews without money, apartment renters, extremely rare in the well-heeled, propertied Columbia Jewish world.

It was about class. I could not really relate to the wealthy Jewish kids. My two close Jewish friends lived like me in rental apartments, and their dads had humble jobs, one a bookkeeper, the other a door-to-door salesman. With David, I bonded about sports, especially major league baseball, and our reading of science fiction. With Herb, who was a student of David Hume, I learned of lofty intellectual things. Unlike most Jewish South Carolinians, none of us went to law school or medical school or into business. We all became, at different points of our lives, college professors.

We had several uncomfortable Passovers because of the tradition of Jewish soldiers stationed at Fort Jackson invited into local homes. 19-year-old strangers in uniform appeared at our dinner table, and they awkwardly sat by while our mom and dad struggled to make conversation. How quaint I thought our parents were! As for the Pesach service: no Peary really knew much about Judaism. Our introverted father struggled to lead a service, reading the Haggadah in English. He spoke many languages—French, Spanish, Italian, Russian, etc.—but Hebrew was not one of them.

Miami Beach 1956

Our family journeyed to Miami Beach for the second summer in a row so our dad could do medical research. We drove from South Carolina in our 1950 Chevy. We also had our dog, Laddie, along. As our father was so uncomfortable behind the wheel, our trip took three days. On our tight budget, we stayed in the cheapest motels all in one room, sometimes without a TV and, even more cruel, always without a swimming pool.

As I've noted, our father had brought home alligators, and in our future loomed a screeching, biting monkey that lived in a cage in our living room and peed on our floor. In Northern Florida, Joe hit the brakes when he saw a large tortoise on the highway. In a moment, it was a rescue on the floor of the back seat, below where Danny and I sat. As we continued southward, our threatened dog, Laddie, put his back legs up into the rear window. He barked furiously down at the tortoise, the barking going on for hours. Meanwhile, the tortoise erupted with diarrhea. We finally lay the tortoise gently on the side of the road so we could proceed in peace to Miami Beach.

We went a bit upscale, moving up from the rooming house of the prior summer to a small apartment, and just a few blocks from South Beach. Let me insert: there was nothing vaguely fashionable about this neighborhood in 1955, especially in July and August. Instead of the old New York Jews who surrounded us the year before, we had blue-collar New England neighbors. There were two young boys, Davey and Bobby, brothers with crew cuts, who were uncouth and uncultured and who would squeal in bliss whenever sighting a familiar license plate: "Hey, Bwobby, there's a Massachusetts caah!" Danny and I had never heard such weird thick accents before, not in our summer in Cambridge. We quickly decided that the dumbest place you could be from in the world was Boston.

By age 11, I had moved up from being a terrible athlete to becoming an average one. I was desperate to play in Little League, but we arrived in Miami Beach too late for me to try out. Instead, I was assigned, along with the Little League rejects, to a minor league team playing our games in Flamingo Park. Somehow, I was made a pitcher and I could throw one pitch, my attempt at a fastball. One day the best actual Little League pitcher, a redheaded, freckle-faced kid named "Hawkins," no first name, sat in the bleachers and observed our lowly minor league game. I was pitching, and Hawkins was impressed enough to invite me to his home for lunch. What an honor! We walked to his apartment, and nobody was home. No mother to greet us. Instead, Hawkins opened up a can of chili and heated it up for both of us on the stove. Wow! I'd never seen a kid cook; I'd never had chili in my life. Among the greatest meals ever!

Here was another horrible summer of going to the beach with our mother. This got exponentially worse with Laura's Russian parents coming from New York to stay with us. Our grandmother, Babushka, though the sweetest person, was even more hysterical than her daughter. She also couldn't swim, and, with the thickest glasses ever, seemed on a path toward blindness. There was the exasperation of being on a Miami Beach street with Babushka who, I believed, was the slowest walker on earth. It felt like a quarter hour for us to manage one block with our grandmother. One step. Stop. Another step. Stop. AAAAAGH!

Our Miami Beach rental came without a TV set, which meant no compulsive watching, as the summer before, of *The 64,000 Dollar Question*. I must have checked out lots of books from the library. What else was there to do in our small apartment? There was the occasion I brought home a coconut that had fallen in a nearby alley, a day with a screwdriver and a hammer trying to burrow through the fibrous outer husk. My brother, who turned 7 in August, hung a bed sheet over the back of the couch and played underneath in what he called Danny's Adventure Club. For his one-person gathering, he came up with an anthem to be sung to "Ta-Ra-Ra Boom-De-Ay" circus music. His song went something like this: "It's Danny's Adventure Club, It's Danny's Adventure Club, It's Danny's Adventure Club, It's Danny's Adventure Club."

In our neighborhood of Miami Beach there was an old-school burlesque theater and I, 11 years old, would walk by it with heavy breath. What possibly went on in there? Several times when I was without parents, I'd slip to the side of the building and then to the alley around back looking for a place to peek. Like a workingman's pub, there weren't any windows. But out front by the entrance was something truly mind-boggling: glossy photos of several of the strippers with pasties and tassels on their mostly revealed breasts. There is more: Danny reminded me that he and I were Peeping Toms that summer, watching from our bedroom window a couple of naked young women in an apartment house across an alleyway.

Because of the overwhelmingly elderly Jewish population, live vaudeville persisted in Miami Beach. A free show! Several summer nights, our family walked to a park in South Beach where we sat on bleachers and where acts simulating the old golden days were featured on stage. There were stand-up comedians with Jewish jokes and crooners of sentimental tunes, often in Yiddish. One evening a young woman singer went through her repertoire and then turned and addressed the audience: "Hey there, what number should I do next?" Some in the crowd shouted back, "Do 'Hey There!'" and she, feigning surprise and delight at the request, belted out, "Hey there, you with the stars in your eyes…" At 11 years old, I had my eyes opened wide. How manipulative was that singer! How did the audience fall for her cheap trick, and answer her like sheep?

The hottest I got in my life? There was that scorching, humid summer day in Miami Beach, when my family walked from where we lived, around 10th Street, up Collins Avenue to a Howard Johnson's around 20th Street. How did all of us, young and old, make it those ten blocks, baked by the torrid midday sun? I don't know if Howard Johnson's was air-conditioned or only "air-cooled" in those days. Whatever, it was a lifesaver when we pushed through those doors into the cold. Finally, the payoff: 28 flavors of ice cream! Which of my favorites did I go for, pistachio or butter almond? And how, when we'd finished our treats, did we turn around and manage to get home? Our very frugal mother would never have allowed for a taxi.

The first eye-opening, conspicuous wealth I ever saw was in the shape of the luxury hotels of Miami Beach in the summers of 1955–56. I was awed. Our father never had the tiniest interest in anything material, so this stuff meant nothing to him. Our mother was much more impressed, as she would be later in life by those who were, in her phrase, "big millionaires." We looked at the fabulously glamorous Fontainebleau from afar, but the almost-as-glamorous Eden Roc had something in place for gawking outsiders. It was an ice cream parlor on the side of the hotel, and there my family went once for what Danny and I embraced as the ultimate in luxury: an ice cream sundae heaped a half-foot high with an ostentatious skyscraper of whipped cream. And a maraschino cherry on top.

In March 2004, Amy and I had a honeymoon in Miami Beach. I would have liked to find where the Peary family had lived in the 1950, but one faded Art Deco building looked like every other. We checked out trendy South Beach, which had no resemblance to the mundane place where I swam in my childhood. To venture where I'd never been before, I insisted we have supper at the Fontainebleau. The mighty had crumbled, as we dined at painful expense on the most insipid, uninspired tourist food.

I had arrived in Miami Beach in 1956 with *Rebel Without a Cause* as my new favorite film. I couldn't get enough viewings of that alienated teen trio of James Dean, Sal Mineo, and Natalie Wood. But *Rebel* fell to an honorable second place with my viewings, on four Florida afternoons in a row, of the John Wayne-starring Western, *The Searchers.* Danny, equally impressed, came along for several of the movie screenings. The director, John Ford, would become my favorite filmmaker, and I would talk of *The Searchers* in reverent intellectual terms, as a modern *King Lear* and as having an unconscious Marxist structure. But at ages 11 and 7, my brother and I had never seen anything as troubling and intense as when little Debbie, a child Danny's age, was captured by Indians in full war paint.

It is in the record books, a truly historic night, August 7, 1956: the largest gathering ever for a minor league baseball game. There were 57,000 strong, and three of our family were among the crowd. For Danny's seventh birthday, we got our father to bring us to this game played at the Orange Bowl. We saw the Triple-A Miami Marlins take the field on an evening with a gala variety show featuring Cab Calloway singing "Minnie the Moocher" and the all-female band of Ina Ray Hutton. That was great entertainment, yet most special was a gala appearance in the game by Satchel Paige, the truly fabled ex-Negro League superstar. Danny remembers him arriving by helicopter and sitting in a rocking chair on the mound. Paige not only pitched and won for Miami but, even more delightful, hit a double and ran the bases. At age 50!

9th Grade

I was back at Hand Junior High School, where the shaky Darwinian experiment that had started in 7th grade went even further. Those of us who had been assigned to the highest section, 7–20, were now deemed worthy to skip 8th grade altogether and move straight to 9th grade. To 9–20. Several students in my class dropped out of the experiment. Was this the right idea for me to buy into it? I had already skipped 3rd grade, and now I would be entering 9th grade several months before my 12th birthday. Was I screwing myself up forever, as I would graduate high school at 15 (and, potentially, college at 19)? To this day, the jury is still out.

Though I'd mostly been a cooperative student, in 9th grade I was changing, beginning to act up. In biology class, I was less interested in dissecting a frog than squirting formaldehyde onto my lab partner. When we were required to submit a project to our schoolwide junior high science fair, mine was the laziest: a couple of rocks, some clumps of grass, and a turtle put into a see-through bread box. A "balanced terrarium." Here was a flagrantly cynical way to separate myself from my biology professor father. I did make some kind of amends by, at one point in biology, getting caught up by the science experiments of the Augustinian friar, Gregor Mendel. For an assignment, I drew and colored an elaborate version of his pea-plant genetic charts. I was pleased to show these to my father, and he was very proud of me, the rarest occasion when we were on the same page about anything.

How even now can I process that, in a school assembly show at Hand in 1956, I, 12 years old, took part in a two-person blackface routine? My parents were surely not aware of it. I assume a teacher thought it up, but I don't think I was coerced. A classmate, Ray, and I strolled out on stage in coveralls and our faces painted black, in minstrel show fashion. I still remember our "Negro" lines. Ray said, "I sho' am tired." I said, "I tired too!" Ray said, "I twice as tired as you is because I twice as tall as you is." And we turned and walked offstage. That was it.

At the 50th anniversary of my graduating high school class, another student who had been in the auditorium that day drilled me about it. A half century later, he still remembered the discomfort of watching. I sheepishly shrugged. I had no explanation for the most overtly racist moment of my long life.

Our 7–20 class was supposed to have the highest IQs at Hand Junior High but our boys touch football team was the worst, losing to other classes every single time. When we got to 9th grade and became 9–20, there could only be improvement. We actually won one game, thanks a bit to me. The score was tied, we were on the goal line, I stumbled and turned around and a five-yard pass fell into my arms. Touchdown! Just to make sure my pigskin achievement was immortalized, I went over to the cub reporter covering the game and pushed her to take down my name. My finest moment in sports came the next morning over the school's PA system. Our principal, in his daily report on football intersquad games, announced the score of our victory and said, "The stars for 9–20 were… and… and GERALD PEARY!" Life can't improve on that.

"Would you join my Boy Scout troop so I can win a free compass?" asked Ned, my classmate. I went to one meeting, was given the Boy Scout Handbook to study. Then I accompanied Ned's troop on a day hike into the South Carolina woods. After several miles, the boys dropped their packs and built a campfire from scratch. They cooked a lunch over it, hamburgers in a Scout frying pan or hot dogs on a stick. I'd brought from home a can of spaghetti and meatballs. I opened it and ate it cold. A few days later, I dropped out of the Boy Scouts, after making sure that Ned got his precious compass.

I hid in my room when my mother shouted up the stairs, "Gerry, come down and watch! It's a Leonard Bernstein's Young People's Concert on TV!" However, I was won over, enraptured, when a violinist, Rubinoff (one name), came to our school for a solo performance of his flamboyant shtick. When his concert ended, I boldly walked up to thank him. He suggested I should hear him play in the evening at a new Columbia nightclub. Much complimented, I persuaded my thrifty family to buy tickets, including one for Danny, 8. When had the Pearys ever been to a nightclub? Where we were seated by the hostess had, I remember, a white tablecloth. Rubinoff was just stupendous, including the uncanny imitation on his violin of the sound of a bumblebee. He even called me up on the stage and serenaded me! He claimed to be playing on a $100,000 Stradivarius and that he'd given concerts at the White House. Who was I to doubt the great Rubinoff?

Wikipedia has confirmed that his claims were true. And he had a first name: David.

My allowance was $1 a week when I was 12 years old, and I spent it almost always in the same way. I would take a bus into downtown Columbia (25 cents round trip), buy a paperback novel (25 or 35 cents) at the Capitol, the city's only newsstand, and see a movie (15–25 cents). One day, I had a sly, ingenious idea of how to get some spent money refunded. I saw a film beginning to end I'd paid to see. The second time it began, I stood and shouted across the theater the name of my friend, "DAVID!!!!!" Promptly, two ushers came down the aisle, took me by the arms and pulled me outside. Exactly my plan. So I said to them, "I want my money back for missing the movie." They shook their heads at my arrogance and stupidity. They left me standing on the sidewalk. Foiled!

I was a kid lucky to be growing up among the radiated insects, flying saucers, and creatures from deep space of 1950s American science-fiction films. Often, I would meet my friend David at a Columbia downtown theater for a sci-fi or horror film. One Saturday, I couldn't make it until the second showing of the horror movie, *Curucu, Beast of the Amazon.* As I paid and walked in with anticipation, David exited the first screening and blurted out, "The Curucu isn't really a monster. It's a man dressed as a monster!" I went in anyway, and, sure enough, the scourge of the Amazon was revealed to be a disguised Brazilian native.

65 years later, David apologized in an e-mail for his Curucu *spoiler.*

David and I, devoted sci-fi readers, spent money almost every week on the newest paperbacks. Quickly, three writers moved to the top of our reading list. We liked Ray Bradbury for his poetic writing in *The Martian Chronicles* and the gothic *The October Country*; Richard Matheson for his frightening end-of-the-world *I Am Legend* and for his philosophic masterpiece, *The Shrinking Man*; and the far less known Robert Sheckley, for his great short story collections.

Flash ahead to David and me at 15. We were in New York City and found Sheckley's address in the telephone book. Unannounced, we appeared at his West Village apartment and buzzed his doorbell. His wife opened up, looked us over, two eager nerds. She said, "Sorry, my husband isn't home." Perhaps true. Or maybe, as David and I have long suspected, our favorite author was hiding in the next room.

An extra treat of the sci-fi movies I feasted on as a kid were the female co-stars. Besides Julia Adams, bosomy and in short shorts in *Creature from the Black Lagoon*, there was Anne Francis, so cute and blonde prancing about barefoot in *Forbidden Planet*. And all those large-breasted women hanging out of their blouses like low-lying fruit in *The Horror of Dracula*.

What did Danny and I buy as gifts for our mom? My brother remembers us once getting her a slip. Strange! Laura knew we couldn't afford expensive presents, but she definitely wanted birthday and Mother's Day cards with poetry provided by Hallmark. The more sentimental the poems, the more prominent pictures of flowers on the cards, the more our mother loved them. Celebrating our father was harder, as Joe had no wants except having his family around him. He wouldn't want to be taken somewhere on his birthday. He didn't notice what clothes he was wearing, and the only reading he did was the newspaper and science periodicals. How many times over the years could we give him a necktie or a new wallet? Not that he ever complained!

Our father could not cook a hot dog or make toast, and he never shopped for food. So what propelled him one day to arrive home with a ripe limburger cheese, something he'd enjoyed when a child in Europe? Our mother went into literal hysterics at the rancid smell. And I, who'd never tried anything beyond Kraft's American and Swiss cheese, joined her in fleeing to an upstairs bedroom, shutting a door to the hideous aroma. My memory ends here, but our father surely backed down and flushed his beloved limburger down the toilet.

I would go to my friend Herb's apartment several times a week for exactly the same supper from his mother. It was a hamburger on a bun and what we called "a little salad" in a side bowl, with iceberg lettuce and a tomato slice and Wishbone French Dressing. I was more than OK with this dinner. Herb's family had very little money so, in 1956, they could afford for Herb only the smallest Bar Mitzvah at Columbia's Orthodox shul. I was one of the few guests. When the Bar Mitzvah concluded, there was no reception. His mother handed Herb a dollar, and the two of us took a bus downtown and he treated me to a 25 cent screening of Cecil B. De Mille's *The Ten Commandments*.

At age 12, I would put in hours on the telephone with David gossiping about the students at our junior high or Jewish temple, or chatting on about Major League baseball. Most often we were absorbed in the latest rankings on our Ugly List, and what unfortunate persons had risen to the top five. The Ugly List was constituted of the most disgusting-looking, *Mad Magazine*-like grotesques whom we sighted as we walked about Columbia. For a long time, nobody could be homelier, more revolting than the woman we saw hobbling about town and called The Pig Lady. But one day, we looked up into the window of a local bus at a big-eared, slow-eyed buffoon with his tongue hanging low out his mouth. We had an all-time winner. For several years, we little snobs made cruel jokes about—Number One on The Ugly List!—the sorrowful Man on the Bus.

The lovely head librarian at the Columbia Public Library allowed me to check out books at age 12 from the adult section. I immediately sought out novels with dirty words and sex scenes. I brought William Saroyan's *My Name is Aram* to my 9th grade class, and my friends bookmarked a certain page and sent it around to all the girls. Would they blush at the word "whore"? Meanwhile, I'd purchased a 50 cents paperback of Grace Metalious's *Peyton Place*, which, the cover promised, would "lift the lid off a respectable New England town." I telephoned Herb and read him aloud the most obscene passages. The best was when a loose teenager, Betty Anderson, asked Rodney Harrington if it was "good and hard." When Rodney acknowledged that he was ready to go, Betty turned on him, "Well, go stick it in Allison MacKenzie!" Hot!

Because our family still could not afford a roof antenna, we continued in 1956–57 with the frustration of a TV with only one station, the NBC affiliate. That meant we were not privy to such popular programs as *Alfred Hitchcock Presents*, *Perry Mason*, and *Gunsmoke* on CBS, *The Danny Thomas Show, Maverick,* and *The Adventures of Ozzie and Harriet* on ABC. That meant Danny and I were left out of conversations at school when our classmates raved about their favorites. I would stand there silent. How could I explain to my junior high peers, "Sorry, we're too poor to have an outdoors antenna"?

Fortunately, the channel available on our television was superb. NBC! Danny and I continued with our perennial favorite, *Your Hit Parade*, but we had a new love, the utopian family drama of *Father Knows Best*. Then there was *Caesar's Hour*—Sid Caesar, Nanette Fabray, Carl Reiner, Howard Morris—the greatest sketch comedy ever. As for quiz programs, I have never been as absorbed in my life, in a constant sweat, as when watching *Twenty-One*. (Yes, it proved a fraud, Charles Van Doren and all that.) Finally, I tasted the avant-garde with *The Steve Allen Show*, featuring progressive jazz artists plus the conceptual comedy of Don Knotts, Bill Dana, Louis Nye.

In 1956, a blue-collar family of four moved into the apartment next to ours in the duplex on Waccamaw Avenue. Extremely unusual for South Carolina, they were Catholic and Polish-American: the W family. They were also big-hearted, informal, and, a key to amicable relations, didn't give a hoot that our father taught at black colleges. The younger W son, Jimmy, 10, was very sweet but a little slow, and he bonded with Danny, 7. The older, Peter, was 14, and he was terrifically smart. I, turned 12, was flattered to be company to this brash, funny, non-conformist. One day, we took a bus into town to see a movie, and, whenever any male on the ride put a hand into his pants pocket, witty Peter would point a finger and shout out, "Pocket pool!"

I thought I was invited for dinner before Peter and I went to a movie. Instead, Mrs. W whisked us into her car and stopped by a drive-in restaurant for a takeout of two cheeseburgers in a paper bag. When we got to the theater, she handed Peter the bag with no explanation. He bought our tickets, we sat down, and the film began. It was 7pm by then, way past our family's 6 o'clock suppertime. I felt I was starving. Were both cheeseburgers just for privileged Peter? I was too timid to ask. My poor barren stomach! Maybe at 7:30, Peter casually reached into the bag. His hand emerged with a cheeseburger for him and then—yes!—the other for me. I wolfed mine down, the best damned burger of my whole life.

After a few months as great neighbors, the W family vanished overnight without a goodbye. We wondered if they'd run out on their rent. I also pondered for many years what happened to Peter, whom I've not seen since 1957. I investigated him on Wikipedia. He became a mathematics professor, and the writer of a popular science-fiction novel which I read, with a Robert Heinlein-like conservative bent. From what I can ascertain, he's living in Northern Florida and, in his late seventies, is some kind of rightist guru.

Almost everyone jokes that they can't imagine their parents having sex. Even more true with my parents. They called each other

"Darling," and Joe would kiss Laura affectionately on the top of her head. But neither was ever caught by me or my brother in an erotic moment. Neither cursed, neither ever made an off-color remark, neither ever flirted with anyone. I didn't feel repression because lasciviousness just wasn't in their brains or loins. When I was 12 and 13, it was time for a talk about what was called in the 1950s "the birds and the bees." The Facts of Life were never brought up by my parents. It would have never occurred to them to have this discussion. When I was 16, my father found my stash of hidden raunchy magazines. He just turned and silently walked away. He had no way to process my sexual desires.

How on earth was I one of the four students on a panel on dating when I was 12 years old and in the 9th grade? Was I hand-picked by the teachers? Or did I up and volunteer? If the latter, that was a most brazen thing to do considering that I'd never vaguely been on a date. Our gang of four sat behind a table in the school auditorium, and the bleachers were filled up with 7th, 8th, and 9th graders. I only remember one thing I said, when asked by the moderator about one's perfect date. "Well," I noted, "first of all it should be a girl." The crowd roared, it really did, at my comical riposte.

At age 12, I could be a little show-off. We made a second visit to the nightclub where we'd seen the violinist, Rubinoff. The featured performer, a pop singer, called me up from the table where our family sat and—part of her nightly routine with a youngster?—crooned a love song to me. I grabbed the spotlight by crossing my arms in a coy fashion and then throwing them in her direction as if rejecting her. The adult audience laughed heartily, my brother was nauseated at my acting up. After the show, I dragged our parents backstage for an autographed picture. Danny says it was the first glossy photograph he ever saw. But the signed photo is lost, and neither of us have an inkling of the singer's identity.

What a parade in downtown Columbia! Waving to everyone from a float was South Carolina's first Miss America, blonde, white-gloved Marian McKight. She had captured the title with, in the talent section, a spot-on Marilyn Monroe imitation. Danny and I loved her, watching her often as a celebrity on local TV. But the prime excitement for us in the parade were the guest appearances of actors Duncan Renaldo and Leo Carrillo, Cisco and Pancho on TV's Mexican cowboy series, *The Cisco Kid*. As they greeted the crowds on horseback, their horses, Diablo and Loco, pooped all over Columbia's Main Street.

It never occurred to our parents to censor what we watched. And so it was that Danny at 7 and I at 12 sat before our television absorbed in *The Gillette Cavalcade of Sports*, a euphemism for the Friday night fights. Our favorite boxers were all African-Americans. Clean-cut, nice-guy Floyd Patterson, heavyweight champ; that lean machine of repeat knockouts, Sugar Ray Robinson; and Tommy "Hurricane" Jackson, a wild-ass anarchist who walked fearlessly into his opponent's punches.

Unrepentant boxing fans into the early 1960s, we witnessed from our den two televised murders: Emile Griffith killing Benny "Kid" Paret and Sugar Ramos killing Davey Moore. We also read in the newspaper that "Hurricane" Jackson, after too many bouts of being pummeled, was shining shoes in Harlem.

It was a startling moment of TV, seeing at age 10 Baron Leone in a leopard skin, his wild hair down his back, tossing opponents around the wrestling ring. Danny and I became enamored of the disparate star performers: Abe Jacobs, the kindly, boring Jewish champ; Ricki Starr, proudly effeminate in ballet slippers; the foul and awful Australian tag-team, the Kangaroos. I once saw Haystacks Calhoun, all 300 pounds of him in coveralls and barefoot, walking down a street in Columbia, a woman under each pillowy arm. But was the sport real or fake? My friend David had heard that a wrestler who supposedly had broken his leg in a bout was sighted on a train without a cast. I guess I didn't really care if it was all an elaborate act. For a birthday, I made our father take me to see it live, a night that good-guy Chief Don Eagle was the headliner. As wrestlers got punched out, slammed to the mat, Joe sat there unmoved. As with anything not involving science, he passively watched and occasionally nodded off.

I have no explanation for why Danny and I could sit with our mother for a whole hour each week of *The Lawrence Welk Show*. Was it a crush I had on one of the Lennon Sisters? Still addicted to *Your Hit Parade*, I was growing up with conventional white boy's taste. My first record purchase was the double-sided Perry Como hit, "Hot Diggity" and "Jukebox Baby." What I played the most were treasured LPs of Pat Boone and Doris Day. But listening to a jukebox in summer 1957, I had my insides ripped up by the primal African-American screeching of Little Richard. The road from "Long Tall Sally" and "Tutti Frutti" led, delightfully, to Chuck Berry, Fats Domino, and the Coasters. Still, I had a toe in white schmaltz. My first Elvis purchase was not "Heartbreak Hotel" or "Hound Dog" but an EP featuring "Old Shep," a cloying C&W song about a dying dog. I would listen to it over and again, melodramatically holding back tears as I lay on my pillow.

At 12 I bought a paperback novel called *The Catcher in the Rye*. I'd never heard of it, but, like countless other boy readers, I was dazzled and hooked by J.D. Salinger. I totally related to Holden and his loathing of phonies. God, I hated them too! It was in the middle of Leon Uris's *Battle Cry*, a sticky lovemaking episode, when I had a different epiphany that "This is really bad writing." After that, I steered away from war novels and even my beloved science fiction. I pledged to read only what I deemed "real books." And so began an obsession with John Steinbeck. I was smitten with Lennie and the rabbits in *Of Mice and Men* and then plowed through about ten Steinbeck paperbacks in a row. When I visited New York, I checked the Manhattan White Pages and there was J. E. Steinbeck. Surely, him! I lifted the receiver, but then I froze. I hung up. I was just too chicken to dial my favorite writer in the whole world.

I can say it now: my grotesque middle name is Mozart. Not the composer. When I was born, a rabbi, recently from Europe, had assured my immigrant parents that was the correct English for the Ten Commandments guy: Mozart and the Burning Bush! When I became cognizant of my horrible name, I hid it from the world. Nobody but my family knew. Until... May 1957. Just before the end of the school year, my homeroom teacher passed out a mimeographed list of all her students and their telephone numbers. Here's the rub: she included everyone's middle names. The students began reading aloud the handout and chuckling. "Gussie!" they said, and all pointed to a blushing Carol. And then the whole room in chorus uttered a single word: "MOZART!" And they looked gleefully my way. I was outed! For a pitiless last week of 9th grade, my classmates addressed me as "Mozart" as many times as they could during the school day. I couldn't have felt more soiled and shamed. I don't think I contemplated suicide, but summer mercifully arrived.

Relatives

About 1957, our mother's sister, Paula, and her husband, Abe, asked our parents to assist them in leaving Israel, where they had emigrated from Romania. They wanted to come to America and qualify for citizenry. The proper strategy was to request an influential representative in Washington to write a letter of support to U.S. Immigration. But what would be the response of avowed segregationist Olin D. Johnston, our veteran South Carolina senator? I remember our father's anguish in petitioning him. But to our astonishment, Johnston's office wrote back that they would be pleased to provide the needed documents. Paula and Abe arrived in the United States and, through a Romanian friend already in the building, got an apartment in New York at 215 West 88th St. In Columbia, Laura and Paula were united for the first time since our mother left Romania in 1941. Paula bonded with Danny by singing "Love Me Tender" and saying she was an Elvis fan.

Uncle Abe had been a high-powered lawyer in Bucharest with, our mother bragged, "a dozen secretaries." In a famous litigation, he represented the company of a Romanian liner that sank with many passengers drowning. Still, when he and Paula wanted to leave for Israel, Abe was required, he said, to get the signatures of ten Christians attesting to his good character. Systemic anti-Semitism under Communist rule. In the U.S., Abe started over. At age 50, he was accepted at NYU law school to get his American certification, and he graduated first in his class. Soon, he was a corporate lawyer again, and a successful one. Having no children, he urged me, his nephew, to think of a law career so I could someday join his firm. I pledged I'd do that, not knowing that the worlds of the arts and academia would derail my mercenary plan.

Our mother's parents only spoke their native Russian living in Bucharest. Paula and Abe, the next generation, conversed in Romanian. When Danny and I visited them, we were often met by their *nouveau riche* Romanian-Jewish friends. The men left little impression. We were turned off by their flamboyant wives wearing shiny gold jewelry and with too much rouge and mascara, looking like fading Elizabeth Taylors. There were several with bulging eyes and sagging necks whom Danny and I labeled "the frog ladies."

In the 1950s, all four of our grandparents were living in New York City. Our mother's parents made the rent by taking in tenants in their apartment on West 95th Street. I remember Steve and George, taxi drivers, who had small rooms there. When our family visited from South Carolina, the four of us had to sleep in the living room on two cots. Our paternal grandfather, Sam, a lawyer in Europe, was now a diamond salesman in the USA with rich clientele. I don't know that our two grandmothers ever met, having nothing in common, and our paternal grandmother, Dussya, being a consummate snob.

Our father's divorced parents, Sam and Dussya, remained sort of friends in the USA. But Dussya continued to be impossibly quarrelsome, alienating everybody with rudeness and coldness. She fought in America even with Marc Chagall, Sam's boyhood pal from White Russia, and ended everybody's friendship. I have been told that there is a small painting somewhere on earth by Chagall of our grandfather, but, sadly, who knows where?

I don't think we were upset when our grandmother moved back to France in the 1960s. She should be fine there. She was the co-owner with my grandfather of a cozy apartment which, rare for Paris, had a lift. But it was the era of the Algerian War, and there was a day when the Algerians threatened to bomb France by air. Papasha was visiting us at the time. I watched him closely to see if he was anxious, but he appeared unconcerned about either the fate of Paris or that of his ex-wife.

What was her fate? Several years after, a dire telegram from the U.S. Consulate in France came to our father. His mother, our grandmother, had been found sleeping on park benches. Dussya had become a shopping bag lady! She died soon after in a Paris hospital. I have no knowledge if she was cremated or of her burial whereabouts.

Sam, my Papasha, was a lover of night life, as comfortable out and about in the world as his son, our introverted dad, Joe, was a stay-at-home. Sam would meet friends and colleagues at his favorite Manhattan restaurant table, where he lingered many evenings doing his business papers and sipping beer in a glass. Several nights, I met him there as a teenager, so impressed by his enjoyment of life. He was a spiffy dresser and, a compact 5'2", considered himself a ladies' man. I once saw him bring flowers to a lovely singer standing high above him on the stage. Did she even know him? She had to squat clumsily, get down on her knees, to claim her bouquet from this flirtatious little man.

When we later lived in New Jersey, our Papasha took Danny, age 11, to the Miss America pageant with Bert Parks. They arrived in Atlantic City for the preliminary "night before," and saw the entire show, including the young ladies parading on stage in their swimsuits. But Sam was completely surprised that he and Danny could not just come in without a ticket for the final night of the competition. They were stopped from entering. Our grandfather was not defeated. He and my brother watched *Miss America* with enjoyment on a TV in their Atlantic City hotel lobby. When he was once in a New Jersey hospital, Papasha confided to me at his bedside, "I told the nurse she was BB. Not Brigitte Bardot. She is beautiful and bountiful!"

When I saw him in New York, Papasha would call for taxis by shouting out "Yoo-hoo!" I was embarrassed, and yet the cabs would somehow stop. He never ceased in the USA being a Parisian dandy. When visiting us, he would take over our only bathroom for a whole hour for his "toilette," treating himself to a sensuous hot shower and then a slow shave and a dabbing on of cologne. As in France, he took long walks, he called them "constitutionals," and we once intercepted him as he blithely began his stroll through our neighborhood in slippers and a bathrobe.

Sam had not been particularly kind to my father when Joe was growing up, but my Papasha always adored me. He'd sent me jeweled postcards of Paris landmarks when I was 7 and 8 and, when I was in college, he agreed to ship me from France banned-in-the-USA Henry Miller novels. With the package containing the Olympia Press editions of Tropic of Cancer *and* Tropic of Capricorn, *Sam included a gentlemanly note: "Personally, I prefer Mark Twain."*

As for our mother's parents: Our grandfather, Djedushka, was stiff, old, in his sixties, and didn't communicate much with anyone. We felt pretty neutral about him, giving all our attention to our grandmother. Somehow she and I conversed, even if Babushka grasped twenty English words and I knew ten Russian ones. Not formally educated, she was a lover of Tolstoy and Pushkin. With our mother translating the Russian, our grandmother offered her favorite literary anecdote. Pushkin was on his horse. Someone on foot below ridiculed him, accusing the famous writer of riding in a conceited way, like a captain commanding his ship. Whereby, Pushkin held up the tail of his stallion and said, "Would you like to enter my cabin?"

A warm, caring woman, our big-waisted Babushka. In her mid-80s, she was talking with affection about her beloved grandchildren, me and Danny, the moment that she fell to the floor and died instantly of a heart attack.

Our mom's older sister, Paula, twice married, was a feisty presence who lived to 98. She was the only woman in our family who was not fearful of water. On a family gathering, she and I swam together in Walden Pond. When I visited New York, she always prepared for me rare roast beef, and, for Passover, she made gefilte fish from scratch, combining pollock and whitefish.

In 1960, our mother's youngest sister, Tania, her husband, Sylviu, and their son, Marc, became the last family members to make the trek from Romania to Israel to America and New York. Paula and Tania lived in the same building on West 88th Street, NY, and they were seamstresses together. Their clientele were rich, lonely Jewish ladies who would stay the afternoon slowly having their clothes altered while everyone spoke in Romanian. Often, the ladies would decide their outfits weren't worth the trouble to fix and they would just leave them with my aunts. Though neither Paula nor Tania went anywhere fancier than a grocery store, they had closets full of Paris-designed couture.

In later days, Paula was the sole relative to challenge our mother, exasperated by Laura's bragging and sometimes dubious and often repeated stories. They bickered for years. Tania was the quietest, gentlest, and by far the most modest of the three Chaitan sisters, and she tried to keep the peace between Paula and Laura. Actually, she adored Laura and told me, "Your mother is a wonderful person." Always patient, she listened to my mother gab on and on in their almost daily phone calls. Whatever did they talk about, since often neither had left their apartments since their last conversation?

Abe, Paula's husband, was the only religious person in our whole family. He would don his yarmulke and go alone to pray in an Orthodox synagogue. And he would host long and boring formal Passover services for the entire family. As Abe was a reserved man, I would struggle for conversation as he sat behind a magnificent cherry desk lined with law books. At the time I was an anti-war student protester, he became a Democrat for Nixon.

The most vivid memory Danny and I have of Abe was when he took us for a walk one day in Central Park with our cousin D, whose Jewish family had become Christian Scientists. In a sudden storm, there was a torrid explosion of thunder. Stupidly, we ducked under a tree. Two people very close by were killed by lightning when they took refuge under another tree. From fifty yards away, we saw medics and the bodies on the ground. I remember wondering irrationally if D was somehow marked by this moment when a few years later he died of AIDS.

As a corporate lawyer, Abe became the only wealthy person in our family. But an uncanny mystery happened that would take a Sherlock Holmes to solve: our uncle, seemingly in excellent health, was discovered at his law firm dead in his sixties of a heart attack. Was this caused by a sudden overwhelming anxiety in his life? Had he been bribed for some indiscretion? Abe left no money to his wife Paula: his bank accounts were all wiped out. Inside the vault in his law office was only one item: a tiny photo of my brother, Danny.

10th Grade

On paper, I was a precocious lad, entering 10th grade in fall 1957 before my 13th birthday. But at Dreher High School, I continued my junior high downward path. B- and C+ grades were typical, as I only perked up and worked hard when I loved the teacher. Hardly ever. Ironically, this mediocre student had no tolerance or compassion for those I deemed mediocrities standing before me in the classroom. Simply, I wouldn't cooperate. I would not do the homework. I would get zeroes on quizzes, being totally unprepared. I did have an amusing social studies instructor in 10th grade and an enthusiastic psychology teacher in 12th grade. That was it, my only two As in three years of high school.

What did my mom and dad say about this? Oddly, for Jewish parents, not much at all. An occasional reminder from my mother about how smart I was, how I could accomplish so much. But Laura and Joe were numb about what to do. They realized, sadly, that they had little influence on my obstinate behavior. As for the actual 10th grade classes: why did I need plane geometry? And chemistry also alienated me by its absolute uselessness, plus the teacher, prematurely bald, was a boor with lethal BO. And a weirdo. Somehow, he didn't get in trouble with the school administration when he sent the girls out in the hallway one day so he could tell us boys a couple of dirty jokes.

Months of my sophomore English class were taken up diagramming sentences, which I concede was a worthwhile discipline. But in surveying American literature, the class went awry with florid verse from 19th-century Southerners such as William

Cullen Bryant and Sidney Lanier. The selections of Whitman were, of course, not his queer erotic poems. And we were given the lightest of Emily Dickinson, so I mistook her for a sentimental poet. I walked around mocking her, reciting in a sarcastic voice, "I'll tell you how the sun rose/a ribbon at a time." Every single writer we studied was white, Dickinson was the only woman, and nobody, teacher nor student, thought about it in 1957 or questioned the canon.

I, the adult, am a straight shooter befuddled by head games and turned off by anything involving disguises, including costume parties and Halloween. It's hard for me to reconcile the 13-year-old trickster version of me, who popped up both at school and away from it. I got off on prank phone calls and utilizing funny voices. One day when David was visiting, I located a Mrs. Pigg in the Columbia White Pages. I dialed her, she answered, and I (camouflaged voice) said, "Mrs. Pigg? How are all the little Piggs?" Ha-ha! I hung up, with David and I much amused by my cleverness.

At Dreher, any substitute teacher should beware if I was in their class. When he or she turned to write on the blackboard, I'd lead my classmates in "accidentally" knocking our heavy books to the ground. Also, I would coax someone nearby to switch our names, and, starting with roll call, I would respond loudly and often with my adopted appellative, as the other students giggled at my daring. Oddly, my favorite instructor of all was a frequent substitute, a bouncy, charismatic woman from Brazil whose exotic accent and excitement about practically everything won me over. When she took over my class, no tricks and I answered properly to "Gerry."

My most elaborate pranking, and the most insensitive, involved my Beginning Spanish instructor. For the first months, I was absorbed learning a new language: "Picaro es un burro!" But in mid-November my teacher got married, and I blamed that on his becoming complacent, lazy in the classroom. I was angry and wanted revenge. I came to class early one day so I could flip all the desks around, facing toward the back. The students took their seats the way I'd arranged them. The teacher arrived and, without losing his cool, suggested that everyone turn chairs to the front, which they did.

OK, what next? The following day before class, I had the stronger boys hoist my desk atop a huge cupboard at the front of the room. Then I was boosted up. The teacher came in to me sitting at my desk 7 feet in the air. He chose to ignore me and conduct the class as usual. But I made stupid faces, threw down spitballs, and made such a nuisance that he had to stop his instructing. He ordered me to lower my desk to the others, and then climb down. Kindly, he didn't expel me or even send me to the principal's office. But I remained petulant, refusing to put in any effort. I got a C for the rest of the school year. In 11th grade, as we were required to take a foreign language, I switched from Spanish to Beginning French.

I was not the wisest in picking other students to admire. There was Branwell, from a well-heeled, distinguished South Carolina family, and he fabricated delicious excuses every day for why he hadn't brought in his assignments. I feel he was the original person, back in 1957, to explain, "My dog ate my homework." Also, there was John, from the wrong side of town. His hair was swept back in a ducktail like the early rocker, Eddie Cochrane, and his pegged pants hung self-consciously to the bottom of his shoes. He would use a rubber band as a slingshot, casually hitting his victim with a rolled-up chewing gum wrapper. John was often my companion in after-school detention hall. I was there for talking back in class, John was there for being a juvenile delinquent.

I always kept a lookout for boys reading *Mad Magazine* at their desks. In 10th grade I bonded with a guy named Willard with greasy hair and a zipper jacket over our extreme amusement at Alfred E. Newman and a lesser *Mad* oddity named Melvin Cowsnofsky. I made a more serious friendship with a Jewish kid named Jeff Denberg about our love of professional sports, especially baseball. A contest we invented was to choose any Major League baseball team and name the players on its roster, back and forth, until one of us was stumped, usually at player 22 or 23. Jeff was more than a trivia dilettante; he was the hardboiled sports editor of our school newspaper. At 15 or so, he had journalism in his veins. He had the right looks and demeanor: jowls like Edward G. Robinson, a thick neck, a bark to his voice, though I never saw him take out a cigar and light up.

I could talk sports for hours, so surely I could write about them. I asked Jeff for a school newspaper assignment. He wasn't as cocksure as I was about my innate journalist capabilities. It was football season, and he started this novice at the very bottom. I would not cover the varsity but an away game of the raw "B" squad of eager 14- and 15-year-olds. It was to be played in a small South Carolina town, and I went there in a car with my friend, Patrick, a guard on the team. We were driven by his father, a red-faced Army sergeant with a proud handlebar mustache. Mr.

Mulcahey dropped us off, as we'd be with the team on the school bus for our ride home.

Pat asked me to keep hold of his jacket when I sat in the stands for the game and took notes for my article. A bad day for Dreher's "B" squad. They were mercilessly stomped on, and I joined the forlorn players and the very pissed-off coach on the school bus. Everyone wanted to get out of there and go home. Just as we were pulling out of the parking lot, I screamed out, "STOP!" I had left Patrick's jacket in the stands! The bus backed up, and the coach, disappointed, glared at me with loathing as I passed by him to retrieve the jacket. Anyway, I wrote up my story on the football game, and brought it typed to Jeff. He read it, and he likewise glared at me. He shook his head and rejected my article. Could it have been because I penned the dullest lead in the history of journalism? "The B Squad consists of 35 Dreher High freshman and sophomores."

Jeff Denberg became a revered sportswriter for the Atlanta Constitution. *He died of brain cancer a few years ago, and I'm sorry we never met again after high school.*

Outside of High School

In summer 1957 we moved across Columbia to a rental closer to my high school. It was the corner home on a swampy, isolated street called Colin Kelly Drive, named for a WWII hero killed in airplane combat. The only other home on this unwanted block held the Averys, a single mom with two straw-haired daughters in elementary school, Rosemary and Caroline. Danny was invited over for lunch one day and got deathly sick on a heaping plate of rice and brown gravy. There was also a toddler in the family with the strangest name my brother and I ever had heard: Iziloo. Iziloo Avery.

What a turn-on when I saw in the *Columbia Record* the movie ads for *Baby Doll*. There'd been nothing like it, so glaringly sexual: nubile Carroll Baker in a slip lying prone in her boudoir, sucking on her thumb. At age 11 I wasn't allowed by the theaters to see that controversial movie. But I dared at age 12 to walk up to the box office at Columbia's Five Points Theater and plunk down 25 cents, the going price, for "sex kitten" Brigitte Bardot in *And God Created Woman*. Delicious tween viewing, including a fleeting look at BB's bare bosom. It was the first time (certainly not the last) that I went to a movie for no other reason than its prurient content.

Also at 13, I felt the pressure to start dating. How about beginning with a double date with my friend David? I asked out a chubby rich girl with whom I had nothing in common except we were both Jewish. David telephoned a girl who was his chum at our Reform temple. My father drove the four of us to a movie, and picked us up afterward. I rode shotgun and David sat with both of our dates in the back seat! In the theater lobby, David overheard the two girls whispering that they regretted that they weren't out with other boys instead of us. No matter the humiliation, that counted as a date.

I kept a list of how many dates I had through high school. About seven or so. Several were with the same chubby wealthy girl. Several more were with a skinny, non-Jewish girl with glasses whose father taught with my dad at Benedict. Her family had moved to South Carolina from Kansas City, Kansas. We went to a county fair together and rode the Ferris wheel. But no hand-holding, no hanky-panky. In truth, all seven of my dates were asexual ones, with not the slightest desire on either side.

I had one game I was pretty great at, and that was ping pong. Table tennis. I put a thumb behind my rubber-covered paddle and pushed the ball hard at my opponent. I rarely tried to slam, as my special talent was defense. At 13, I had great reflexes, and anything hit at me, no matter how hard, I would manage to return. My place to play was an indoor recreation hall at a local park. I'd be there three or four days a week after school, sometimes playing in a show-off way, swigging a Coke in my non-paddle hand and with salty peanuts inside the bottle.

Paul and I made a dynamite all-Jewish doubles team. We entered the Columbia City Table Tennis tournament and quite handily took the boys' championship for 14 and younger. Even more thrilling, I won the boys' singles championship, a prize-winner my first time in a ping pong tournament. I beat a guy named Mike, who'd been titleholder the last several years. He was an ugly kid with a huge head like a gargoyle, and he had a mighty slam. But when he slammed, I always returned it, until his shots began to miss the back of the table. What a victory!

I saw myself as the ping pong pride of Columbia after winning it all. Flying so high, I looked confidently to the South Carolina singles championship for boys 14 and under several weeks later.

Victors from towns around the state met on a Saturday in a giant armory filled with dozens of tables for the great run-off. I won at least one 2-out-of-3 match, maybe two, and I found myself, deep in the afternoon, in the semi-finals. Beat this opponent and the next and I would be—yes!—South Carolina State Boys' Champion. The Crown Prince of Table Tennis! However, life is cruel and unjust.

The day of ping pong matches had been going slower than the judges wanted. They wished things to end so they could go home. Out of nowhere, they instituted an arbitrary rule to quicken things, announced over the PA system. From that moment, the server must win the point in ten volleys. If he hadn't, the volley was stopped and the point went to the opponent. WHAT? That rule change went every way against my defensive-minded game. Serving, I now badly rushed things. I tried to win with slams, and my shots hit the net or flew off the table. Glumly, I fell far behind. I lost badly. Head down, I walked away from the table. That day, I could have been champ. I wuz robbed.

One afternoon, Danny and I came upon a massive table of jacketless 45s at Sears and Roebuck for 10 cents each. We hadn't heard of a single tune, A-side or B-side. The biggest singing star available was a quite minor one, Georgia Gibbs. The most famous celebrity was *The Honeymooners'* Art Carney crooning, "Sheesh, What a Grouch!" But we splurged on about 15 records for $1.50 in all, and then played them to death. We're probably the two people in America who knew the words and music of such campy ditties as "Let's Go Fishing," "Blueberries," and the pricelessly titled "Two Thirds of the Tennessee River." The only record we purchased with any cachet was "Say Hey (The Willie Mays Song)." But "Two Thirds of the Tennessee River" was ours and ours alone.

In March 1958, Danny and I went to the annual exhibition game which brought to town the Cincinnati Reds, that year playing the Philadelphia Phillies. We were waiting afterward for our dad to pick us up when we sighted Phillies shortstop Chico Fernandez and first base prospect Frank "Pancho" Herrera. Danny: "They were the first celebrities I ever spoke to, and I'm sure it was all babbling. We asked if our father could drop them off at their hotel. They said politely, 'No thanks,' that a ride was coming. We didn't comprehend that they, being of color, were going to a hotel away from the white players. Fortunately, their ride did show up and they didn't rely on us. In typical fashion for our dad, we got a flat tire on the way home."

A Summer Break

In 1958, our dad Joe once again uprooted his family when he took a three-month gig doing science research in Buffalo, New York. We rented a small house across the border in Canada in Fort Erie. The most momentous event was Danny and I going to the first amusement park of our lives, Crystal Beach Park on the shores of Lake Erie. I was 13 and Danny was almost 9. Standing at a strategic spot by the exit of a funhouse, we were treated to women with dresses flying upward and their underwear revealed when hit from below with a gust of blown air. Fabulous! And we were definitely spooked by a fright house trip in a rowboat through a darkened lagoon with apparitions leaping out at us.

Just as scary were the classic Universal horror movies of the 1930s and 1940s, shown each week on Buffalo TV and which Danny and I watched, to be even more terrified, with the doors shut in a pitch-black laundry room. Our introduction to Boris Karloff, Bela Lugosi, and Lon Chaney, Jr. Our favorite picture that summer was *Frankenstein Meets the Wolf Man*. It had everything ghoulish we could have wanted, including the titular battling monsters. Danny could barely sleep after any of these movies. An impressionable boy, he had screamed out "Japanese! Japanese!" having a nightmare after viewing *Rodan,* the flying Tokyo-based behemoth.

Three distinct memories of this summer in Ontario. Seeing teenage girls flirting with the boys in a soda shop and feeling it in my 13-year-old body. Playing baseball on a neighborhood lot and actually having 18 kids fielding all the positions. Sitting on our front porch and relaxing, doing absolutely nothing on a mellow July afternoon.

The same porch, and there in a metal chair is Djedushka, our mother's gruff, incommunicative, Russian-speaking father. Danny is below him on the ground. Every minute or so, our grandfather reaches down and flicks Danny on the ear and then sits back, acting innocent. Danny is puzzled, looking up. Is our grandfather actually doing something playful? Connecting with us? Danny looks away, Djedushka flicks him on the ear again and sits straight, pretending to have done nothing. Danny shakes his head, slightly annoyed at the teasing. And then Djedushka does something I'd never seen before. He smiles at me, acknowledging the joke.

11th Grade

My washout junior year. Switching from Spanish to French, I had as a teacher a hip, bemused woman whom I really liked. But I fell behind because of the verb wheel I was unable to master and the strange Gallic tenses. What in the world was "the pluperfect"? Also, I'd gone from Algebra in 9th grade, which I liked, to Plane Geometry in 10th, which I didn't enjoy, to Trigonometry in 11th grade, which I despised. A truly useless course. Recently, I had a recovered memory, transporting me back to that Trig class of 60 years ago. I read somewhere these three words I'd buried forever: "sine, cosine, and tangent." What horror! Sine, cosine, and tangent.

I remember far less of the actual school year than of any other, going back to 1st grade. Unfortunately, I do recall a shameful, devilish moment of my worst behavior. My poor Trigonometry teacher, a harmless little lady! She didn't deserve in any way that I took out on her my hatred of the class she taught. As she stood before me, I leaned toward her and said, of the sharp-pointed compass she was holding, "Why don't you stick it in your throat?" My teacher was so shaken by my terrible words that she paled but did nothing. Absolutely, I should have been thrown out of school.

I can't imagine there were book reviews in the *State* or *Record*, Columbia's dailies. But somehow after failing as a sportswriter for Dreher's student paper, the *Blue and Gold*, I had the chutzpah to reinvent myself as a book critic. For several months in 11th grade, I provided a column of my own clever invention: Peary Picks the Pockets. "Pockets" referred to the soft-cover publisher, Pocket Books, but it was also to paperbacks in general. I read soft-cover novels by the dozen, and I recommended the cream of my discoveries to my fellow high-school students. I don't recall a single title I wrote about. I do remember a lead sentence I felt particularly pleased with: "One book sure to catch the reader's eye is…"

I was 13 turning 14 and had never been kissed. The sexual difficulties between Lady Brett and Jake in *The Sun Also Rises* went over my head. Nor could I get what was implied in *Death in the Afternoon* by Hemingway's assertion that, "I know only that what is moral is what you feel good after and what is immoral is what you feel bad after." My favorite Hemingway novel by far was *For Whom the Bell Tolls*, so stirring and romantic, and a match in my affection for Steinbeck's impassioned *The Grapes of Wrath*. I was clearly a precocious reader then, but I just wasn't equipped for some of the supposed classic books. *The Great Gatsby* fell flat, meant nothing to me. It was no *Catcher in the Rye*. And I wrote a book report in my English class saying, "*Lord Jim* is the most boring book I've ever read."

As a 6th-grade dropout from Hebrew School, I never had a Bar Mitzvah. The not-so-impressive substitute, on a Friday night at the Tree of Life Reform temple, was a confirmation service. On stage with Rabbi G were the handful of us, boys and girls, turning 14. I do know I worked hard and long on my speech, and it was soundly applauded. More than 60 years later, my self-consciously pretentious opening words still ring out, though I don't quite understand what they mean. "Now more than ever," my oratory soared, "it's important for Jews and Christians to achieve a firm basis of understanding." That's correct, "a firm basis of understanding."

My literary taste was in line with the 1950s, sexist to the core. I'd been for The Hardy Boys but not Nancy Drew, preferred Alcott's obscure *Little Men* to *Little Women*, and, as a tweener, chose exclusively male science-fiction writers. I think I read only two novels with female authors, Grace Metalious's *Peyton Place* and Agatha Christie's *And Then There Were None*. The non-fiction writers I picked to read were all guys. Thor Heyerdahl with *Kon-Tiki*. Morey Bernstein with *The Search for Bridey Murphy*. I learned about liberal Judaism in the Deep South through the essay collections of Harry Golden, and I was made cognizant of class relations not from Marx but from Vance Packard's *The Status Seekers*. Who knew it was better to be an Episcopalian for your social position than a Southern Baptist?

Hail Daniel P. Mannix! He was my favorite non-fiction writer as a 14-year-old. Never heard of him? The author of the zesty autobiography of his carnival days, *Memoirs of a Sword Swallower*? Ballantine Books was the go-to publisher for his original paperbacks; and Mannix's talent was penning freaky subterranean cultural histories, to which I gravitated. Among them were *Those About to Die*, gross-out details of the Roman games, and *The Beast,* the decadent life and times of occultist Aleister Crowley. On a cross-state Greyhound bus ride, I saw a man across the way reading a Mannix volume. My comrade! We talked through the night about our love for those colossal books, and also of a Dr. Frank S. Caprio, who specialized in seedy, supposedly scientific studies of deviant sexuality. I remember my companion beaming and sighing, "Ah, Frank S.!"

For three years our parents had tried to buy a house in Columbia and couldn't find a seller because my father taught at black colleges. In early 1958, a liberal family from the Jewish community agreed to let us purchase their modest brick home on Ellison Avenue in a middle-class neighborhood. I believe the cost was $9,000 and, as an army veteran, my father financed it the usual 1950s way with a GI Loan. Danny and I had tiny bedrooms right next to each other, and we had a bit of a lawn and even a very small den, where we put our television. This was our first owned property. Danny reminded me recently: our father, Joe, reverted to his old bad habit of bringing home strange, unwanted pets. This time it was a pair of chinchillas, which didn't last long in our den, detested equally by our angry mother and Laddie, our flipped-out dog.

How I lost my religion in less than half an hour. I invited my friend, Herb, to our newly bought home. Like rabbinic scholars, we strolled back and forth across the front lawn as Herb, a 15-year-old serious reader of philosophy, challenged my Jewish religious beliefs. As Herb explained in terms that I could grasp, on the TV show, *The Adventures of Rin Tin Tin*, everyone bowed and scraped before the sainted German shepherd. Isn't that how we all genuflect before an alleged God? "It was!" I agreed, and became a non-believer on the spot. And without any anxiety about it. I never looked back.

A half a century later, I again met Herb, who was a psychology professor in Vermont, and thanked him for freeing me to become an atheist Jew. Herb didn't seem proud of his achievement. In fact, he's retracted a bit and was now only an agnostic Jew.

My parents voted for Adlai Stevenson in 1952 and 1956, so Danny and I grew up in a family that identified as Democrats. But our father and mother didn't talk much about such matters at home. And for someone who has been obsessed with politics since JFK's triumphant election, I don't recall any deep passion during my high school years, 1957–1960. One might assume that my father teaching at two black colleges would have made me an ardent integrationist. I think I accepted the Jim Crow world as fixed, immovable, the wrong-headed thinking of other white Southerners.

I learned much later that African-American students at Benedict College and Allen University participated in sit-ins of Columbia's segregated lunch counters in February 1960, my senior year. Why didn't I know that? In those days, civil rights activity often was "blacked out," unreported in Southern, white-run newspapers. But surely our father would have told us what happened on his campus, in the city where we lived? My amnesia about these valiant acts of civil disobedience is a mystery to me. I do know that my consciousness had not yet been transformed, as it would be soon after by the civil rights movement. I learned of the "black-out" when making a podcast, *The Rabbis Go South*, about rabbis from the North arrested in St. Augustine, Florida, trying to desegregate the city. This story was covered nationally in the *New York Times* but not in the *St. Augustine Record*.

Our mother, Laura, was only a high school graduate, attending a music conservatory when she grew up in Bucharest. But somehow she was hired to teach both a French class and beginning piano at Benedict College, joining there my father, a legitimate Ph.D. Danny and I have the hardest time imagining her in the classroom. She spoke rapidly, she had a trying foreign accent, her English wasn't exactly coherent. Our mother had never taught anything in her life, and she knew nothing of the ways of American education. She agreed to do it because our family needed to pay the bills. Wasn't she afraid? Our mother always possessed a strange confidence and cockiness. She would talk to anyone and say anything. One day, W. E. B. Du Bois came and lectured at Benedict. Our mother bluntly asked him if he was a Communist. "He said he wasn't," she told us over dinner.

In a middlebrow way, our mother, loved classical music. She would listen raptly whenever a Met opera bigwig like Jan Peerce belted something sudsy and grandstanding on *The Ed Sullivan Show*. She'd tried without success to make me love classical music also, and suddenly she had a grand opportunity. Because she was teaching beginning piano at Benedict, we got a used piano at home. I agreed to take lessons from her, but only if I could start with popular music. My learning of piano lasted only a couple of weeks. We had shouting arguments because I couldn't abide the way she instructed me to play the Marty Robbins tune, "A White Sport Coat (and a Pink Carnation)." That was my whole repertoire, performed clumsily and impatiently, before I quit forever. Meanwhile, our mother tired our ears by endlessly practicing "The Moonlight Sonata."

Our new home was the site of a death in our family, my mother's Russian father, Djedushka. He was as mysterious and far off from Danny and me when he succumbed as he'd been in life. He and Babushka came down from New York and, for several months as he weakened from stomach cancer, he took over our parents' bed. They slept in a fold-out couch in the front of our house. One day, he left us. An ambulance came and took the corpse away while we remained in our bedrooms. Bye-bye, Djedushka! Our mother had a histrionic reaction, declaring loudly like a professional mourner, "I want to die! I have nothing to live for!" Djedushka was buried in New York, though my brother and I stayed in Columbia at the time of the funeral.

At Dreher, there were no art history courses. I was on my own discovering the majesty of art. I bought postcards of 19th- and 20th-century masterworks and pasted them into a spiral notebook. Below each picture, I copied words about the painting and the artist from encyclopedia entries. I also wrote down definitions of art movements which excited me: Impressionism, Surrealism. For the first time in my life, I had a favorite painter, Monet. And I was crazy about Salvador Dalí and so surprised when I went to the Museum of Modern Art that "The Persistence of Memory" was such a tiny work. On that super MoMA visit, I came across what instantly became my most beloved painting in the world, Henri Rousseau's "The Sleeping Gypsy." Sixty-five years later, I am strangely unmoved by most Impressionism or Surrealism, and I especially loathe that poseur Dalí. But "The Sleeping Gypsy," still hanging at MoMA, remains a mysterious delight.

The county fair each fall was a big deal in Columbia. I went there not for the rides: I have a lifetime phobia of anything beyond a Ferris wheel. But I enjoyed the crowds and the pretty girls and eating caramel-covered apples and corn dogs. One high-school year, I attended with Herb, my intellectual friend. For our hours at the fair, Herb feigned being very stupid in a Jerry Lewis way, and I was the Dino straight man. We conned the carnies working the games by making them repeatedly explain the rules to my impossibly thick friend. Finally, Herb would pretend to "get it," for instance, the knocking over of piled milk bottles to win a prize. Handed a baseball, Herb threw it wildly, insanely, forcing the carny to scramble for cover. "Get the hell out of here!" we were ordered, and we took off, snorting with laughter, heading for another booth and more havoc. Herb and I: what a comic team.

All the fellows at Dreher were whispering about "Dixie Lee," "Dixie Lee." They were boisterous and crude in describing what they'd witnessed. Dixie Lee was a stripper at the county fair. She got naked in front of the male crowd and willingly did unspeakable things. My mouth was wide open. I was 14 and had never heard anything like this before. I'd seen Brigitte Bardot on film and a *faux* documentary set on a volleyball court at a nudist colony. That was it. I got to the fair alone, not wanting to be caught by anyone. I located the strip show, and stood in front for a long time, hyper-ventilating. At last, I addressed the man selling tickets, asking him, absurdly, what was inside. The man leaned down to me and said, "For a dollar, you get to see a woman's _____. Does that sound good?" I didn't know, but I paid the dollar (no questions about my age) and, sure enough, Dixie Lee strutted about and I saw her _____.

Our mother had an emergency gall bladder operation, meaning she had to rest afterward. She declared herself too fatigued for what she'd always done, make three meals a day for her family. She'd only prepare two meals, but lunch was too much. How could we handle this, with our father helpless in the kitchen? We didn't have the money for it, but my parents had no choice but to join Columbia's Jewish Center. I would now go every day and swim in the pool. After swimming, I'd always have the same lunch at the canteen of a kosher all-beef hot dog on a bun with a squirt of Gulden's Mustard. Danny ate there his first pastrami.

The Center's lifeguard, Raymond, was a 16-year-old with a homely face but a really buff physique, and some thought he was a candidate for the Olympics as a swimmer. "And Jewish!" people marveled. My only other memory there was of a sketchy kid named Andy bringing in pornography, very rare then, for the teenage guys to check out. This was 1958, and I believe I almost fainted at my first sight of such doings, in this case Mexican pros-titutes and their johns all in black Zorro masks. Meanwhile, our time at the costly Jewish Center was short-lived. Our mother got better, she could make us lunch, so we gave up our membership after about two months.

The Last Summer Away

In June 1959, our family left Columbia for the leafy middle-class suburb of Fairfax, Virginia, so our father could work in Wash-ington, D.C. He must have been paid decently for once. Danny and I couldn't get over the handsomely furnished ranch house that we rented. It was so much fancier than any place we'd ever lived, and with a back yard that stretched out probably sixty yards. Mowing our property took much of an afternoon. I was 14 and found myself for the first time meeting and hanging out with teen-agers. There was a cool, ironic guy named Malcolm, 15, who lived across the street. His mouth was wired shut, he explained, because he'd been making out with a girl and fell out of a hammock onto his jaw. He claimed he now drank meat-and-chicken milk shakes. He would end a conversation by saying, "I'm going home now to watch *The Mickey Mouse Club* and Annette's boobs."

We were not the only outsiders in placid Fairfax. A family from Appalachia, hillbillies, rented a nearby house. There were three teenage boys, and the two older were unapologetically crude. They bragged that they'd attended a party at a rich person's home and both peed into a bathroom sink. The most civilized of the brothers was Harry, 15. He was also the cutest, and one of the sexiest girls I'd ever seen was all over him, she in white short shorts and with painted toenails. Whatever, I had my own erotic interlude. I spent an afternoon of smooching in a dark garage with Linda, a pretty girl with bangs. At 14, it was the first make-out session of my life. By the end, our lips were bruised from all that kissing. But I didn't have the daring to venture farther, no run at second base.

12th Grade

Starting my final year at Dreher in fall 1959, I had to acknowl-edge that at times I wished for some mainstream acceptance. For a school talent show, a kid I knew, Eddie, had memorized the *Inside Shelley Berman* comedy album, and he recited a chunk of it, making everyone in the assembly laugh. How nice, I thought, to be so popular. The final act that day was a boy band of haughty Dreher rockers with drums and guitars and red sports jackets and identical thin ties and a catchy, sexy song, "Oh come, yes come, to the house on the hill!" I marveled at their confidence as they strolled about on the stage. And, of course, the girls went crazy. Where was a place for me in such a throbbing, intoxicating teen world?

I saw a heavier Eddie, probably a retired businessman, standing about with a drink at the 60th high school reunion. I reminded him of his comic appearance in the school talent show. "Oh yes, Shelley Berman," he said and chuckled, quite indifferent about it, not showing the slightest surprise that I remembered his ten minutes of celebrity six decades later.

My heady pal, Herb, was going now to another high school, not Dreher. My close friend, David, was as loyal as ever, but I'd brought him to literature, to science fiction and John Steinbeck, never the other way around. Who could instruct me in something valuable? Teachers were useless. The person who'd perhaps mattered most in my intellectual development was the kindly woman at the Columbia Public Library. Not only had she allowed me early to check out adult books, she was properly enthusiastic when I babbled to her about my literary discoveries. But let's return to Dreher High: my life was about to change sublimely.

I finally found my crowd. My clique. My people. It didn't seem possible in such a conservative school in such a conservative state. But there it was: a small group of Dreher students who understood and appreciated my sensibility. Why hadn't we hooked up earlier? I had noticed the famously smart fraternal twins, Jimmy and Johnny, but lacked the nerve to approach them. Susan, who was a painter, was new to me, and also Rita Ruth "Rue," and our spiritual leader, Marshall. How did we teenagers start hanging out? I can't remember something so important in my life. But soon we were meeting, often at the home of the twins and irregularly at Marshall's or Susan's. Most of us were big readers, and all acted artistic and, in 1959–60, each of us was stirred by what we knew of the Beat movement. If we had a canonical text it was Lawrence Ferlinghetti's *Pictures of the Gone World*.

It was incomprehensible to me how such average parents had birthed such brilliant sons, Jimmy and Johnny. The parents were kept to the upstairs of their split-level home. They never dared venture to the large, cozy den below, where our gang hung out. What a place for emboldened 15- and 16-year-olds to make our own! Jimmy played piano, and both twins favored classical music, so that's what was always on the hi-fi. Often Beethoven's Third and Ninth. The twin brothers would go upstairs and return with treats for us: freshly popped popcorn and Pepsis on ice in tall glasses. Best of all was a large chessboard with foot-high carved wooden pieces, and we could play for hours. Or stop and discuss literature! The only interruption on a choice afternoon would be the twins' father at the top of the stairs calling down abrasively, "Johnny! Jimmy! Come to supper!"

When we went to Marshall's house, we settled in for music listening in the big living room. And there was Marshall himself, barefoot and in blue jeans, cross-legged on the floor digging his modern jazz albums. He started me easy with The Dave Brubeck

Quartet. But the album that transformed my taste forevermore was Thelonious Monk's 1957 *Brilliant Corners*. Explosive African-American jazz! It was an out-of-body moment when I heard that opening title track with Monk's intricate shifting piano rhythms and the screeching harmonies of saxophonists Ernie Henry and Sonny Rollins.

There were only two girls in our floating group and up to eight guys, so the females were much coveted. That's when Jimmy and Johnny swooped in. A discreet relationship developed between Jimmy and Susan, There was a rumor, never verified, that he crawled into her bedroom window. That left Rita Ruth, "Rue," who wore little heels and tight skirts and eyeliner and had the most wild, unruly hair imaginable in this Sandra Dee teen era. I had a quiet crush on Rita Ruth and Johnny did also. It was a weekend afternoon at Susan's, and classical music was on the record player when Johnny made his move. I was the heartbroken witness as Johnny edged closer and closer on the couch to "Rue" until they were madly kissing. What choice had I but to give her up to my good pal? They were 16, and I'm sure it was the first love for each.

And the last? They would marry some years after, have a daughter, and stay together for half a century until "Rue" died of cancer.

So far away in South Carolina, my high-school pals and I dreamed of San Francisco and North Beach and the Big Sur. We read with awe *The Holy Barbarians* and *The Beat Generation & the Angry Young Men* and the half-dozen Kerouac novels which spilled out to the public between 1957 and 1960. Marshall, a son of churchgoing Christians, was the most spiritually advanced of us, introducing our set to Alan Watts and *The Way of Zen* and the Buddhism of Kerouac's *The Dharma Bums*. In 1959, I saw Kerouac—pained, vulnerable, unsmiling—on *The Steve Allen Show*, but how magisterial he was reading aloud from *On the Road*. For me, he was the real thing. And a *Time* magazine putdown of Gregory Corso backfired for this 15-year-old. I adored the very lines in "Bomb" which *Time* mocked: "Ubangi BOOM, orangutan/BING BANG BOMB BOOM bee bear baboon."

It was Lawrence Ferlinghetti's *A Coney Island of the Mind*, with its open invitation to free verse, that coaxed me and others in our group into trying poetry. These are florid words from a particularly heated poem I penned in 1960: "Swiftly moving, never stopping, over the Sands of Time he stumbled" until, lo, fourth

verse, "He met Truth, glistening and glowing in the gory night."
The alliteration!

*About 2005, I shared an outside breakfast in San Francisco with a
table of men, including Ferlinghetti. At the end of the meal, I went
over to where the poet sat and, standing above him, gushed about
his influence when I was a teenager. He listened politely, had no
reaction, as he'd probably heard a version of my speech five thousand times. Then he rose and rode away on his bicycle. I didn't
recite for him my poem above with its blistering conclusion: "Truth,
goddammit, you LIED!!!!!"*

I have not talked once about my wardrobe. Growing up, I NEVER
thought about clothes. I was in line with my woefully dressed
father. Probably my mother purchased everything for both of us
without consultation. I didn't care. I do recall one shopping trip
with mom to Sears and Roebuck and my requesting pants in my
favorite color: green. I got them: green pants. So what happened
my senior year in high school, when several of my self-consciously bohemian friends went about in black turtlenecks, like
budding French existentialists? My drab clothes remained the
same. However, I had one modish month as a 15-year-old affecting
the smoking of a pipe, reaching into my pouch of mellow British
tobacco. But I coughed too much to be cool, and my pipe kept
going out because I failed to pack it tightly enough. So much for
my Holmesian fashion statement.

Not one of my artsy crowd gave a damn about sports like I did,
so there was no talking about my beloved Kansas City Athletics
baseball team or the college basketball championship I carried in
my heart from listening to it on radio: the 1957 triple overtime
victory of North Carolina over the Wilt Chamberlain-led Kansas.
The star of North Carolina was Jewish, the great Lennie Rosen-
bluth. I started having pride in Jewish athletes, Sandy Koufax,
of course, and the Cleveland Indians' all-star third baseman, Al
Rosen. Yes, I was an atheist but a Jewish atheist, so it warmed me
to celebrate even the most obscure Hebraic ballplayers.

I persuaded non-athlete Johnny to participate in a baseball
game, and Danny, 10, was somehow the shortstop in a contest of
older kids. Danny: "Johnny hit a grounder so hard and fast that I
can still hear it sizzle. I put up my glove, not quickly enough, and
the hardball hit me squarely in the face. I dropped to my knees. It's
amazing I wasn't killed, and Johnny felt guilty about what he did

for years. My eye blackened and the whole right side of my face was discolored. The girl I liked in school spoke to me for the only time. She said, 'You look like Bugs Bunny.'"

There was one boy on the periphery of our high-school gang whom I didn't much care for, Susan's acquaintance whom she had pushed into our group. F, prissy and supercilious, was active in our school theater. I saw him with powdered white hair and a German accent in an overacted Dreher production of *You Can't Take It With You*. Nobody was gay in 1960 in conservative South Carolina, but it was suspected of F. His personality rubbed me wrongly, but, more, I didn't know him as a serious reader. To be properly in our clique you had to care deeply about literature.

F, so rare for a South Carolinian, moved to New York, where he became a writer of opera reviews and, later, an editor at a gossipy soap-opera magazine. So I've heard, he came out. And became a devoted reader.

Jaws dropped among my bohemian friends with the appearance in our high school mid-senior year of a new and most mysterious young man. He wore to his classes a buttoned suit with a tie, and his eyes couldn't be seen behind dark shades. The consummate hipster! When we actually spoke, Harmon lived up to whatever we'd invented about him. He came from Wisconsin, and he'd been in a juvenile facility for, I believe, stealing cars. He was quiet-spoken and, at 17, referred with amusement to his earlier trail of crime. Anyway, we were quite taken by Harmon, and welcomed him to hang around with us. He gave us authenticity. Here was someone whom Dean Moriarty could have befriended on the road. Whenever I conjure up Kerouac's eponymous apparition, Doctor Sax, I always see him as Harmon.

Among my high school bohemian chums, there wasn't a lover boy in the bunch. That could be why Peter only circled us. Maybe he'd share a dark beer with us at the one tavern which served us, but would never join in. He was simply too cool. Red-headed and handsome and a confident abstract painter, Peter at 16 had girlfriends who were already in college. Assuredly, he slept with them. I once asked if I could borrow his copy of *Sexus*, Henry Miller's banned opus which he had imported from Paris. "Sorry, Gerry," he said, patronizingly. "That would be like me lending you my mistress."

We imagined big things for Peter, him leaving the backwaters of South Carolina for a flashy New York art career. I guess it never happened. Almost sixty years later, a friend reported that she'd been at a yard sale in Columbia and saw, across the tables checking out the items, a familiar-looking toothless old man.

I don't think it was because some of us had read *Thus Spoke Zarathustra* and, at 15 or 16, become taken with the idea of the Superman. Nor that we'd been influenced by *Compulsion*, the 1959 film about the Nietzsche-bent child murderers, Leopold and Loeb. But for whatever reasons we thought ourselves, in small matters, beyond the law. We became, for a few months, shop-lifters, and felt impervious to getting caught. Several of my friends had pouches under their coats, perfect for lifting books and LPs. Mostly we'd jam paperbacks into our belts beneath a sweater. We were adept little thieves. And none of us were arrested for our illegal deeds. How do I feel about it 60 years later? Not good at all about robbing the little store, the Capitol Newsstand, where I'd religiously bought books for years.

Someone in our group opened an unlocked desk drawer in the high school's administration office and came away with a list of the Stanford-Binet tabulated IQs of our Dreher classmates. Could there be anything more inappropriate and damaging to fall into the hands of students? I don't remember if that list was mimeographed by us after being outright stolen. But it was passed among my friends with gaiety. Soon we'd be walking down the halls and run into someone whose Intelligence Quotient we'd cruelly memo-rized. "Hello, 114," we'd shout out smirking, or far worse, "Hi, 98!" Oh, the poor student, not understanding how he or she was mocked. The comeuppance was uncovering my own just-OK IQ. Was that all it was? I had crashed from my boyhood intelligence in West Virginia, from being a "boy genius."

At Dreher High, skipping school was taken seriously and had consequences. So when Marshall and I and another friend, L, decided not to show up, we knew we would be punished. The next day the three of us were summoned from our various classes to the Assistant Principal's office. Mr. Witt was known to be a decent man and to possess a sense of humor, so we put on a show for his benefit. Each of us pretended to be surprised that the others had skipped school also. What a coincidence! Mr. Witt laughed at our antics then sent us for several weeks to after-school detention hall. We decided it was worth it for that one day burst of freedom. It was *Ferris Bueller's Day Off* 25 years earlier, the exaltation of his truancy.

How absurd that anyone called us that. But the hearsay that there were "beatniks" among them spread through the conservative Dreher student body. Even those who'd known us for years looked at us strangely, with fascination and also repugnance. For a time, my friends had gathered without disturbance in a certain classroom after lunch. Suddenly classmates flocked to peer through the doorway at us, as if we were zoo specimens. How could we battle back? It was my idea to sell to the moronic oglers "Beatnik" toothpicks, on which I'd penned down the side the B-word in tiny capital letters. I probably sold six or seven at a penny a toothpick. I wonder if anyone kept them over the ensuing years. Could they be offered now on eBay as memorabilia of the Beat Generation?

My first public display of social consciousness occurred on May 2, 1960, the day that Caryl Chessman was to be executed in California. Sentenced to death as a kidnapper and rapist, Chessman had become a cause célèbre in the fight to end capitalist punishment. A repeat criminal, yes, but he hadn't killed anyone, and he penned several tabloid autobiographies which I had read in paperback. When news came across the radio that he had been put in the gas chamber, I marched classroom to classroom chalking on the blackboards, "Caryl Chessman is dead!" Teachers didn't like that nor did most of the students. It was a disrespectful "Beatnik" act.

More impactful was what my friend Marshall, a student of Zen, did on the sly. He put up graffiti all over Dreher announcing, "Buddha lives!" What blasphemy in our deeply Christian public school, and one without a single Asian student. There was a faculty meeting called by the top administrators with the object to squelch this anarchic Beatnik explosion. It came to naught. They suspected that the heretic was someone in our crowd. Who else would it possibly be? Yet short of bringing in the police, they had no way to find the student, foul and loathsome, who had stood up for Buddha.

I'd played chess casually since I was 9 or 10, not aware of a world of serious, committed professionals. It was a Jewish family friend, Rubin Slater, a dentist and colonel in the Army stationed at Fort Jackson, who educated me. Dr. Slater was nationally ranked in correspondence chess. With his inspiration, I checked out books from the Columbia Public Library, which told the history of chess and which included move-by-move bouts between grand masters. Soon I was caught up in the lives of Paul Morphy, the 19th-century

American champion, and the Cuban maestro, Capablanca, and, above all, Alexander Alekhine, who'd been part of my grandfather Sam's Russian-Jewish cadre in Paris during the 1920s and '30s.

At 15, I started playing out famous games from the past and some contemporary ones also, the Soviet battles for the world championship between the titleholder, Mikhail Botvinnik, and challenger Vasily Smylsov. I lifted and lowered my chess pieces, white and black, exactly as the masters had maneuvered them. My heart raced when I imitated the most uncanny, unexpected, and winning moves ever, dramatized in the chess books with boldface and exclamation points: **BxKc4!!!**

I was a wretched school citizen at Dreher High School, never once on the honor role, never considered for any class office, and, until senior year, not participating in a single extracurricular activity. The Dreher Chess Club saved me from complete anonymity and oblivion, a tiny identity I could register next to my geeky picture in the yearbook. In three or four months of rigorous chess, I'd surprised myself by becoming a quite skillful player. I beat both of my twin friends, Jimmy and Johnny, on the way at 15 to the high-school chess championship. I got a trophy!

One day, the South Carolina state chess champion, Lanneau Foster, came by our club and played a round robin match, challenging all of us as he walked between tables. To his chagrin, I had him down a pawn in our game. Having quickly dispatched the others, he sat down before me and, with great pride, battled me for an hour until I was forced to resign. What I remember most was that, because of his determination to win, we played through lunch hour. That day I went to my 1 o'clock class famished, desperately hungry. How did I manage to make it until supper? I don't think I've missed lunch another day in my life, including on Yom Kippur. There was an upside. Mr. Foster invited me to join the South Carolina chess club. For several months, I went and played matches against a bevy of eccentric elderly men.

And then I never played chess again in my life, until, in 2013, being cast as a chess master in the American independent film, Computer Chess. *For the movie, I faked playing quite effectively. Afterward, a journalist for an airplane magazine set up my first real game in over 60 years so he could write an article about it. It wasn't much of a match, as I was quickly stomped on, forced to resign within ten moves.*

At 15, my music taste was all over the place. I embraced progressive jazz. I knew nothing of classical music. I dug Harry Belafonte and calypso, as did the whole white world, young and old. The same with the Kingston Trio. Didn't everyone own their first albums of collegiate-sounding folk songs? I was slightly more adventurous with several multi-cultural albums of Theodore Bikel. Who was Jewish! And there was Oscar Brand's *Bawdy Songs and Backroooom Ballads*, more titillating than truly raunchy: "Oh dear, what can the matter be, seven old ladies locked in the lavatory." As for rock, I continued having schizophrenic taste, crazy about Black artists like Lloyd Price and the Platters but also syrupy white singers like Jimmie Rodgers. No, not the yodeling "Singing Brakeman." The Jimmie Rodgers of "Honeycomb" and "Kisses Sweeter Than Wine."

I came home one day to my mother sitting on the couch next to a woman friend. "There he is," my mother announced, disheartened, "my son, the atheist." That I was, never changing my mind after 14 about the non-existence of God. No synagogue for me. But was I missing something in my lack of religiosity? I'd heard positive things about the Unitarian Church, that it was for rational thinkers and without Jesus. So Johnny, a lapsed Christian, and I, a lapsed Jew, attended services a couple of Sundays. It was a compliment, I suppose, that we teens were taken seriously by the adults there. They yearned to have conversations with us about ethical issues. Jesus never came up but I recall lots of to-do about the stately wisdom of Thomas Jefferson. My verdict? Boring, boring. All those earnest people! No Unitarian Church for me. Instead, I sat by a pond on Sunday mornings self-consciously reading the *Collected Sonnets* and *Collected Lyrics* of Edna St. Vincent Millay.

The foreign-language film that we took in as a family: *La Strada*, our parents' all-time best. But for my thirteen birthday, I'd made our father accompany me to see Elvis in *Jailhouse Rock*. I had grown up happily on Hollywood cinema, requiring nothing beyond. That priority changed in one night in New York City, when, at 15, I persuaded my aunt and uncle, Paula and Abe, to bring me to a Swedish double feature. It was a long arduous night for them, pure ecstasy for me: Ingmar Bergman's *The Magician* and *Wild Strawberries*. Overtly spiritual themes, symbolism to unravel, and two magnificent stories. Wow! At that moment, every movie I'd ever watched fell aside next to the transcendence of Bergman.

In Spring 1960, I made a week trip with my family to visit our New York relatives. I skipped away from the Upper West Side and took a subway downtown to the Village for the first time in my life. I was 15, swept away by jazz and the Beats, and I wanted to be in the footsteps of all that was culturally electrifying. I discovered the Eighth Street Bookstore and bought several new volumes of the Pocket Poets series, these coming straight from San Francisco and Lawrence Ferlinghetti's City Lights Books. I found a colossally hip record store, chatted with the owner, and purchased on his recommendation a great album, *Mulligan Meets Monk*. Then I walked down MacDougal Street and peered into clubs where folksingers performed inside, such as the Café Wha?, painted like a circus side show, advertised as "Greenwich Village's Swingingest Coffee House." If only I had the money to pay the cover. But my funds were well spent on poetry books and an essential LP. What a great day in New York! My bohemian friends back in Columbia would be most envious.

During this seminal time, I went four straight days to the Village to hang out by the fountain in Washington Square Park, and then I would walk to the nearby benches to observe some more. Everyone seemed remarkable just by being there. I talked with a scrawny, disheveled painter named Zev who was probably in his forties and lived several blocks away in the derelict Hotel Earle. He brought his paints and an easel each afternoon into the park and also some works to sell. But if a tourist wanted to buy anything, he got paranoid and refused to let go of it. No matter that he had almost no money. Prideful with others, Zev was quiet and gentle with me and didn't mind me being around. I was so honored to associate with a real Greenwich Village artist. We were a pair for several days, and I helped him set up and carry his art supplies. In 1961, I returned to Washington Square looking for Zev, and I heard, with great sorrow, that he had starved to death in the New York winter.

"Hey, brother, we're trying to get some bread together for a little taste." That was me at 15 being hit on, to pay the bulk of the money for a bottle of cheap wine. It would be shared among my new friends in Washington Square. I even took a swig or two, as I was so exhilarated to be among the group of unemployed Black men who hung every day in the park. The leader of the pack was Ray, an ex-boxer from Michigan, who told a great story about being arrested for public drinking and dried out at a Harlem jail. When released, he stopped at every bar on a trail to the Village until he was drunk on his ass back in Washington Square. Anyway, our tranquility ended when teenage punks from nearby Little Italy physically threatened me. Revolted that I was sitting among Black men, they screamed that I was "a faggot." Ray jumped in for my defense, and he and the *Mean Streets* types shouted that they would meet the next day in the park. His black brothers against their gang of young Italian-Americans. Did it happen? I went home to South Carolina without ever learning if, in Spring 1960, I precipitated a Greenwich Village race war.

Nobody today believes this, but through my senior year of high school I had only a dim thought about higher education. I'd signed up for the College Boards, true, but that was about it. The University of South Carolina in Columbia, still segregated in 1960, was known to take any white graduate in the state. Was that where I might go by default, as I literally applied nowhere? Whatever, I first had to graduate high school. That was complicated by the fact that my mediocrity of an English teacher threw me out of her class. While she lectured, I'd been reading a book at my desk which was not her assignment. For several months, I sat in the assistant principal's house, until Mr. Witt finally convinced me to apologize so I wouldn't fail and have to repeat 12th grade. The apology was an insincere one, but I passed English with a "C."

How stupid were our teachers! My friend, Jimmy, was asked to explain on an exam in his English class the meaning of "A rolling stone gathers no moss." He wrote, "When a stone rolls, no moss gathers on it." The teacher marked Jimmy's answer correct!

My bohemian coterie decided they would have a real party, and they rented an apartment on the bad side of Columbia for one night. I paid for the first taxi of my life to get there. I was carrying a large suitcase with clothes, as I'd lied to my parents that I was sleeping over at a friend's. I arrived at a dark, creepy, deteriorating house. Was I at the right place? When I went cautiously up to the door, I heard from inside the comforting, familiar sound of "Bolero" on a record player. I had arrived! Inside, the lights were low, and there were about ten of my acquaintances listening to music and talking in loud voices; and I drank hard liquor until I announced, giddy and happy, "I'm drunk! I'm drunk!" Drunk for the first time. Soon, I was puking in the toilet, miserably sick. May I mention that I was taking my College Boards in the morning?

I dragged my bulky suitcase the next morning straight from the party to the place of the College Boards. "Is it all right to put my suitcase next to my desk?" I asked an official. And one more question: "Could I please sit at the front of the room?" I needed a lavatory nearby in case I started vomiting again. I also was exhausted and had a hangover. But as I settled in, I decided that I was acing the exam, whizzing through the questions with skill and knowledge. Not exactly. As I learned in time, my College Board score was 520 out of 800. Nothing special at all. Moral: one should not party and get drunk and sick and not sleep the night before taking the College Boards.

Did my gang of bohemians secretly crave acceptance from our straightlaced peers? I don't think so. And yet. There was a Homecoming tradition that Dreher would try to steal the flag of our crosstown football rival, Columbia High. I remember prowling the halls of the enemy school with several of my nervy friends looking to bring that flag home to Dreher. Why did we do that, we who were so derisive of the idea of "school spirit"? Probably because it was an adventure. I did attend my graduation. I did pose for a photograph in my rented cap and gown. And my clique, including non-seniors, couldn't resist that same evening checking out the graduation party. It was there that I had a couple of beers and then, somewhat drunk, walked up boldly to Dreher's lead cheerleader, a gorgeous blonde, and planted a lascivious kiss on her mouth. She smiled. I raced back to my nihilist friends and deliriously announced, "I kissed Molly McKenzie!"

At my fiftieth high school reunion, I saw Molly and told her this story. She was charmed by it, and that time she gave me a big kiss! At my sixtieth reunion, I sighted Molly and told her the story again. I had pushed my luck. She smiled wanly and looked uncomfortable at my silly confessional.

It was May 1960, and I had no idea if I was going to college in the fall. Who would want me with my 520 College Boards, my C+ cumulative high school average, and Chess Club as my only high school activity? And a reputation as a bit of a troublemaker? The question of my academic future was answered in a surprising way. Our father, who had been applying for new jobs for years, suddenly was offered one. He would leave Benedict College and Allen University and Columbia for a position teaching biology at Rider College in Trenton, New Jersey. And because my father would be on the staff at Rider, I was automatically admitted... and with free tuition! My failures at Dreher weren't an issue at all. So we were moving North, and I would be, in September 1960, a Rider freshman.

Yes, our family was leaving South Carolina, where I'd lived since 7th grade. We'd be getting out of the Deep South. I spent a final afternoon with David playing a two-men-on-a-side touch football game. I had the most athletic day of my life, as each pass tossed by David over my head I would magically catch and race for a touchdown.

A few days before our departure, I decided on an all-night walk with Johnny through the streets of Columbia, my sentimental "adieu" to the city. It turned into an abominable nightmare, when we were picked up in a car by two muscular football players from our high school team. They drove us about, threatening to beat up us ninny "Beatniks," who were shivering in the back seat. We were finally let out unharmed, but much shaken. That's my last memory of residing in South Carolina: almost being punched out by Dreher's star quarterback, who later played briefly in the NFL.

And then I moved North.

Post-Columbia postscript

My two Jewish friends also went North. David, who lives in Wisconsin, became an engineer, then a college instructor with a Ph.D. He remains angry at Hand Junior High for assigning him to class 7–13 when the highest section was 7–20. Herb, whom I converse with often on the phone, stays up through the Vermont night composing avant-garde music for instruments of his invention. He is a much-published retired professor from the University of Vermont.

I have been back to Columbia four times since moving away more than 60 years ago.

The first time was just a year after I went North. I saw my high school gang again, and it was very pleasant. Several were freshmen at the University of South Carolina. We all went swimming. There was a seeming replacement for me whom I liked immediately, a clean-cut guy who read good books and was a fine conversationalist. But he kept saying, offhandedly, he wanted to commit suicide, and I kept rebutting, "No you don't." He was about 18. I returned to the North and, several months later, he killed himself.

The second time was around 1975, to show a Boston girlfriend where I'd lived. We drove about and only located one of the three residences.

The third return to South Carolina was in 2010 for the 50th anniversary of graduating from Dreher. When I visited my old high school, I was delighted to see African-American students on the sidewalk and sitting on the front steps. Segregated Dreher High had become soundly integrated! Hooray! No longer was the student body dominated by the prosperous children of the white establishment. As for the reunion itself, it was friendly and polite, but I tried to sniff out the few of my ex-classmates who weren't Republicans. I did meet one courageous woman who had picketed George W. Bush when he'd visited her small South Carolina town.

No matter that many at Dreher got superlative College Boards and had the aptitude to go to excellent universities anywhere. As I learned at the reunion, South Carolinians tend to stay in their beloved state. One girl went to New York to appear in Broadway musical theater, and, as I mentioned, F, clearly gay, also journeyed to New York to review opera and edit soap opera magazines. Another student leader boy, closeted gay, committed suicide several years after graduating. More adventurous students moved over the years to North Carolina and Georgia, the most liberal persons dared to take up a residency in wild Atlanta.

My fourth visit was for my sixtieth anniversary of graduating Dreher. Lots of fellow students had died by this point. It was at a country club, and I quickly downed a couple of gin and tonics. Everyone, age 77–80, was politely friendly, but the locals huddled together with South Carolina small talk. However, my night elevated when I shared a table with two men (and their wives) who'd been my classmates in 7th grade and 9th grade. To their credit, they had moved out of Columbia. One lived in Pensacola, Florida, the other in Wichita, Kansas. How different were our lives! They had been fraternity brothers at Clemson University in South Carolina. Both were active always in their church. Both had served long in the army, and one was a proud Vietnam veteran. But they tried valiantly for common ground. They told me of their Jewish friends and African-American acquaintances, and one had gone to the Washington civil rights museum. The other practiced on me saying the word, "L'chaim." We took a photo together, we hugged goodbye, and promised to stay in touch.

My own high-school crowd have not all led bohemian adult lives. The twins, Jimmy and Johnny, became, respectively, a medical doctor and a high-tech specialist. L died in obscurity in Oklahoma, Pat of cancer in Columbia. Rita Ruth, married to Johnny, also succumbed to cancer. Susan still paints and still lives in Columbia but has had some hard medical times. Harmon, the most Kerouac-like of our group, died in 2012 in Wisconsin after years of homesteading, logging, sawmilling, gardening, fishing, writing poetry. Marshall, our 16-year-old Zen leader, continues on his spiritual paths. He was involved for a time in NYC with the American Underground Cinema. For more of his adulthood, he has been a practitioner of the teachings of Gurdjieff. And me? When I saw Rita Ruth in 2010, she asked, "Do you still write poetry?" Luckily for the world, not for sixty-five years.

Postscript

It was a mistake to send our impractical dad to find a place for our family to live in the North. He rented for us an abysmal little house exactly like every other in the planned town of Levittown, Pennsylvania. But in a year, we contracted for a split-level home in Lawrenceville, New Jersey. It was blocks from Rider, where our father taught and where I was a student. Mostly, a good student. Nobody there knew that I barely squeezed out of high school in South Carolina. Some of the faculty decided that if my father was a professor there, his son must be bright and academically moti-vated, and they treated me that way. And I responded, by getting decent marks for literally the first time since 6th grade. I suppose it wasn't very hard to be successful at Rider. The most renowned student in Rider history to that time was Woodrow Wilson's private secretary.

I had never been on stage since 1st grade. At Rider in 1962 I got involved with the theater program. I went on to NYU for a Master's in Drama, and I was close to getting a Ph.D. at the University of Wisconsin when I switched to film studies. I'd been directing plays, which I was good at, but had come to despise actors as babies and brats. What should be my profession? A year after graduating from Rider, I was invited to give a guest lecture in the literature class there of my favorite professor, Kenneth Hempstead. I talked on the Kafka short story, "A Hunger Artist," and afterward, I was taken to lunch and told I would be a great teacher. A teacher? I hate teachers! But that's what I did, teach college for 45 years. I've wished often that Professor Hempstead had seen his prophecy fulfilled, but he died of an open-heart operation at age 36.

In high school, I'd managed only a single makeout session. That I started college at 15 and grad school at 19 wasn't exactly conducive to a robust erotic life. And I was gun shy also, so it was quite a few years until a home run. After that, I was lucky with interesting girl-friends and now marriage to wonderful Amy. And if my sexuality was arrested when young, the compensation was that I'd embraced with continuous passion reading and moviegoing. I became a literate person, and I was ready to go to work when offered a position in 1978 as a Boston-based film critic. When I started to direct documen-taries in 2000, I knew film language from a lifetime at the pictures. In contrast to me, my brother, Danny, five years younger, had plenty of girlfriends as an undergraduate. He also obsessed about cinema and, even more than me, sports. He's the author of twenty-five books on those two topics, including biographies of baseball stars and a world-renowned series on cult movies.

I hold a dim vision from my childhood of being on Long Island and a very drunken man driving me and our mother to catch a train, and our mother begging, wailing to be let out of the car. Hardly anyone except me drank in our family. Not my brother. Not Jewish dinner guests, who, feeling obligated to bring a gift, would bring from the corner grocery a cheap red wine. Our mother, Laura, would pull the bottle from the bag and place it immediately in the refrigerator to cool it. Cold red wine! Our father, an abstainer, once gulped down a couple of shots at a Jewish wedding and soon was performing by himself an inebriated Russian *sher*, a scissors dance, his arms crossed on his chest, his legs crazily kicking out. Until he was gasping for breath.

As I've noted, we always, always ate at home. It is not until I was 16 that I can recall an actual sit-down dinner out with my family. It was at a shopping mall Italian restaurant in Pennsylvania where we feasted on a huge antipasto plate of cheese slices and cold cuts. My first time going to a restaurant by myself was at 19. I met a pal, Alan, on Times Square at a cheapo place called Romeo's for spaghetti and a glass of chianti. The same year, my grandfather, Sam, who ate out daily, treated me and my college friend, Saul, to a lavish dinner at the popular Mama Leone's. It wasn't until I was 22 that a girlfriend's urbane, bourgeois parents, brought me to my first fancy restaurant, the intimidating Cyrano's in Manhattan, where we got the house special, Crepe Cyrano's. Is it any wonder that, growing up in cuisine prison, that I'm so food-crazed, and with a fever for supping out?

Our father and mother were both decent people and proper parents, and I adored them when young. But the great disappoint-ment, in hindsight, was my inability to communicate with them later on. Our father cried about this on one occasion, sobbing that he didn't have one thing in common with his two sons. That was quite true, as he knew nothing about sports, music, movies, popular culture, and we cared nothing about science, geography, foreign languages. What was there to talk about? Especially since both parents were insulated from the world in which Danny and I lived. Our mother wasn't very introspective so she probably didn't notice that I never confided in either her or our father, or asked their advice. Only our father was saddened.

Here's one for our mother, Laura. She was very hospitable to all women Danny and I were involved with, no matter if they were Jewish. And cordial to any friend we brought home. But from adolescence on, Danny got along with her far better than I did. They bonded watching lots of TV together while I'd hide in my room reading. In her later years, I had little patience with her always maneuvering to be the center of attention, talking incessantly, charming outsiders with the tired stories that made me cringe, that I'd heard 500 times. I should have been a more empathetic son, cognizant that, living among Jewish friends and relatives in New York, she was making up for those lonely, displaced years in West Virginia and South Carolina.

According to Danny, our mother once caught her dear husband secretly applying for a job in Tahiti. How funny, but no surprise. Remember, I went to a different school in fourth, fifth, sixth, and 7th grade, as we moved from West Virginia to South Carolina to Pennsylvania back to South Carolina. Our parents seemed finally settled in New Jersey in 1961 with our dad tenured at Rider College. However, in 1967 without consulting with our mother, Joe suddenly quit Rider and took a non-tenured position at a college in San Juan, Puerto Rico. Our mother hated it there. Uprooted again.

Our dad was fine teaching in Spanish and, at the end of the day, joyfully floating on his back in the ocean. But that job in Puerto Rico was soon lost, so my parents returned to the States about 1970 and to our father's final position. He taught biology at a community college in Spanish Harlem. He was not renewed there either, the ignoble end to a frustrating life in academia. But at least Joe and Laura were in New York, where our mother would have wanted to live all along. Instead, she'd moved to Mississippi in 1944 to marry our father, and it took 25 years to get back.

Our mother lived incredibly modestly but she adored parties and meeting rich people and was incredibly impressed by "big millionaires." In her 80s, Laura loved to shop in a vintage clothing store in the Hamptons, getting a vicarious thrill at purchasing items she believed were previously owned by the super-wealthy. And at bargain prices! My brother and his wife Suzanne bought a home in Sag Harbor, and Laura would boast to everyone about her regularly staying in such a fancy spot. Our Jewish mother didn't understand the concept of a Jewish mother, even if she said Jewish-mother-like things: (1) When she balked at joining a bus tour: "I'd be with strangers who I don't even know!" (2) When I took her to tranquil, rustic Walden Pond: "Don't they have a place to get snacks?" (3) She never looked at a map in her life. Self-reliance meant nothing to Laura, so she always asked strangers for directions, even if she was standing beneath street signs.

Our father had no knowledge of celebrities. But he was certainly pleased when, on a trip to France in the 1970s, our parents were invited by Jacques Cousteau for a visit aboard the Calypso. Probably more exciting for our mother was when I took her to visit a filmmaker at the tip of Long Island who lived in a multi-million-dollar estate formerly owned by Andy Warhol. He gave her a tour of his mansion and with a stop at the bed where Elizabeth Taylor had slept. They got along grandly and, as we rode away, Laura told me, "We both agreed that it's not important how rich you are but how you spend your life." Her most thrilling night of all was when a famous documentarian, E.M., invited my parents to a screening of his latest film at Lincoln Center, and then he had them sit with him and his wife at the after-celebration at an expensive restaurant. "It was wonderful," our jubilant mother told us. "Waiters came over and brought the food and your father didn't even have to get up from the table."

In New York in the 1970s, our mother took an office job, employed for a few years at Metropolitan Life Insurance. As with other times she worked, it was to bring needed money into the household. For someone who liked to brag about herself, about what a great bridge player she was, about what a great cook she was, what accomplished children she had, etc., it seemed strange that I never heard her express a regret about having no serious profession. Her proudest employment was certainly her first upon coming to the USA, meeting Hollywood stars as a hostess at New York's Longchamps restaurant. In later life, she was supportive of other women having interesting jobs. Perhaps being the matriarch of our family was enough.

"Ask the taxicab driver why there are so many Chinese around here," our mother once demanded of me. I sighed. We were in Chinatown. Our parents hardly ever left the neighborhood where they ended residing, in Stuyvesant Town on First Avenue, except to visit Laura's sisters on the Upper West Side. Laura and Joe would go occasionally to a generic Cantonese restaurant near their apartment building, which our mother labeled "the best Chinese restaurant in New York." Once, our parents were invited for Szechuan food, not knowing the cuisine. Our mother complained after, "Someone needed to tell the waiter that the food was too hot." But 95% of the time in Manhattan, our parents ate at home as they'd done their whole married life. Finally, our mother could cook up some Eastern European dishes that had been too strange for West Virginia and South Carolina. What was in her recipes? "A little of this and a little of that," she would answer coyly, and add every time, "No fat. No fat at all." I'm proud that there's an acclaimed Russian cookbook whose title was actually inspired by what our mother always said. It's called *Please, To the Table*, edited by Danny's wife, Suzanne.

When she was in her 80s, Laura was encouraged to go to the local senior center for a game of bridge. She had no such desire, as she considered herself a great player and these people were her inferiors; and she was uninterested in hanging out with those she denigrated as "old people." She kept her mind sharp reading the *New York Times*. She walked a bit, did a few TV exercises. But she didn't swim or ride a bike, never went once to a gym, lived to 91. How did our mother do it? (1) Worrying almost every moment of her life. If she relaxed for a second, she got anxious, and started worrying again. (2) Never ever living in the moment. As she put a dinner before me, she would be talking a million miles an hour about what she was cooking the next day. (3) Never shutting up. Making up in spades for a quiet, shy childhood.

In his 80s, our father, Joe, slowly sank into dementia, having suffered a series of minor strokes. He started what he called "editing," marking up printed books and the entire *New York Times* with his cryptic pencil citations, scribbling on every page. He also began drawing again, for the first time since age 14. What he produced came straight from the unconscious, like an uninhibited 5-year-old, and his new work was primitive but sometimes oddly striking, true Surrealism. The famous documentary filmmaker, E.M., collected several of our father's most peculiar drawings, which much thrilled our mother. One day I was sitting with dad on a couch, and he turned to me with a smile and asked, "Did I ever tell you about the time I fought at the Bay of Pigs?"

The jury is still out whether our father was "on the spectrum" in a time when nobody knew what "the spectrum" was. The evidence: like many with Asperger's, Joe was enormously knowledgeable in narrow, factual areas, brilliantly informed about the biological sciences. He spoke eight languages, and had the world's geography in his head. But he had little ability at human relationships, and was like a naïve child dealing with people or doing anything practical. My brother says "No" to "the spectrum," as our father was warm and affectionate and liked being hugged and kissed. "He was always more comfortable with Europeans than Americans," Danny observed. I say "yes" to Asperger's, while agreeing about our father's sweet disposition. As for our mother's vantage: where I now see "the spectrum," Laura saw her husband, "the genius."

In the anti-Communist 1950s, our father was offered an enticing government job one summer, but accepting it required signing a loyalty oath. I'm proud to say he wouldn't sign it. I've inherited from him a sense of social justice and a hatred of racial prejudice. Thank you, Joe. And what came to me from the rest of my family? From our father's crazy, unhappy painter mother, Ida, perhaps my artiness. From our mother's mother, Miriam, a touch, I hope, of her big heart. From our father's extroverted father, Sam, a love of dining in restaurants, of being out in the world, and, yes, admiring lovely, intelligent women. From our talky, uninhibited mother, Laura, an insistence on speaking my mind and rarely holding back, both a good trait and a bad one. And impatience. Finally, I don't know who got our funniness from whom, but I'm been around a whole life of my brother Danny and his quick, infectious, tremendous sense of humor.

Very early in this memoir, I talk about a seminal moment of my life when I entered 1st grade in Philippi, West Virginia, and already had been reading for several years. My teacher declared me a "genius," which my mother believed, and Mrs. McLeod asked with seriousness for my autograph. She declared that I would be world-famous after attending Harvard University. Well, I have at best been slightly known. And with my damning C+ high school average, I certainly didn't go to Harvard. But many years later, I actually worked at Harvard for one year. Does that count, Mrs. McLeod, as I don't want to disappoint you? My mother, not thrilled by many of my life decisions, was appeased by my temporary Ivy

League appointment, one that came with an office. "Now," she said, "when we are on the Harvard grounds, your father will have a place to go to the toilet."

Imagine Hemingway typing the last paragraph of one of his illustrious manuscripts, a compliant wife cowering outside the door, macho friends waiting there with celebratory daiquiris and to take him deep sea fishing. I complete this memoir with my two kittens standing on my keyboard demanding lunch, and my annoyed spouse in my face saying, "Don't you have an appointment? You've got to stop your writing now and wash up!" Whatever, dear Amy. I declare this memoir is finished.

I Was A
Pre-Teenage
Auteurist

Originally published in *Citizen Sarris, American Film Critic: Essays in Honor of Andrew Sarris* (2001), edited by Emanuel Levy.

How can I forget that fateful day in 1965 when, strolling about Broadway in the West 80s, I wandered into Dan Talbot's New Yorker Bookstore, a second-floor adjunct to his legendary New Yorker Theater? There was a circular wire carousel in the middle of the store containing back copies of film magazines. I swung the carousel around, and there before me, with Busby Berkeley chorines on the cover, sat a remaindered issue of an enticing-looking periodical: *Film Culture* from spring 1962.

I opened it and, innocently, commenced reading… the special issue in which critic Andrew Sarris, whom I'd just started following in the *Village Voice*, tackled the American cinema. All of it! He sliced it, diced it, spun it on its ear, and weirdly classified it. He applied something he called the "auteur" theory to several hundred directors, dropping them into immutably Dantean categories. The "Pantheon" cineastes floated on high, along with "The Far Side of Paradise," while "Expressive Esoterica" knocked hopefully at the empyrean gates. "Lightly Likable," "Oddities, One-Shots and New-comers," and "Subjects for Further Research" bobbed in limbo, whereas poor "Strained Seriousness" and "Less Than Meets the Eye" dropped into the devilish muck below.

For me, the gentle reader: lightning bolts! Joycean epiphanies! Proustian flashes! My eyes bulged, my legs shook, standing there in the New Yorker Bookstore. New to Sarris's rhetorical mannerism, his wordplay, his stylistics, I'd never read film writing which described the cinema so colorfully, so unusually, so authoritatively: "Sternberg's films are poetic without being symbolic. We need not search for slumbering allegories of Man and God and Life, but rather for a continuous stream of emotional biography. Sternberg's exoticism is, then, less a pretense than a pretext for objectifying personal fantasies. His equivalent literary genre is not the novel or the short story or the theatrical spectacle, but the closet drama unplayable but for the meaningful grace of gesture and movement."

Wow!

Except for Hitchcock, many of the filmmakers whose names I knew best—Stanley Kubrick, John Huston, Stanley Kramer, Elia Kazan—were disparaged. That was perplexing enough. Yet who in the world were these directors Sarris was pushing in their place, to me unheard of, such as Budd Boetticher, Anthony Mann, and

Douglas Sirk? And then there was this Edgar G. Ulmer, "whose films," Sarris said, "are of interest only to unthinking audiences or specialists in mis-en-scène."

Mis-en-scène! That was for me, whatever it was.

I purchased the *Film Culture* issue and, in the coming weeks, read it through again and again, practically memorizing Sarris's shorthand and delightfully judgmental polemics. I was definitely persuaded. I started recasting my aesthetic, seeking out Sarris-approved "auteur" films on TV's late shows. ("Where oh where is Douglas Sirk's *Taza, Son of Cochise*?" I'd joke with my movie friends.)

As for new movies in the mid-1960s, I now swore weekly allegiance to Sarris and his cohorts in the *Village Voice*. These critics spoke out—and this was *very* radical then—from intensely personal points of view. Gay rights and women's liberation and film history and underground cinema all were in the wonderful mix. I solemnly believe that there has never been a more splendid, talented group of critics working for a newspaper. A Golden Age: Sarris, Molly Haskell, Stuart Byron, William Paul, Tom Allen, and, additionally, Jonas Mekas. Awesome!

But was it a coincidence that I was so swept away by all of this? Or, more likely, character being fate, wasn't it inevitable that I would be smitten?

The Road to Andrew Sarris

Without knowing it, I was a pre-teenage cultist, whose taste as a movie-crazed child was truly madly deeply prematurely "auteur." Many years before Sarris had brought his "Politiques" from Paris, I was already drumming to their Nouvelle Vague beat. The precocity of a future film critic: the movies I loved best as a tiny child were made, almost invariably, by Sarris-designated "auteurs."

In the 1950s I lived in Columbia, South Carolina. At the Palmetto, Carolina, and Five Points theaters, I fell hard for Nicholas Ray's *Johnny Guitar*, Don Siegel's *Invasion of the Body Snatchers*, George Stevens's *Shane*, Alfred Hitchcock's *Rear Window*. If you'd asked me in 1956, when I turned twelve, what were my three favorite films of all time, you'd find a formidable challenge to François Truffaut. I adored Nicholas Ray's *Rebel Without a Cause*, Howard Hawks's *Land of the Pharaohs*, and, most of all, John Ford's *The Searchers*. Enraptured, I watched *The Searchers* four days in a row at the theater at its original release.

When I did learn about directors, it was a different bunch, foreign language masters—Fellini, Kurosawa, Antonioni, Wajda— from avidly reading my first magazine film criticism in the early 1960s: Hollis Alpert and Arthur Knight in *The Saturday Review* and Dwight Macdonald in *Esquire*.

I was reborn as a foreign film dandy. Ingmar Bergman was my most cherished filmmaker and, for several years, *The Searchers* was forsaken for new all-time greatest films, *Wild Strawberries* and *Jules and Jim.* My film taste was rarefied and elitist. The movies which "meant something" had subtitles. I needed to be shook up! So thank you, Andrew Sarris!

We're back to *Film Culture*, spring 1962. We're back to Sirk and Ulmer, and me, regaining my cine-soul, seeing American movies as serious and meaningful as European ones. Bergman might be obsessed with the death of God, but Nicholas Ray, said Sarris, demonstrates that "every relationship establishes its own moral code, and there is no such thing as absolute morality." Sarris showed me that, without abandoning my continental tastes, it was very cool to love and admire *The Searchers* above all.

The Searchers, I learned, was directed by John Ford! In Andrew Sarris's Pantheon.

Pursuing a Ph.D. at the University of Wisconsin, I traveled to the film-nutty town of Madison, Wisconsin, where, in the mid-to-late 1960s, Sarris's aesthetics had already hit big. The film section of the school paper, the *Daily Cardinal*, was totally auteurist. (I was arts editor in 1970.) Most important, we students began our own amateur film magazine, *The Velvet Light Trap*, which combined Sarris-style auteurism with things new: "studio studies" (RKO, Warner Brothers) and also leftist-revisionist film history.

At the "Berkeley of the Midwest," some of the most passionate film freaks were also politically occupied by the War in Vietnam. For several heated years, I felt out of sorts with Sarris's more centrist liberalism. I identified myself as a leftist-auteurist, and I veered toward personal directors whose work had a socially activist bent: Pontecorvo, Godard, Arthur Penn, Hal Ashby.

However, I also remember how the most Marxist-Godardian-left-wing of film aficionados, Tony Chase (now a law professor), brought Sarris back into the fold. One day Chase decided that Sarris's old *Film Culture* categories (by then recast in book form for 1968's seminal *The American Cinema*) went far beyond a way of placing films. Instead, they offered a veritable cosmology, a way to classify anything: friends, American presidents, gods, you name it. Chase proved his abstract point by one day holding in hand an elaborate Sarrisian chart ranking about fifty candy bars! Hershey Bars and Mr. Goodbar were "Pantheon," Reese's Buttercups were "The Far Side of Paradise." Several popular candy bars that Chase disdained were classified as "Less Than Meets the Eye." I remember that "Chuckles" headed the category "Here Come the Clowns"!

From Madison to the World

Australians were eager to know about Sarris first-hand. Flash forward to summer 1995. A literal Tribute to Andrew Sarris, a main event at the Sydney Film Festival. Now working for the *New York Observer*, he was flown from Manhattan to talk, to reminisce. Fortuitously, I was teaching Boston University film students in a special summer-in-Sydney program, so I was asked to host the exciting event.

I stood alone on a huge stage before an audience of rapt Australians. I told my story that began this essay, the discovery of Sarris's *Film Culture* writings that changed my life. And then, to enthusiastic crowd applause, I introduced The Great Man himself. Sarris had a wonderful time in Australia, that I do believe. "Auteurism" thrived Down Under, and the audience listened intently when Sarris, the American critic, was asked to rank Australian filmmakers.

It wasn't long before, by request, he launched into the famous tale of his first meeting ever with Pauline Kael, in which he daydreamed beforehand a kind of *Adam's Rib* banter and attraction. "Alas, Pauline was certainly no Katharine Hepburn," Sarris joked. "But I was no Spencer Tracy either."

Sweet Memories of a Film Addict

Published in *Coming Soon to a Festival Near You: Programming Film Festivals* (St. Andrews, Scotland, 2012), ed. By Jeffrey Ruoff.

"I think it would be a great idea for you to start sending me to Cannes," pleads an alternative-newspaper film critic in Joan Micklin Silver's 1977 independent feature, *Between the Lines*. His editors are not to be convinced. That poor critic remains stuck at the office, no foreign adventures. Lucky for me, my journalist superiors usually have said "Go!" when I've wanted to flee to a film festival; and that's happened many, many times in my more than 30 years writing about movies, the last 14 of those for the *Boston Phoenix*.

It began innocently in 1976. Visiting Montreal, I was told that a film festival was going on (the World Film Festival). Would I be interested in checking out with a friend a movie there? Sure. What I saw was a raw French-Canadian independent work and, though my French is awful and there were no subtitles, there was something so incredibly compelling and romantic about being caught in an enthusiastic Quebecois festival crowd. I was smitten. Two years later, 1978, I had my first job as a film critic for the long-defunct Boston weekly, the *Real Paper*. I was assigned to cover the New York Film Festival. OK! I interviewed Éric Rohmer, met Claude Chabrol. I went to a liquor store with Gérard Depardieu. I sparred during a Q&A with Rainer Werner Fassbinder. My path was set.

What a fun life! Film festivals have been such a vital, essential—insatiable—part of my existence. Oh, the endless memories! Here is an edit of what I recall: snapshots from three delirious decades as a film festival addict.

The New York Film Festival, October 1980

Before the advent of the Sundance Film Festival, the New York Film Festival each fall was the essential fest in the USA. The festival director was Richard Roud, a champion of modernist European masters. 1980 was the year that Jean-Luc Godard and François Truffaut both attended with important films, though the once-Parisian soulmates no longer conversed.

Living in self-exile in Switzerland, Godard came to the Big Apple with his first semi-traditional feature in many years, *Sauve qui peut/Every Man for Himself*, a slimmed-down, lucid, rethinking of his classic 1960s works. The filmmaker professed to like his new movie. "I feel now that I've landed in this beautiful country of narrative for the first time, remembering the full strength of Mack Sennett's arrival in California," Godard said at a NYFF press conference. "Of course, I don't pretend it to be as good."

Who knows what Godard really believes? He acted unconcerned that the New Wave innovations of his *Breathless* (1960)—jump-cutting, stop-action etc.—had been abducted by commerce. "It's a fact that all Eisenstein discoveries are on TV today. Shampoo ads come from *Potemkin* [1926]. What can we do? I'm not against advertisement. I was hired to do a two-minute commercial for a men's aftershave lotion. I gave them two hours [of material]." Was he still, as in the early 1970s, a Maoist-minded revolutionary? "I'm a capitalist," he declared. "I'm a producer. I love money. I love to spend it."

Godard couldn't leave the stage without getting in a dig at his favorite adversary, his ex-pal Truffaut. "When I tell him, 'François, in my opinion, you're not a very good director, but you're a good screenwriter,' he gets shocked!" Would Truffaut fight back? The NYFF press conference after his *The Last Metro* offered Truffaut a chance to respond. "I'm perfectly aware that Jean-Luc thinks all of my films are bad," he said. "I say that all of his films are good." You could feel the bitterness and pain despite Truffaut's attempt at diplomacy. (Truffaut died four years later of a brain tumor. The two giants of the New Wave never reconciled.)

The Jerusalem Film Festival, July 1988

The week before I arrived, Palestinians in the Old City had stoned archaeologists digging close to their holy shrines, and the Israeli police countered with tear gas and arrests. After several days, the confrontations ebbed. The five-year-old Jerusalem Film Festival at the Cinematheque had gotten a quick reputation as a "peacenik" event with a mandate to show films from Arab directors and also from the Eastern Bloc. So this was the natural landing spot for the first delegation of Soviet filmmakers ever allowed by their government to enter Israel. These included Alexander Chervinsky, Jewish, the screenwriter of *Tema* (1979), made at a time when controversial Jewish subject matter was forbidden in the Soviet Union. It was shelved in the Leonid Brezhnev era but resuscitated in 1987 by Mikhail Gorbachev, to be readied for worldwide release. Even to be shown in Jerusalem.

I spoke to Chervinsky about how he had made it from Russia to Israel. He said that Andrei Smirnov, the acting secretary of the Union of Soviet Filmmakers, struggled to have this trip allowed. "He insisted at the Foreign Ministry that the policy of our union is to enlarge the showings of Soviet filmmakers everywhere. In Israel, lots of people speak Russian. Also, it's a film market. There's money!"

Chervinsky's screenplay for *Theme* included a subplot about an unhappy Russian Jew emigrating to Israel, and he believed that was why his film was never released at home. In Brezhnev's time, "a character in a film could be Jewish, but only in a very specific way. He could be in the war, very bold and brave, and die while everyone lives. Or he could be a friendly, funny Jew. I don't have to tell you—it's the same as black persons in American movies."

The Berlin International Film Festival, February 1990

I stood on the Berlin Wall! Hoisted up nine feet, I squeezed among the hundreds standing on one section of the Wall while the Russians bulldozed another. The festivities stretched from the Brandenburg Gate to Checkpoint Charlie, a mile away.

This was the year that the grim February city of Berlin became, both East and West, a gigantic, euphoric playpen. Virtually every filmmaker, journalist, buyer and seller skipped away often from the 40th Berlin International Film Festival. The lazy people—most of us—bought pieces of Wall rock from the myriad entrepreneurs behind makeshift tables. However, for a single West German mark you could rent a pick. For two marks a pair of goggles to guard against the flying debris.

Those who chose to hammer away? An American film critic from Washington, D.C. got scratched, bloodied hands. "It's not easy knocking down a concrete wall," he complained. "Have you ever tried to rip up your sidewalk?"

Meanwhile, the West Berlin-based festival acknowledged the opening of the border with daily showings of forbidden East German films. There were prime pickings especially from 1965 to 1968, when the huffy, intractable Communist government banned virtually every movie produced there. One of those verboten works was *Born in '45* (1965), finally unveiled at the Fest in the year 1990 with Jürgen Böttcher, the filmmaker, present. Did he just walk over from East Berlin?

In 1966, the GDR officials had complained: Why did three of Böttcher's characters have to stand against a black wall? What does that say of East Germany? And why did the hero stare out the window at a building not yet completed? What did that symbolize? In one scene, a tourist bus from West Berlin passed through the frame. Böttcher said: "I was told that the presence of a Western bus insulted the powers above. We should be happy we don't ride on Western buses!"

At several earlier Fests I'd made the depressing trek into East Berlin. I'd visited the awful giant department store, walked into grocery markets where cabbage was the favored vegetable. And I tried to get into Bertolt Brecht's house, a national museum that, frustratingly, was always closed.

Was I surprised that the Wall came down? I'd had a premonition a year earlier. In 1989, I got into Brecht's home. I stood by the single bed in which the playwright died. If BB's home was open at last to the public, so, I figured, Berlin, the Open City, could be next.

The Provincetown International Film Festival, July 2001

What a faux pas, all because I missed a screening of the documentary *Southern Comfort* at the gay-and-lesbian friendly third Provincetown International Film Festival. How could I know, when I met the genial *Southern Comfort* star at a party, that Lola Cola was not a transvestite but a transsexual? I referred to Lola as "him," only to be corrected by Lola's female lover: "Lola is a she!"

I did have a cool metrosexual moment: a heart-to-heart with a drag artist from Minnesota whose nightclub act, he/she (?) noted, encompassed both Celine Dion and Reba McIntyre. Also, I was cruised by a bearded nun outside a sing-along screening of *The Sound of Music* (1965). Is there a better spot on earth for "Doe, a deer" than uninhibited P-town? At the screening, boos and hisses rained down on Christopher Plummer's so-straight Baron von Trapp. Who in the gender-twisting audience could abide such a hetero patriarch?

I checked in at the apartment of filmmaker John Waters, who has been coming to P-town for 37 Massachusetts summers. A fervent supporter of the festival, he's agreed each year to introduce a favorite oddball movie. This time, he chose *Baxter* (1989), a French flick about a bull terrier who bites those who are sentimental about dogs.

Waters was giddy about the upcoming evening featuring 1960s songster Connie Francis with her super-hit 1960 movie, *Where the Boys Are*. As we talked, Waters played volume four of her Greatest Hits. Frankly, I had some trepidation about Francis's appearance. Would she justify the $25 ticket price? Not to worry. After tanned muscle boys pranced through the audience in bathing suits, Connie came on to cheers! "What a joy it is to be here tonight! Welcome to the groovy Provincetown Festival!" she said. Then the film rolled, the mostly boring, inanely written *Where the Boys Are*, only vaguely improved by a 35mm restoration.

Back on stage, Francis confessed how little she'd wanted to make the movie. "I didn't attend the première. I didn't like the way I looked, sang, acted. But *Where the Boys Are* was my *Gone with the Wind* [1939]. The rest of my movies—*Follow the Boys* [1963] etc.—were downhill all the way. I really have nerve being at a film festival!"

The Toronto International Film Festival, September 2001

I was at the Toronto Fest on 9/11. That morning, I walked out of a theater in the middle of a tedious screening (it was a film from India) to come upon people with eyes on TVs wherever they could find them. Horrific images from NYC. On the fourth day of the festival, the world appeared to be ending. The many Americans I knew there—press, publicists, directors, movie stars, and so on—stumbled about in collective shock, moving from watching CNN on monitors to struggling to get through to New York and LA on cell phones. Eventually, they formulated patchwork arrangements to traverse the Ontario-U.S. border and arrive home—hopefully, without encountering a second wave of terrorists.

A typical plan: six California show-biz people pooling money for a minibus and a three-day drive to Los Angeles. On the other hand, there was a solipsistic Hungarian filmmaker who called worried from Budapest: would his screenings at the Museum of Modern Art in New York be affected?

The TIFF closed down for about 40 hours, and then, cautiously, started up. Slowly, those who had disowned the cinema on Tuesday began, on Thursday and Friday, to watch movies again. I too. Exiled in Toronto, we could do nothing about crashed planes or the downed World Trade Center. Inside theaters, those who so wished could escape a bit in the dark. But wouldn't you know it?

There was a film, Denis Chouinard's *Tar Angel*, so close to real events. It climaxed at a rural airport with a confrontation between Canadian police and young Muslims, labeled by the government as terrorists. The only violence came from the cops, who beat to death an unarmed Muslim. (Not unexpectedly, *Tar Angel* never played post 9/11 in the United States.)

The Midnight Sun Film Festival, June 2002

It's certainly surreal, the sun blazing at midnight in Lapland, home of a zillion freezing lakes, where, buzzed on 120-proof Finnish vodka, I run from a sauna and jump into one of them. Each year, one American journalist is invited to the Midnight Sun Film Festival, and I was that special guest in 2002. And who's that bearded, naked man in a towel on the sauna porch? It's Francis Ford Coppola, another happy-on-vodka camper. Earlier, clothed, he led the gathered in off-key singing of "Avanti Popolo" and then soloed on a wobbly, screechy "God Bless America." Welcome to a VIP party at the June-set Midnight Sun Film Festival. Coppola was won over by a retrospective of his films, which reclaimed such neglected works as *Tucker* (1988) and *Gardens of Stone* (1987).

Sixteen years earlier, three Helsinki-based filmmakers—Timo Malmi and Aki and Mika Kaurismäki—envisioned a utopian European festival. They'd been at enough compromised ones to realize what they didn't want. "Filmmakers use limousines, stay at five-star hotels, and the people attending never talk to them," Mika Kaurismäki complained to me. "A festival in Helsinki would be too normal. We wanted something strange." The search for a setting ended in the polar region a 12-hour drive north of Helsinki. The tiny Lapland municipality of Sodankyla, a place known for alcoholism, suicides, unemployment, and coal-dark winters. Understandably, the town's mayor was eager to talk business.

Malmi and the Kaurismäkis saw possibilities in this three-street, one movie-house spot. It was geographically exotic, 100 kilometers above the Arctic Circle. And yet each June, transcendence: it was tee-shirt warm, and the sun stayed out 24 hours a day. The Midnight Sun Film Festival was born in 1987. The first guests, French film-maker Bertrand Tavernier (*Round Midnight*, 1986) and American "B" cult director, Sam Fuller (*Shock Corridor*, 1963, *The Naked Kiss*, 1964), got, as promised, 35mm screenings of their films. "Sam never slept" said Kaurismäki. "On the street, if you saw the cigar smoke, you knew Fuller was there, talking about movies."

Filmmaker guests have included Michael Powell, Krzysztof Kieślowski, and Terry Gilliam. Still, there was only one Fuller and, after his 1997 death, a Sodankyla street was named after him: Samuel Fullerin Katu/Samuel Fuller's Street! Standing in June at that anointed street corner, l tried to imagine cruel February in frozen, lonely Lapland: just forlorn locals around, and, in the deep snow, the street sign of Sam, with reindeer everywhere. As I said, surreal.

The Cannes Film Festival, May 2003

"Life is short, Cannes is long," quipped an exhausted American film critic days into the seemingly endless 61st annual film festival. What bedazzles and seems so glamorous on TV—the azure French Rivera, the red carpet at the Palais, toothsome international movie stars— makes for the most sleep-deprived, 12-day, workaholic time of the year for the 4,000 journalists in attendance. They scramble from screening to cell phone to interview to press conference to computer to e-mail from 8:30 am to deep into the night. Yes, there are lush parties down by the sea, each après-midi and evening, but these are mostly a gulp-a wine and gobble-some-hors-d'oeuvres tease.

On-the-job reporters are quickly back to work. The Riviera beach? No critic worth his/her salt has gone swimming in years. Sex under the palm trees? Maybe for starlets and collegiate interns, not for the deadline-obsessed fourth estate. Is that awful enough, dear readers?

In 2003, the Cannes jury deserved commendation for rejecting all prizes for the mean-spirited film predicted for the Palme d'Or winner: *Dogville*, the female-bashing, people-loathing, Amer-ica-despising tome from Denmark's Lars von Trier. Legions of auteurist-worshipping Europeans were angered when header Nicole Kidman took no Best Actress, Trier no Best Director, and *Dogville* no Best Picture. For me: hallelujah!

At the *Dogville* press conference, I challenged the Danish cineaste with a hostile question "In three recent films, you have had your female stars, Emily Watson, Björk, and now Nicole Kidman, tortured, raped, imprisoned, chained, murdered, or some variant of the above. Why always are your victims women, women, women?"

"That's a superficial way to look at the story," Trier answered. "That's not the way I look at the story. I don't think it's important if the victims are men or women. I'm sorry you don't like it. There are other people who do like it." But dear Lars, if it doesn't matter, why not a couple of guys instead of gals strung up and anally attacked? That'll be the day!

And then there was Vincent Gallo's self-starring ego-trip, *The Brown Bunny*. Smugly assured before his screening, Gallo shriveled a bit due to the scornful laughter during the public screening; and that was followed by the torrent of negative reviews in the English-language press. Who could fathom why Gallo squandered that much screen time on himself doing practically nothing: shaving, combing his hair, pumping gas, sleeping, driving, driving, driving? Finally, the scene arrived for which every dirty-minded person was waiting (count me in): Chloë Sevigny doing a Monica Lewinsky on his erect member. The blow job was authentic on her part, yet rumors started quickly that what we saw sticking out of Gallo's zipper was a large piece of rubber. Apparently, such an object was missing from the set of Claire Denis's *Trouble Every Day* (2001), in which Gallo starred.

"I apologize to the financiers of the film, but I assure you it was never my intention to make a pretentious film, a self-indulgent film, a useless film, an unengaging film," Gallo said in Cannes the somber day after. He added that the fact that some French critics liked *The Brown Bunny* "is almost like salt in the wound!"

The Bangkok International Film Festival, January 2005

Would it be obscene to hold the Bangkok International Film Festival just weeks after the Thai coast had been done in, and so many drowned, by the tsunami? A decision was made: the 11-day show would roll on, bankrolled mostly by the Tourism Authority of Thailand. However, the opening-night celebration was canceled, and proceeds from the festival were announced as going to "tsunami aid." As for the much-anticipated appearance of the Thai royal family at the closing night: Princess Uboltrana couldn't attend. She was in mourning for her son, who'd been vacationing that fatal day by the ocean.

The lavish festival moved ahead with a thoughtful tribute to Mexican cinematographer Rodrigo Prieto (*Amores Perros*, 2000; *Frida*, 2002; *21 Grams*, 2003). A career award was bestowed on

Hollywood schlock maestro Joel Schumacher (*Lost Boys*, 1987; *Batman Forever*, 1995; *Phone Booth,* 2002). He unveiled there his dubious-achievement musical, *The Phantom of the Opera* (2004), without fear of audience chortling. Thai citizenry are famously polite.

David Hockney was a no-show because he couldn't get a visa to Thailand for his boyfriend. "I told David, don't worry, you can find plenty of boyfriends in Bangkok," a festival organizer confided. Maybe Hockney was put off by the travel time to Thailand? It couldn't have been worse than mine: with woeful connections, it was 36 hours from Boston's Logan, including a nightmare 3am switching of planes in Fairbanks, Alaska, where reindeer sausage was on the early-bird breakfast menu.

But what's to gripe? I was president of the five-person International Critics Jury; and probably nowhere on earth was a jury of the press treated with such luxury. We stayed at a five-star hotel, swam in the pool between screenings, toured ancient Buddhist sites, ate in tasty, spicy Bangkok restaurants. Our jury duty was to select the best Southeast Asian film among 15 candidates. We watched three a day in a plush little theatre in a multiplex supplied with lean-back armchairs, blankets and pillows.

And what did we see? The first film we'd ever encountered from under-siege Burma (Myanmar), a naive, inept work about some Burmese in Japan who learn that their homeland (no mention of the military occupancy) is the place to be. Three horrid Philippine melodramas. An intriguing Vietnamese neo-realist film about water-buffalo herders. A Thai tearjerker with a husband dying of a brain tumor. Our winner? *The Beautiful Washing Machine*, 2004), from Malaysia's James Lee, a deadpan sex comedy somewhere between Luis Buñuel and Ming-Liang Tsai.

Bergman Film Week, June 2010

Each July and August, tourists pack the Swedish island of Faro (pronounced 'foreh," with a rolling 'r') for hikes, bicycling and jolting leaps into the brisk Baltic Sea. But winters are desolate and fierce, and under 100 residents remain. A sole filmmaker resided year-round on Faro and died in August 2007. That was Ingmar Bergman, 89, the island's most famous citizen.

It was in 1960 when Bergman first arrived on Faro for the filming of *Through a Glass Darkly* (1961). The craggy, stormy ambience—and the truly extraordinary light—fit perfectly with his vision. Bergman told his cinematographer, Sven Nykvist, that he would buy a house and make more movies there. Someday, he would move permanently to Faro. And he wished to die there. The promises of half a century ago were kept, including the home and the filming of such masterpieces as *Persona* (1966), *Shame* (1968), *The Passion of Anna* (1969), and *Scenes from a Marriage* (1973). Bergman sold his Stockholm apartment in 1993, transferred all his belongings to the island. Living alone at the end, he expired in his Faro bed. He's buried in the graveyard of Faro's only church.

Bergman honored Faro. How could Faro honor him?

In 2010, I was one of eight international journalists brought to Faro by the Swedish Institute. We would participate in Bergman Week, an annual summer film festival. Also, we would see where on the island Bergman shot his famous films. Most enticing of all, we would be the first press group ever to watch movies in Bergman's private theatre and tour Bergman's house.

Our initiation to Faro was a conversation with Liv Ullmann, star of four key Bergman features made there, starting with her dazzling film debut in *Persona*. When she was romantically involved with her director, they resided for months each year in Bergman's Faro house. Said Ullmann: "I had almost five years here with him, and a daughter, and an incredible creative relationship. It's who I am: Faro, the people I met, the strange seasons, the light in the middle of the night, the barren winters with no colors."

Lin Ulmann, the Norwegian novelist daughter of Ullmann and Bergman, brought us to a converted barn which, several miles from his home, had been Bergman's private screening room. It was equipped for 16mm and 35mm showings and with a projectionist on call. "My father would meet us outside on this blue bench," she showed us. "We'd see two films a day, at three o'clock for the hard-core: an artistic film, often a silent one. At 7:30, there was a film for a bigger audience, sometimes even with children." In awe, we ventured inside. We looked about, so deeply thrilled: a tapestry on a wall of Bergman's *The Magic Flute* (1975), pine-wood walls, and 16 plush chairs in three rows. In the front: the chair where Bergman always sat, supplied with a wool-covered back pillow. We stared at Bergman's seat but stayed obedient to the holy house rule: it's only for the Swedish master. For evermore.

We did more sleuthing in a rushed trip through Bergman's house, pushed through by impatient guides. Some of us lingered in his library to check out his books: lots by playwright August

Strindberg, his hero. Several Bibles, of course, and, surprising to me, many novels by Isaac Bashevis Singer. Bergman's huge VHS collection had predictable classics—Andrei Tarkovsky, Fritz Lang, etc.—but also random films revealing, perhaps, an unexpectedly eclectic movie taste. Did this high modernist really watch *The Blues Brothers* (1980), *Blood from the Mummy's Tomb* (1971), *Elvis! Elvis!* (1976), and Adam Sandler in *Anger Management* (2003)?

We stood solemnly at the double bed with a white cover where the filmmaker died. Later, we were taken to Faro Church, where Bergman, often angrily doubtful of God, apparently worshipped. He is interred in a private spot far from other graves. His burial place is shared with his last wife, the non-actress Ingrid Bergman. She had passed on before him, but her body was exhumed and brought here.

Bergman carefully planned out the 2007 funeral with his woman minister. "He picked the wood for his coffin, and the carpenter," our guide told us. "People were to be dressed in black, and there should be red roses." And what about journalists? The guide laughed. "The press had to be 100 yards away, in a field where the lambs stand."

An Interview
with Bill Marx

It's a bit daunting trying to figure out how to frame an interview about a lifetime of moviegoing.

A few years ago I was asked to do a stage interview with composer Philip Glass about the music he'd provided for various films. I was very anxious as I'd never met Glass before, so I wanted to know from him precisely what he wished discussed, what film clips he was comfortable with, and in what order to show the clips. And Glass replied, "Let's wing it. Whatever movie clips you want to show, that's fine with me. Ask any question you want, that's also fine with me. Surprise me!" It turned out to be a great evening because it was spontaneous and Glass had lots of fun having no idea what I was going to throw at him. So, surprise me!

All right, we'll just go into it and see what happens. Could you talk a little bit about when you first embraced cinema?

I was always, always deeply into movies. From early childhood. In contrast, critic colleagues have told me that they didn't care about cinema until they took an inspiring film course in college, or at 19 they read Pauline Kael and fell head over heels with her writing and her opinions, or they saw Roger Ebert and Gene Siskel dueling about movies on TV and that made them want to be cinephiles. But I was film crazy from probably 5 years old when I was a child living in the hills of West Virginia in rural America. I frequented two theaters on the Main Street of Philippi, the small town where we lived, especially the one which regularly showed "B" Westerns.

I've written several times about seeing my first movie at 3, around 1947–1948, a live-action *Goldilocks and the Seven Bears.* I was completely enraptured, especially by a scene in which the characters, human and animal, had a pillow fight, and feathers from the pillows soared in slow-motion through the air, a moment akin to that with the schoolboys in Jean Vigo's 1933 surrealist masterpiece *Zéro de Conduite.*

But seemingly the film that I am confident I watched does not exist! I wrote an essay for a book about this seminal cinema experience and the editor of that book, film critic Peter Keough, decided to fact check. And he was shocked, chagrined, amused or whatever because he could find no record anywhere of this film that I was raving about. An animated "Goldilocks" yes, but absolutely no live action version. But I *know* that film is out there...

At least in your own head.

It's more than my head! Someday a print will be found in the dusty basement of some film archive and I will be vindicated!

I want to probe a little bit your initial attraction to cinema. Pauline Kael has made the case that early moviegoing for her had an element of the illicit, "I'm seeing something that my parents would not want me to see." Was moviegoing illicit or delinquent in any way for you?

Do you mean when I was 13 and blushing at the ticket booth paying to see Brigitte Bardot's nakedness in *And God Created Woman* [1956]. Or my embarrassment as a teenager sneaking into some soft-X pseudo-documentary with bare-breasted nudists playing volleyball?

I mean when you were still a child.

Then the answer is "no." My parents never said, "You can't see certain movies." They never censored me in any way. They had no interest in the illicit, no knowledge of the illicit. But they believed that whatever your kid wants to do is okay. So I was seeing whatever movies I wished to see and I was reading whatever books I wanted to read and that was fine with them. No guilt.

But if not illicit, going to movies as a young child was certainly a thrilling adventure. In the early 1950s, children like me went all by themselves to the cinema, which is just unimaginable in our time. The cinema was a safe place. Even my worrywart Jewish mother didn't think that somebody seedy was going to molest me or kidnap me. So there *was* something alluring and sexy about being a little boy sitting alone in a movie theater. And gasping at what was up there on the big screen.

Are you describing the education of the future film critic or a fan? Movies obviously reflected a reality that you were not living. You had that fantasy of seeing the adventurous heroes, glamorous starlets and so forth, which must have been pretty attractive, right?

I don't know that I saw things differently from others. Everyone likes cute starlets and screen adventures. I was just part of the crowd, and whatever I was seeing was pretty appealing to me.

Unless it was adults on screen talking too much and too much kissing. But I was placated as long as there was filmic activity, like cowboys galloping on horseback across the range or Native Americans whooping it up with bows and arrows. I adored swashbucklers, *Three Musketeers* types of stories with lots of sword fighting. I loved guys with feathered hats stabbing each other with pointy swords! That was great.

The beginning of the 1950s was still an era when there were serials at the movie theaters, at least in rural West Virginia. And that, for me, was a primal surrealist experience. Seeing people tumbling from skyscrapers or into crocodile-filled waters and having people blown up by dynamite and almost drowning in floods, and things just swirling around you! Just a constant super-adventure with scary things happening to the characters every second. Wow! I felt that delirious spirit again years later with early James Bond movies like *Dr. No* [1962] and Fritz Lang's *Dr. Mabuse, the Gambler* [1922]. Georges Franju certainly captures that spirit with his homage to serials, *Judex* [1963]. And Spielberg did all right by me with *Raiders of the Lost Ark* (1981).

Did you become more interested in movies than books? Though you're an avid reader, did movies win out in that competition?

I don't think they won out. My whole life, I've been schizoid, jumping between the one medium and the other. Even now I ask myself several times each day, "Should I read a book or see a movie?" I sometimes say that if I were on that proverbial desert island, I would take a book over a film. Books probably win, but it's really, really tight. But what a wonderful choice: do I open a book or do I watch a movie on my computer? Or do I listen to music—jazz or country or rock—or see a Boston Celtics basketball game on TV? I was not bored as a child and I'm never bored as an old person because of all these grand choices open to me without my leaving my house.

Did you watch movies naively as a child or did you begin to develop a critical sensibility?

My first moment of a critical sensibility was when I realized that serials were often a fraud. If you saw a serial one week, the ending showed that it was impossible for the characters to escape the peril they were in. Death was imminent. But the following week when you saw the final scene repeated at the beginning of the serial's new chapter, you noticed the insertion of a couple of shots which allowed the characters to get free. And live on. I correctly felt cheated.

You felt you'd been fooled and you were pissed off. The beginning of the critical impulse. Did you decide after that you'd have to look at movies far more carefully?

I doubt if at 7 or 8 I had that conscious thought, but I got that movies weren't perfect. They were just romantic objects. They had flaws like everything else. And obviously later as a critic I saw many flaws in movies and realized that movies were rarely perfect.

Besides Westerns and swashbucklers, what other kind of movies did you like as a kid?

Stupid comedies for sure. Abbot and Costello and the Bowery Boys were just phenomenal. That goofy Huntz Hall! A bit later, Jerry Lewis and Danny Kaye.

When puberty hit, I assume you became interested in the sexual elements in films.

Certainly by age 12 I was aware of attractive women in films. My male gaze was afire! I first noticed Virginia Mayo, that leggy blonde actress, and I remember staring hard at a poster outside a theater of bosomy Jane Russell. And I felt an erotic tingle seeing Anne Francis prancing about barefoot and in the shortest skirts in *Forbidden Planet* [1956] and shapely Julie Adams bobbing in the water in *Creature from the Black Lagoon* [1954]. Was I some kind of a fetishist? I was taken by Grace Kelly in a slip in *Dial M From Murder* [1954] and Elizabeth Taylor also in a slip shedding her stockings in *Butterfield 8* [1960]. So yes, I felt the sexuality of movies and I liked that. I still like that: Eros and cinema.

You do realize you aren't being politically correct, tooting your own horn about your heterosexual desire?

I can't deny that it's part of my sensibility, including when I'm reviewing films. I think it's absurd that male heterosexual desire is dismissed in our PC age as having no validity, or for being intrinsically creepy. But having desire isn't the same as acting out in life as a sexist pig, which is not acceptable. Anyway, I'm for most kinds of sexual desire being expressed in cinema and not repressed, and that includes queer desire and trans desire. Some favorite films of mine are manifestations of queer sexual sensibilities from Jean Genet's *Un Chant d'amour* [1950] to Rose Troche's *Go Fish* [1994] to Pedro Almodóvar's *Law of Desire* [1987].

Besides becoming sexually aware, did your taste in movies become more sophisticated when you were 12 and 13?

My taste expanded to horror films and crime movies. But as a teenager I was not suspicious at all of costume dramas, one of the funkiest and campiest of genres. I didn't notice anything funny or stupid when I saw *The Ten Commandments* [1956] or *Ben-Hur* [1959], two movies which I now find absurdly bad. My favorite costume drama by far was *Land of the Pharaohs* [1955], a disparaged film which I still enjoy. I understand it was also a Martin Scorsese childhood favorite, though neither of us were cognizant that it was co-written by William Faulkner and directed by Howard Hawks. When I really adored a movie, I would see it three or four days in a row. *Land of the Pharaohs* was one of those pictures I watched repeatedly. This viperous woman played by Joan Collins screws around on her pharaoh husband and he locks her alive in a closed-off pyramid to die. What an inventive revenge!

Yes, one of the great death scenes with the sands slowly moving room to room in the pyramid. To bury Joan Collins forever.

That was mind-boggling. For *Land of the Pharaohs*, we've got to thank Faulkner for writing some of the scenes, maybe that scene.

Were you talking to other kids as you're watching these movies? Were you saying to others, "Here's what I think, what did you think?" and beginning to have a critical dialogue about the cinema?

When I was 12 and now living in Columbia, South Carolina, I had a friend, David, who was also a movie fan. David and I took the city bus to see films on Saturdays, and usually we gravitated to horror movies. We were lucky enough to see the original runs of *The Incredible Shrinking Man* [1957] and *The Fly* [1958] and

Invasion of the Body Snatchers [1956]. But did we talk critically about these movies? I doubt it. We were just fans.

The other person I saw movies with was my little brother, Danny Peary. He was five years younger than me. Sometimes I didn't want him around because he was an annoying younger brother. But we did see *Land of the Pharaohs* together, for sure. And we saw the most important movie of both of our childhoods, John Ford's *The Searchers* [1956]. I watched it when it first came out in summer 1956, which would make me 11. And my brother, who was 6, came along for three or four days in a row. I'm sure we didn't have critical discussions, though Danny also grew up to be someone who wrote seriously about movies. Among other excellent books, he's the author of the highly influential *Cult Movies 1, 2, and 3* and *Guide for the Film Fanatic*. Many important filmmakers swear by Danny's works as getting them into cinema.

Again, you talked to nobody critically about the movies you saw?

That's correct, and certainly not to my parents. But the strange thing was that I had astonishingly developed movie taste. Where that came from I don't know. I've written about this in several places, and I still scratch my head at this, but almost all the movies that I really loved turned out to be from directors who later were claimed as auteurs. That includes Hitchcock, Ford, Hawks, Nicholas Ray, Fritz Lang, George Stevens, Joseph H. Lewis... just on and on. I didn't have the vocabulary to note camera movement or editing or any visual component or to articulate how movies were shaped. I was only dimly aware of film direction. But all I can say is that my instincts were to pick really first-rate Hollywood movies. I did go with my parents to see two favorites, *Shane* [1953] and *Rear Window* [1954]. But what other 10-year-old went by himself to see *Johnny Guitar* [1954]?

I know John Ford is a key director in your own personal pantheon and The Searchers *is among your favorite films, so seeing it at 12 was quite a leap from those sword-fighting films you'd been lapping up.* The Searchers *is ten times deeper than, say,* The Mark of Zorro *[1940]. Did you feel, "This is the real deal"?*

Swashbuckler films have almost no psychological life. It's just witty banter and fun sword fights and pratfalls and that's about it. But *The Searchers* was this disquieting movie with deep and terrible psychological things going on. It certainly was a primal viewing experience from the very first act, realizing that the Natives were going to massacre this nice family. And then watching Debbie being separated from them, crawling outside, and then the moment which scared the dickens out of me, the dark shadow of Scar falling over little Debbie and then Scar in warpaint blowing this discordant note into his horn. Debbie, a child like me and my brother, was being stolen away! I felt that in every bone and in my brain and gut.

That was very, very different, being so shaken up sitting there in the movie theater. Far from *Scaramouche* [1952]! Even with four viewings, it didn't register for me to notice that *The Searchers* was directed by someone named John Ford. The only directors whom I was aware of when I was 12 or 13 were the two who really self-promoted, Cecil B. DeMille and Alfred Hitchcock, whose names were above the title. I knew of DeMille when I saw *The Greatest Show on Earth* [1952] and *The Ten Commandments* and Hitchcock for a bunch of 1950s films. And then Hitchcock hosted a television program. But John Ford? I had no idea where *The Searchers* came from. It just came out of the air.

Besides knowing of DeMille and Hitchcock, when did you begin noticing the names of directors?

Probably three or four years after *The Searchers* experience, when I was 15 or 16. I slowly learned of directors because I started to read film criticism. My parents subscribed to a culture magazine called *The Saturday Review,* and every week there was a film review column shared by Arthur Knight and Hollis Alpert. Knight was a film professor at the University of Southern California and Alpert was a New York critic. They were somewhat intellectual and at least mildly critical. I read these columns with interest. They led me to smarter Hollywood films and also some foreign-language films.

Wasn't what you're describing very much part of the critical cultural assumptions of the 1950s? That culture was a ladder. You could educate yourself through universities but also through critics to improve your taste and nurture your cultural sophistication.

Something like that. *The Saturday Review* was there to gently prod my aesthetic choices and improve my taste. I probably used

Knight and Alpert as a step to more dynamic and forceful critics. They certainly served a purpose; they were okay guys. Thanks, Hollis and Arthur, for being there for me in the late 1950s.

Did reading The Saturday Review *critics make you think you'd like to write movie criticism?*

Not at all. But I did briefly write for my high school newspaper a column of short reviews of books I'd been reading. There was a paperback publishing house called Pocket Books and I named my column "Peary Picks the Pockets." Clever, huh? And the alliteration! I recall that I was using critic cliches, which I must have picked up from daily newspaper critics. I distinctly remember penning this immortal phrase, "One book sure to catch the reader's eye..." I must have read that somewhere and conveniently borrowed it. Whatever, that was my first critical writing.

You were reading film critics, and like it or not, you were beginning to absorb their language and their perspective. Was there yet anyone with whom to discuss your aesthetic interests?

I had always been a kind of an intellectual loner, but not one who pined about it or felt sorry for myself. I just thought that's what life is like: reading books and seeing movies and thinking to yourself about them. Several times, I hooked up with nerdy guys who read sci-fi and *Mad Magazine*, and that was nice. But in my senior year of high school, I was befriended by a very, very important group of people for me, a bunch of self-proclaimed beatniks at my high school in South Carolina. I was introduced to jazz and to competitive chess, and we started reading poetry out loud especially Gregory Corso and Lawrence Ferlinghetti. And I started writing some florid poetry myself. This group of friends were incredible readers. They liked film, but they weren't passionate about film like they were about literature. So, pushed by them, I read about 150 books my senior year. Reading became something that I not only thought about but talked about with my very smart friends. It was, I guess, the first time that I conversed critically about the arts.

And what was the reaction to your book column in the school paper?

I don't think anybody read my column seriously or took up a book that I recommended. I do have a memory of being a little bit disappointed in my fellow high-schoolers. What philistines! And you know, this disappointment has carried through much of my life as a critic. I'm always a little pissed off that the crowds don't immediately race off to the movies that I'm recommending or fall down and thank me for my brilliant insights sending them to a great film. I'm mostly joking saying this. But not entirely joking.

It's interesting to hear about this beatnik group in high school that took you in and with whom you talked with excitement about the arts. Would it be safe to say that when you embraced this cultural underground, it was a step toward later a rejection of being a mainstream critic? Early on, you had outsider mentality.

Everything you say is true. A good observation. And I was even more of an outsider being Jewish in Christian West Virginia and South Carolina and having parents from Europe with thick foreign accidents. The final nail in the coffin was that my father, a biology professor, taught at two black colleges in Columbia, and that was the most dishonorable job you could have in the deeply segregated 1950s South. People would shun our family. Maybe it's time to note that I was an awful, awful high school student, completely alienated. I was kicked out of classes as a disciplinary problem. I barely graduated and didn't even apply to any universities. I was just reading on my own and hanging out with my captivating friends. But then my father got a job in New Jersey teaching at a place called Rider College. In 1960, we moved north from South Carolina. And I got into Rider simply because my father taught there and I got free tuition because he taught there. And the fact that I had terrible high-school grades didn't matter. That was the last time I ever lived in the American South, and from that point on I was mostly a decent student.

Up to your time going to college, had any people you met influenced your film taste? Helped you decide whether a film was a good or bad one and why?

I think intuition still reigned, even with reading the critics in *The Saturday Review*. I don't remember being very reflective about the cinema. I surely talked about movies with these beatnik friends. But I am much more aware of our passionate book discussions than speaking of cinema.

And you got nothing from your parents?

My biologist father knew zero about movies. Zero. I do credit my mother, Laura Peary, for being a bit of a movie fan. If we ever went to a film as a family, it was my mother who decided, "Let's go see *Rear Window*! Let's go see *The Trouble with Harry*!" She liked Hitchcock. She kind of liked movie stars. Her favorite as a girl was Pola Negri. My parents being from Europe, I went with both of them in South Carolina to see several foreign films, a first for me. I saw some Italian cinema, and I became slightly aware of another director, Vittorio De Sica.

It was 1960 and you were a college student. That must have begun to shape your film taste.

I had skipped two grades in elementary school and I was just 15 starting college. And now, the big book which affected my life: the posthumous collection, *Agee on Film*, James Agee's estimable reviews for *Time* magazine and *The Nation*. I don't know how that book ended up in my hands, but it was truly revelatory. I was in such awe of the beautiful, even poetic writing emanating from this critic. Different from the measured, fairly impersonal words in *The Saturday Review*, Agee offered a passionate argument for cinema as something marvelous to ponder. Yet he also said caustic and dismissive things about some of the movies that he reviewed. Perhaps the most important thing for me was that I tasted "auteurism" before the "auteur theory" would come from France to America. Agee clearly was an auteurist, and he wrote with a special conviction about two film directors, John Huston and Charlie Chaplin, both of whom became his friends.

His essays on Chaplin and Huston totally knocked me out. I was absolutely moved by what he wrote about *Monsieur Verdoux* [1947] and *The Treasure of the Sierra Madre* [1948], neither of which I'd seen. This was the first time that reviews made me desperate to see movies endorsed by a critic. These films as described by Agee sounded incredible! I was a transformed person because of those reviews.

Can I just make a quick flip back to a movie you had seen and I know you felt passionate about: Rebel without a Cause *[1955]. I'm wondering whether part of your love for that film was recognizing at least some aspects of yourself in that story, your own experiences.*

Absolutely! *Rebel without a Cause* was another film I saw four days in a row when I was 11 years old and without being aware that Nicholas Ray was the director. It told of alienated kids who have their own little world and they try to flee from the stupidities of parents and the pressures of 1950s conformity. I don't think I intellectualized those things, though I did respond emotionally to the bonding of that sensitive threesome of Natalie Wood and Sal Mineo and James Dean, and to James Dean's mutterings and confusions. I was touched by what he said: "If I could have one day in which everything went right…" Yes, I definitely felt all of that. The little beatnik group that I eventually joined up with in high school, that was the equivalent of hanging out with the trio from *Rebel Without a Cause*. My wish come true.

Another thing very important to me then was sports and especially major league baseball, both for me and my brother Danny. I have a theory that males of our generation had an easy time memorizing the names of the actors and directors of films because we had so much experience as children and teenagers learning the names of every baseball player. Interestingly, I'm not a fan of sports movies. They're too corny and sentimental, and baseball movies don't register for me. *Bang the Drum Slowly* [1973] is the very rare baseball picture that actually moves me. I loathe *The Natural* [1984] and *Field of Dreams* [1989]. The first is dishonest, the second is mush.

So we'll go back to Agee. He also was a political critic. I don't know whether you thought of that consciously when reading him, but the fact is that he had a certain moral/political perspective that he brought to reviewing films.

My parents were liberals, Adlai Stevenson Democratic voters in the 1950s, and I was also a liberal. But I don't think I viewed culture during my high school years in the deep South with a political consciousness. But living in the North in college, I was now reading James Baldwin and cared deeply about the civil rights movement. However, I'm not aware of connecting my political beliefs to my embrace of Agee. I did learn from Agee how Chaplin was screwed by HUAC, the House Committee on Un-American Activities.

Agee appreciated well-done entertainment. But he argued also for films that actually said something about society. He was a Catholic,

and there's a religious sensibility and spirituality there as well, his
sympathy for the poor and downtrodden, shown in his reviews of
foreign films such as Shoeshine *[1946].*

I think I was somewhat conscious of Agee's moral sense, his earnest
humanism, which I did respond to. I've never been an earnest writer,
but I do think my reviews many years later can reflect an Agee-like
moral sense. Except when they don't. I'm also attracted to transgressive amorality. Jekyll-and-Hyde in one reviewer... me? I should
mention one other film critic from the early 1960s whom I really
loved: Dwight Macdonald, who appeared monthly in *Esquire.* He
famously derided middle-brow culture and I'm completely with
him on that. He was a brash elitist who wrote about Fellini and
Antonioni and he was very funny and his reviews had bite and sting.
I liked Hollywood movies far more than he did, but I hope there's
some acerbic Macdonald wit in my writing. Also, I plead guilty to
Macdonald-like snobbism in my rejection of soft bourgeois cinema
and my lack of interest, and sometimes disdain, in recent years, of
much of Hollywood-fabricated popular cinema.

What about Agee's spirituality?

I absolutely missed that reading him. And I don't know if that
would have appealed to me. As a 16-year-old, I was already a
proud atheist, totally secular, a Jew who rejected going to shul.
It was decades later before I had the revelation that spiritual and
religious cinema was actually avant-garde, so weirdly different
from the 95% of cinema which is secular and earthbound. Only
then was I ready, though still an atheist, to genuflect before *A Man
Escaped* [1956] and *Ordet* [1955]. I thank Paul Schrader and his
Transcendental Style in Film: Ozu, Bresson, Dreyer for helping me
to see the light.

So after reading Agee and Macdonald, any thoughts of you being
a film critic?

Maybe it's time to announce that I was a real latecomer to writing
reviews. A great portion of my life happened before I became a
film critic. My gestation period goes on for years, far into adulthood. Agee and Macdonald did not make me want to be a film
critic, but they did make me want to see better movies and more
worthy and weighty movies. At the same time, I was happy to

watch practically anything. Though I was in college in the early 1960s, I still lived at home. And this was the halcyon days of older American movies on television, the *Late Show.*

My brother Danny and I watched many, many, many movies starting at 11:30pm interrupted by commercials into the deep night. We watched pretty much whatever was playing. If we had any critical help in choosing films it was the Steven Scheuer paperback *Movies on TV*, a book of alphabetized mini-reviews which predated Leonard Maltin. Did he even list the director's name? Maybe I should have known better by then, but I still watched classic Hollywood pictures without noticing who the director was. I continued watching them for the story and for the actors. But I do believe I was cognizant of John Ford for the first time, not for *The Searchers* but by seeing on TV *The Informer* [1935], which I loved, and learning he had won the Best Director Oscar.

There was also a critic named Judith Crist who wrote in *TV Guide*, which was mailed to our house, and she had a column of "Movies of the Week." Like Knight and Alpert in *The Saturday Review*, she had a bit of taste and she kind of guided you in a functional way. The best thing was just all the movies I saw, a self-education. Again, I think my intrinsic good taste was there. I liked movies that were actually good and didn't like movies that were bad. But I wasn't writing about them, or taking notes, and I wasn't having discussions with my brother about them. We would just watch movies to the end at 1am or later, go to bed.

Didn't the commercials drive you mad? You'd be getting deep into a movie and then, BOOM, an ad would crash in.

I didn't like the commercials but that's just the way the movies were shown on TV. Danny and I accepted that as being the biosphere of 1961, 1962. Once again, our parents did not object to us being up late watching movies almost every night. Whatever my brother and I wanted to do was fine with them.

You said that Agee and Macdonald pushed you to see better and more worthy movies.

I would do that when leaving New Jersey to visit my relatives in New York City. My grandparents lived on 95th Street in Manhattan, the same street that housed the legendary Thalia Theater, which played lots of classic Soviet cinema. With my Russian-speaking relatives, I'd see an occasional film there, though these were stiff and not a lot of fun. But one day in New York City, I found a magazine; it might've been a free magazine, called *Cue*. And this magazine had paragraph reviews, 50–100 words, of every movie playing in New York that week. These reviews were well executed by a guy named William Wolf. He praised idiosyncratic works which we would now call "cult movies." He would write enthusiastically about them. A big moment for me was reading Wolf writing hyperbole about *A Face in the Crowd* [1957] and about its director Elia Kazan. Well, I got excited by this review, and I went downtown and saw *A Face in the Crowd* and loved it. Here was a direct connection between a reviewer and me following the advice of his review. Somebody who knows more than me, whose taste I trust, leading me and guiding me.

Many years later when we were both critics, I became acquainted with "Bill" Wolf, a very nice guy, and I thanked him profusely every time I saw him. He was humble about it, he chuckled about it, but boy was that important to me, his *A Face in the Crowd* review. So did I decide I wanted to be a critic too? Not one bit. Not for a second. But when I finally got to be a reviewer, I wanted to speak to my readers the way Bill Wolf did, get them motivated to see movies which I cared about.

So now you were in college. My repeated question: Did you finally make a friend with whom you could talk seriously about cinema?

I did make such a friend! Suddenly this guy came along, Saul, whom I met in my sophomore year at Rider. A devoted English major, he used to read "J. Alfred Prufrock" aloud. We started going to foreign films together at a theater near our New Jersey campus. It played movies by major European directors after their New York runs. And Saul and I, budding thinkers, would actually discuss their "meaning" after seeing them. The first time in my life!

About the same time, my aunt and uncle in New York City took me to a double feature at my request: my first Bergmans, *Wild Strawberries* [1957] and *The Magician* [1958]. My dear relatives were forced to sit through four hours of this heavy stuff, but I was in ecstasy. I'd never seen movies like these, so overtly artsy and symbolic. I felt they were on a completely different plane than the Hollywood movies I'd grown up on. Weren't they so superior to American movies?

I knew for sure that my aesthetic had been drastically altered when I went twice in two weeks to the movies with boys from my neighborhood. First we saw *The Guns of Navarone* [1961], which the guys loved and bored me. The next week, I somehow got them to go to the local art house for *L'Aventura* [1960]. No surprise, they hated me for foisting it on them. What did I think? The issues of Antonioni were totally foreign to this virginal 17-year-old. I didn't understand alienated love or any kind of love, but I claimed that I loved *L'Aventura*.

Yes, I was changing. I'd been caught up in the visual mastery of Bergman. What does Antonioni or Fellini mean? In my sophomore year at Rider, I managed my first film paper ever, an analysis of *La Dolce Vita* [1960]. I wrote about "alienation in the modern world" and got a very good grade. That was fun to write. I thought critically on paper about film, but then I didn't do another review for a few years. That was it. One review.

How lucky were you to come of age as a moviegoer at a time when you had such great foreign films in the theaters?

I was completely fortunate to be a young person uncovering the wonders of cinema exactly at the moment of the French New Wave and a vibrant Italian cinema and the British New Wave, all at the same time. Every few weeks, there would be a new Godard, a new Truffaut, a new Fellini, a *Saturday Night and Sunday Morning* [1960]. A new Polanski! And that was normal 1960s filmgoing! It was all so incredible.

So at this point you were no doubt considering directors?

I was learning directors for sure, especially with foreign films. After Bergman, Truffaut was my favorite European filmmaker, and *Jules and Jim* [1962] the film which really got to me emotionally. If I had a favorite American director in the early 1960s, it was the person Agee championed, John Huston. I'd finally seen *The Treasure of Sierra Madre* and it was splendid, everything that Agee had promised. And of course I liked Hitchcock and rushed to see *Psycho* [1960] in its first week in the theaters. I had no idea what would happen to Janet Leigh when she stepped into the shower.

Can we continue your biography?

After graduating Rider as an English major, I went in 1964 to NYU for a master's degree in drama. At that point I became a committed drama person, reading plays and acting in them, directing them. But my first choice had been to be an English professor. I'd tried to get into Columbia University for graduate school because the famous Lionel Trilling taught there. I don't know why I was impressed by his presence; I certainly hadn't read him. I also applied to Penn. Two Ivy League colleges for their English graduate schools. Probably because I went to unheralded Rider College, I was rejected from both. If I'd been accepted by either, I would have had a different life. I would now be a retired tweedy English professor. Probably I never would have been a film critic. Instead I went to NYU to study drama for a master's, with a view to a new life. I would now aspire to be a theater director. I was not thinking film director.

This is the first mention of theater in your life.

Rider College had one thing that was first-rate: a theater depart-ment with a talented director named Lee Yopp, who really taught me a lot by observing him. Rider did lots of musicals but also semi-cultured things like *Inherit the Wind* and *Joan of Lorraine.* And *Compulsion.* I acted mostly small roles but really liked the theater experience from the inside. When I went to NYU, I started going to theater in New York City when I could afford it. And because of Lee Yopp, I wanted to be a theater director also.

In New York, you must have seen really some amazing things. It was the heyday of Off Broadway.

I remember seeing the famous Off-Broadway production of Brendan Behan's *The Hostage* and a great version of Molière's *Tartuffe.* The most dazzling thing was Zero Mostel starring in *Fiddler on the Roof.* I don't remember ever in my life applauding so hard for a perfor-mance. At NYU, I directed my own one-act adaptation of Flannery O'Connor's story "A Good Man is Hard to Find." Also at NYU, I took a course on criticism. It was dramatic criticism, but we were allowed to write about film, so I wrote my second essay ever on a film, on Godard's *Contempt* [1963].

This piece was far more sophisticated than what I had written about *La Dolce Vita.* Graduate school versus undergraduate school. I had some original ideas, the first time I began to explore what a film can do, the parallel narratives here of the heroic Homeric

Odyssey being filmed and the anti-heroic modern-day Odyssey being lived. Anyway, I was a very young person at NYU in graduate school. I was 19 years old and it was a night class in which the average age was probably over 30. I was completely intimidated as a raw youngster. But I was surprised to receive the highest grade in the class from the demanding professor, an A-. So somewhere in my brain was implanted this idea that I could write film criticism and maybe had some talent. But that was stored away for years.

Did you think of switching your major to film?

I don't know that NYU even had a film school then. It was that long ago. No, I had not one thought about a switch. Theater was very romantic and fulfilling to me at that point. And I was deeply thrilled to have a celebrity, drama critic Robert Corrigan, as one of my teachers. He was astonishingly exciting talking about modern masters like Brecht and Dürrenmatt. He led me to reading Jan Kott and Eric Bentley's *The Playwright as Thinker*. Both so important to me.

But what about Andrew Sarris and The Village Voice?

Of course, this is where all our talk is headed. While at NYU, I start to read—devour!—*The Village Voice*. Hallelujah! The promised land! I couldn't wait for the new issue to arrive at the newsstand to read the film section. I become completely caught in the competing worlds of Jonas Mekas and his promoting of the American underground, and Andrew Sarris championing non-underground auteurist cinema and for teaching me that holy term, "auteurist." Also here was Molly Haskell, the first critic I ever read who was writing, and so brilliantly, from a feminist vantage. There was Stuart Byron, who came at films from an auteurist queer perspective. He once was critiquing a movie and somehow the review segued to how he'd been distracted giving a blow job allowing someone to pick his back pocket. I thought that digression was beyond awesome. I was so impressed that something bold and transgressive like that could be thrust into a movie review. Finally, a priest wrote reviews for the *Voice* named Tom Allen. We talked earlier about spirituality and James Agee. Here with Allen was the first critic I ever read who led with his spiritual and religious connection to cinema. A final *Voice* critic was William Paul, who would write books on Lubitsch and on screwball comedy.

But the key person at the *Voice* was the editor of the film section, Sarris himself. As we all know, he brought auteurism from France, and he used his column to proselytize for off-beat, adventurous American directors. At this point, mid-1960s, because of my love of Bergman and the French and British New Waves, I'd switched my priorities to European cinema. Sarris kind of switched me back to appreciating Hollywood movies again and getting pumped up about Hollywood cinema when it was made by filmmakers with a personal vision.

Recall that for many years as a movie watcher I barely noticed the names of directors. I was there for the stars and the story. Now I fell fully in line with Sarris: the director was everything. The "auteur." A totally romantic way to look at cinema. Through Sarris, I learned that I'd been loving Nicholas Ray and John Ford since childhood. He introduced me to a whole slew of American directors whose work I had never seen. Who was Douglas Sirk? Budd Boetticher? Frank Borzage? Edward G. Ulmer? I got to know their films only because of Sarris, first with his *Voice* column, then with the publication of his 1968 tome, *The American Cinema*.

I believe what you're talking about is a love of movies expressed through the prism of New Journalism. You wouldn't have seen this fresh way of writing in The Saturday Review, *or in* Time *or* Newsweek *or* The New York Times.

I didn't know what New Journalism was. That term didn't mean anything to me until much later.

But you were reading examples of it, nothing like the academic papers you wrote on La Dolce Vita *and* Contempt.

When I finally became a film critic, Sarris and Molly Haskell influenced me with their auteurism and feminism. And I certainly am a first-person film critic with, I hope, a voice that is immensely mine.

I would contend that you express your passion for cinema in your reviews in a way that earlier film criticism would not have allowed you to do.

Definitely. The "I" would become essential for me to utilize, and, as in *Voice* reviews, I use slang and exclamation points and the language of the day. But except for dealing with sexuality, the *Voice* critics were not especially political. I wasn't bothered at the time by that because the rest of the *Voice* was extremely socially conscious. I absorbed all the political articles around the film reviews. Later, with the Black Power movement and opposition to the war in Vietnam, I thought hard about the place of politics in writing about the cinema, but in the mid-1960s living in New York, it was auteurism which I cared about.

How do you feel about Sarris's categories in The American Cinema?

More mixed as the years have gone by. The best thing is that Sarris putting certain forgotten or underrated directors into the favorable categories has raised their profiles immeasurably. Who today would be studying the films of Sirk if Sarris hadn't labeled him The Far Side of Paradise? Or who would be watching André de Toth and taking him seriously if Sarris hadn't called him Expressive Esoterica?

What I like less and less is Sarris's denigrating of some directors, including some extremely fine ones, by assigning them to the dustbin categories: Strained Seriousness, Less Than Meets the Eye. It's appalling that Sarris wrote so disparagingly about John Huston, William Wyler, Fred Zinnemann, just to mention three superb directors, and hardly reneged on his criticism. Shame on that. I mean, Huston is not only an immensely skilled filmmaker but a 100% auteur. So many of his films are about the same subject: men on a quest which will always fail, blow up in their faces. But what a quest! From *The Maltese Falcon* [1941] to *The Treasure of Sierra Madre* [1948] to *The Asphalt Jungle* [1950] to *The Man Who Would Be King* [1975]. In my auteurist pantheon, John Huston is a king.

You have mentioned two books that people must read if you really care about film. One is Sarris's American Cinema, *the other is Pauline Kael's* I Lost It at the Movies. *Talk a little bit about Kael and Sarris.*

I learned far later as a critic that you were supposed to choose sides, swear an allegiance to one or the other. Although I was in my soul a Sarrisite, I started out embracing both of them. I liked what everybody likes in Pauline Kael: her perky style, her exuberance, her confidence, her bouncy language. Again, New Journalism in a way, such personal writing. I didn't see the things about her that I got to dislike over the time. I felt she was an open and excited critic.

But wasn't Kael undercutting a lot of what Sarris had to say about auteurism, which she considered silly and adolescent? Note her essay in I Lost It at the Movies *called "Circles and Squares."*

I read her essay attacking Sarris, but I don't know that I was angry about her for writing it. I found the essay quite provocative, though it didn't steer me away from auteurism. I thought Kael had one valid point in questioning auteurism, that just because a director has the same theme in a bunch of movies doesn't mean the movies are therefore good. That's not just a virtue in itself, a repeated theme.

For me in the mid-1960s, Kael is good and Sarris is good. They're both good, though I leaned more to Sarris. Before you ask again: I was by then an enthusiastic reader of film criticism, an advanced reader of film criticism. All this film stuff was bubbling in my head. But I still did not have one thought about being a film critic myself.

You haven't mentioned the most influential critic at the time: Bosley Crowther.

I was also reading Crowther in the *New York Times*. Later on I was taught that he was a horrible, horrible critic, despised by both Kael and Sarris as The Enemy, this befuddled out-of-his-elements guy who didn't get *Bonnie and Clyde* [1967] or the French New Wave and had no feel for the formal elements of cinema. I didn't particularly feel negatively about him when I first read him. He was literate, he seemed okay. I was a political liberal, he was a political liberal. He was anti-racist and dared to attack the blacklist and he stood up for human rights. Crowther often equated a good film with one which had progressive values. I certainly don't feel that way now, but I would start to lean that way as the 1960s went on.

You mean when you went to the University of Wisconsin-Madison to begin your Ph.D. The Berkeley of the Midwest?

This was the next chapter in my life and, for my life journey, so extraordinarily important. I arrived there in the summer of 1966 and remained for almost a decade. My desire was to be a theater director, and I guess I vaguely wanted also to be a professor.

I didn't know anything about the University of Wisconsin except that it was supposed to be a good school. It turned out that it wasn't especially distinguished for theater. The best theater in Madison was mostly done outside of academia. On the other hand, the university was a hotbed of anti-war resistance, with demonstrations bringing thousands of people into the Madison streets. A thrilling place for me to be. Steps away from Wisconsin's conservative theater department I was surrounded with self-proclaimed radicals. I moved leftward and joined the mass demonstrations. I was certainly enmeshed in the anti-War movement. And so my politics became very, very important.

The second thing about Madison was that it turned out to be an epicenter of film culture. I knew nothing at all about this before getting there. My first pleasant surprise was outdoors screenings of silent movie classics, my second was discovering the Wisconsin Film Society with its auteurist programming. There I saw on screen *Citizen Kane* [1941] and Renoir's *La Marseillaise* [1938] and, for the first time, *It's a Wonderful Life* [1946]. The series was curated by a precocious undergraduate, Joseph McBride, later a world-class film biographer and acknowledged expert on Welles and Ford. And then there were filmmakers brought to Madison to speak: King Vidor with *The Big Parade* [1925] and Harold Lloyd with *The Freshman* [1925]. This was around 1966 when I was 22, and those two were the first film personalities I ever observed in person. I dared stand near Lloyd and saw him do in person his quirky handshake greeting from *The Freshman*. And then a very old man walked up to Lloyd and introduced himself. He was a Wisconsin resident, Roy Aitken, brother of Harry Aitken, both financiers of *The Birth of a Nation* (1915).

It sounds like you were losing your interest in theater.

Not at all. My major time was spent taking the theater classes required on the way to a Ph.D. and teaching many sections of Intro to Theater, great plays from Aeschylus to Ibsen. To my delight, I found that I was a popular and skilled teacher. Something new! At Madison I also directed a Yeats play and in 1969–1970 secured my first full-time job as a theater professor. I was hired at the University of Wisconsin-Whitewater about 30 miles from Madison. Alas, my contract was not renewed after one academic year because of my on-campus anti-war activities. In my brief time at Whitewater I directed stage productions of Dürrenmatt's *The Visit* and some Pinter short dramas. And I taught the first cinema course in my life, a film history class. That was very enjoyable.

At Whitewater, we started an anti-administration under-ground newspaper called *Good News*. And therein I contributed in winter 1969 my first published film review. At last, at age 25! It was a sympathetic reading of Arthur Penn's *Alice's Restaurant*. Unfortunately, I have no copy of that review.

After being made to leave Whitewater, I returned to Madison in summer 1970 for far more intense involvement in movie culture than even before. Now I *did* reject theater. The drama students at both Whitewater and Madison were in my view maddeningly apolitical. I just didn't want to direct them anymore. As for writing a Ph.D. in drama: though I had taken only two film courses, one film history and one 8mm production class, I somehow got my department to sign on to me writing a dissertation in film. I would do my thesis on the rise of the American gangster film, starting with early silent cinema and ending in 1931 with *Little Caesar*.

So I had a thesis topic and I slowly researched it. But I spent far more hours of the week in Madison procrastinating, doing things more immediately pleasurable. I became the arts editor of Madison's campus newspaper, the *Daily Cardinal*. I did write mini-review blurbs in the *Cardinal* called Screen Gems about the films which would be shown on campus each day. I can say that with 40,000 students at the university those blurbs were widely read and greatly influenced movie attendance. I'm sure I was never that influential again when I became a professional critic.

Can you say more about the film culture in Madison at the time?

Wisconsin was the only university in America with a 35mm theater in the student union. I became part of a student committee that picked the films to be shown there. And the State Historical Society of Wisconsin was given a momentous gift: 16mm prints of Warner Brothers and RKO films spanning 1913–1954. For a few years, I was among the avid cineastes who projected these films for our own pleasure. Finally, Madison gave birth to more than a dozen pop-up film societies, which then would rent space in university buildings to show 16mm films. I ran one of those, the

Tar and Feathers Film Society, with Patrick McGilligan, another future film biographer of acclaim. My brother Danny had come to Madison as an undergraduate, and he co-ran the Pinocchio Film Society. A guy named Bill Banning ran the most financially successful film society, and he later operated the Roxy Theatre in San Francisco.

I say this seriously: in 1970, the two greatest places on earth to see movies were Paris and Madison. There were at least 15–20 films shown on campus every week. And the choices went from very popular art films by Truffaut and Fellini to really obscure works from the 1930s and 1940s. This was a film-loving campus for sure, but within in there was a loose circle of about 50 or so students who were completely film crazy.

When Russell Campbell, a graduate student from New Zealand decided to start an off-campus film magazine, many of us were eager to write for it. It was called *The Velvet Light Trap* and in 1971 I appeared in issue no. 1, "Warner Brothers in the Thirties," typed and published in Campbell's student apartment. This was my second published film review ever, a super-auteurist essay about the Hawksian elements in Hawks's *The Crowd Roars* [1932].

The Velvet Light Trap (*VLT*) had a decided auteurist bent— there would be a John Ford issue—but it was more seriously political than other auteurist publications from *Cahiers du Cinéma* to *Movie* in England to *Movietone News* in Seattle to *Focus* in Chicago. American films were usually viewed in *VLT* not only through the vision of the director but in a historic context, like seeing the Warners 1930s films against the background of FDR and the Depression and the New Deal. And *VLT* was unabashedly committed to feminism, thus an early issue on *Women and Cinema*. For that issue, I co-wrote with Karyn Kay my third movie review-essay, this on Dorothy Arzner's *Dance, Girl, Dance* [1940]. And I branched out from Madison for a companion essay on Arzner's *Christopher Strong* [1933] for *Cinema* (California).

Let me complete the picture through the mid-1970s. I wrote essay-length reviews on two Hollywood works from the 1930s, on *Doorway to Hell* [1930] for *VLT* and on *Son of Kong* [1933] for *Film Heritage*. I did several shorter reviews of contemporary films, *Juggernaut* [1974] and *The Bad News Bears* [1976] for *Jump Cut*, *Westworld* [1975] for *Take One*.

The reviews were piling up. Weren't you a film critic at last?

I never used that term or thought of myself that way. I probably called myself "a film studies person" or "a film historian." *The Velvet Light Trap* was a delightfully unpretentious amateur's magazine. Nobody got paid and it was hawked about Madison for 50 cents an issue! I was an amateur writing for free about movies I loved and not a film critic.

Where does sexual politics come into all of this?

Feminism was in the air in Madison, and I had Molly Haskell in the *Voice* as a model for noting feminist issues in cinema. My work with Karyn Kay on Dorothy Arzner was motivated by our desire to show that a woman could be an auteurist also, and that the themes which repeat in Arzner's movies are female-oriented: women struggling to find their voice in a male-dominated world. So obvious now, but we were pioneers in the mid-1970s writing about this stuff around a woman Hollywood director. Arzner, whom we also interviewed, deserved far more than to be placed in Andrew Sarris's non-category, "The Ladies Auxiliary," or to be ignored altogether by Kael. I'm also very proud to have written for *VLT* the first article in America about Alice Guy-Blaché, and I was the discoverer on microfilm in the university library of her astounding essay, "Woman's Place in Photoplay Production," which then appeared in *VLT* and has been often reprinted since.

How did you meet Dorothy Arzner?

When Karyn Kay and I saw *Christopher Strong* and *Dance, Girl, Dance*, which nobody had written about into the early 1970s, we were so stirred and thrilled. I have no memory of how we got her telephone number, but we cold-called Arzner at her home and she actually answered. We blabbed some kind of effusive praise her way. At first Arzner was suspicious, then slowly warmed up. We had several more phone calls after that. And one day to our total surprise, Arzner telephoned us! She agreed to a mail interview. We sent her lots of questions and she mailed us back her answers handwritten on a yellow pad. She also agreed to send her private photos to *Cinema* magazine in LA to accompany my article on *Christopher Strong*.

A follow-up interview was conducted in person by me without Karyn but accompanied by Joseph McBride. Arzner invited us into her La Quinta, California, home for maybe an hour-and-half visit.

She was very nice in a formal way as Joe and I plied her with more questions. The combination of the two interviews is what was printed in *The Velvet Light Trap*, the most consequential interview that Arzner ever did. Sadly, I never saw her again, but Arzner did pay me the ultimate compliment. When film festivals wanted her to be their guest she declined but would tell them "Invite Gerald Peary instead. He knows more about my films than I know."

May I mention that on our trip into the California desert, Joseph McBride and I also stopped at the home of Howard Hawks for what became a five-hour interview? What a contrast to Arzner, being with this manly man who didn't think to offer us even a glass of water! We realized that Hawks liked to steer his interviewers to the same stock anecdotes, so Joe and I were determined that we would stop him cold when he started to tell them. We would make him tell new stories, never before published. Although that interview totally exhausted both of us doing it, kind of like wrestling with our subject, we came away with a wealth of Hawksiana which became the basis of a lengthy *Film Comment* interview called "Hawks Talks" and which takes up many pages of McBride's book, *Hawks on Hawks*.

Neither Arzner nor Hawks are vaguely left wing. What about your other film interviews at the time?

I was part of the leftist zeitgeist of Madison, so when I turned to interviewing filmmakers there is no doubt that I usually sought out directors and actors with anti-establishment, left-of-center points of view. Warren Beatty passed through Madison for the progressive George McGovern campaign, and he talked to me and Michael Wilmington, future *Chicago Tribune* and *LA Times* film critic. It was the only interview Beatty did in a bunch of years. A scoop! I interviewed for *Cineaste* a fairly unknown Swedish filmmaker, Johan Bergenstrahle, who made engaged films and objected to all the praise for the apolitical Ingmar Bergman. Also for *Cineaste*, I talked to Howard Alk, the director of *The Murder of Fred Hampton* [1971], because that documentary dealt with racism and police violence. And for *Film Quarterly*, Patrick McGilligan and I did a long interview with someone we both deeply admired, the African filmmaker great Ousmane Sembène.

When Maureen Turim and I spoke with Marcel Ophuls for *The Velvet Light Trap*, I was at my most politically strident. Rather than fall on our knees in thanks to Ophuls for the monumental *The Sorrow and the Pity* [1969], we young Turks bashed him for not letting women have enough voice in the film and for what we saw as his bourgeois politics. We were embarrassingly arrogant and impolite.

Into the 1970s, the Madison film community broke informally into two groups, what Michael Wilmington called the "politicos" and the "aesthetes." I was in the first group. There was a strike of cafeteria workers and we were bitterly divided over whether we should shut the Play Circle movie house down in solidarity of the workers, which was my position, or have movies as usual, which is what the "aesthetes" thought should happen. Things got so bad that Michael Wilmington and I had a fight in the student union, jumping on top of each other. It took us some years to be friends again but we totally made up. We even got over a second fight, not a physical one, when Michael and I went to see Howard Hawks's *Rio Lobo* [1970] and I thought it was ridiculously awful, which greatly angered Michael because he thought it an auteurist masterpiece.

While at Madison did you interview other film critics? Did they make an impact on your writing?

Robin Wood came down from Canada to speak in Madison. I did the first interview with him ever, published in *Film Heritage*. I certainly learned from Wood how to do close analyses of films from an auteurist perspective, especially from his tremendous book about the films of Hitchcock. Also for *Film Heritage*, I interviewed Peter Wollen, who was teaching at Northwestern and married then to Laura Mulvey. In this case, I became pals with both of them, and I and my girlfriend Karyn Kay would visit them in Evanston, Illinois, and they stayed at our place in Madison. When I interviewed Wollen about his famous book, *Signs and Meaning in the Cinema*, I worked hard to ask intelligent questions about things like structuralism. I didn't understand much about film theory then, and still don't. Wollen's writing had no influence on my writing at all, but his intense love of cinema certainly was felt by me.

I can see why your Madison years, though half a century ago, continue to make an impact on the way you look at movies, your stance as a critic. Any last memory of Madison before we move on?

I did want to mention two long reviews I wrote for the *Daily Cardinal*, pretty cool ones, because they were of theater productions by Madison undergraduates who later on became esteemed filmmakers. My first review was of a play directed by future horror director, Stuart Gordon, who did *Re-Animator* [1985]. Gordon produced a startling outdoor production of *Titus Andronicus* with cavemen and their dogs in a dug-out pit. It was utterly fantastic. My second piece was the first review ever, a rave, of a comedy ensemble of college kids from Milwaukee called Kentucky Fried Theater. They then went to LA, switched to film, and made *Airplane!* [1980] *The Naked Gun* [1988] and other Hollywood hilarities. Jerry Zucker actually asked me if I would like to join their troupe and go West with them. But I said no, and remained in Madison. I could maybe have been a madcap screwball performer. My conciliation was that Zucker, also director of *Ghost* [1990], framed my *Daily Cardinal* review and had it on the wall in his office at Paramount Pictures. The high point for this still non-critic.

Were you going to ever leave Madison?

It had to happen. I was 30 years old in 1975, time to stop being a slacker and leave my cocoon. Time to be a college professor and finally complete writing my burdensome Ph.D. thesis. Graduate students at Wisconsin found it difficult to get teaching jobs because of the radical reputation of the school. Ironically, Wisconsin's radicalism and my firing at Whitewater for anti-war activities worked in my favor. A Marxist-Leninist film professor at Livingston College, Rutgers University, arranged to have me interviewed by his English Department colleagues. Livingston was the so-called "experimental college" of Rutgers, its ugly campus built quickly in response to the 1967 Newark riots. It was supposed to be a place with a racially diverse student body and faculty. Somehow, this young white man got hired because the African-American novelist, Toni Cade Bambara, took a liking to me when I was interviewed.

So bye-bye, Madison.

Yes, bye-bye. I drove East with Karyn Kay and our two cats. When I actually arrived to teach in the fall of 1975, Bambara had moved on. I was dropped into the middle of the most contentious ideological faculty all demanding alliances, from fierce Black Power advocates to self-righteous Marxists. The chairman of the department was one of the few conservatives and he would see that my contract was not renewed after three years. In the meantime, I taught some interesting film courses, including team-instructing a class in German cinema with the esteemed feminist essayist Ann Snitow, a lovely person. I also co-taught with Roger Shatzkin a class in "Hardboiled Film and Fiction." Many years later, *Borat* [2006] filmmaker Larry Charles contacted me and said he'd been in that class and that it influenced his career. When he wrote and produced *Seinfeld*, several of the programs had "noir" elements which he'd absorbed in our course. Nice! A Livingston highlight: Wim Wenders was paid $100 to drive out to New Jersey from New York and show *Alice in the Cities* [1974]. Afterward, he went out for a beer with me and the students, and he chose to stay at some seedy motel along Route 1, just the kind of place inhabited by Rüdiger Vogler in his movie.

Your time in Livingston seems also to have been a fertile time for you and book publishing.

That's true. My first book in 1976 was a breezy study, *Rita Hayworth*, one in the endless Pyramid Series on Hollywood actors. I thought Rita Hayworth was sexy and I guessed it might be fun to see all her movies for my film education. And I might elevate my writing by doing a long-form project. In the mid-1970s, before video stores, the immense challenge was to trace down Hayworth's pictures in 16mm. I was introduced to a movie club which convened in a small private theater in Manhattan. For my benefit, the club agreed to show their members, all white male seniors, a Hayworth "B" film from Columbia Pictures. When I arrived, I was handed a xeroxed sheet listing all the actors in the cast. I mean maybe thirty or so, literally whoever appeared on screen. When we were watching the film and Rita Hayworth's taxi hit another car and the person in the other car popped on screen for two seconds, those around me proudly shouted out his name! If I didn't know it already: everyone watches his/her private picture. This movie club convened for the joy of knowing the identity of all actors in the films they saw. Quite eccentric!

Having one book accepted probably gave you the confidence to approach editors about additional books.

Also true. Because Ted Sennett at Pyramid Books was such a nice guy, I found it much easier to approach Stanley Hochman at Ungar with an idea for dual anthologies, *The Classic American Novel and the Movies* in 1977 and *The Modern American Novel and the Movies* in 1978, both co-edited by my Livingston colleague, Roger Shatzkin. As I explained earlier, I've always cared equally for literature and cinema. Therefore, I've tried forever to read the book before seeing the movie, keeping a toe in both fiction and screen. These anthologies reflected my lifetime interest in the process of adaptation. The first book began with essays on adaptations of Cooper, Hawthorne, Melville, the second ended with Vonnegut and James Dickey. I was particularly proud of two scoops. Who knew that Philip Roth was a film critic for the *New Republic* for a brief time in 1957? I reprinted his very funny review of the lame Tyrone Power-starring *The Sun Also Rises*. It was written by Roth as an acerbic parody of Hemingway style. I'm also pleased to have commissioned an iconoclastic article on King Vidor's version of *The Fountainhead* [1943], in which the writer, Kevin McGann, read the various Ayn Rand screenplays and discovered that the famously non-compromising author compromised in every way.

After that, I went to a bigger publisher and met with Cyril Nelson at E.P. Dutton. Karyn Kay and I co-edited in 1977 for Dutton the first anthology published of feminist film essays, *Women and the Cinema: A Critical Anthology*. Our book included our article on Arzner's *Dance, Girl, Dance*, our Arzner interview, an appreciation of Lois Weber, the first contemporary interview with Ida Lupino, the first anthology appearances of Susan Sontag's brilliant take on Leni Riefenstahl, "Fascinating Fascism" and Laura Mulvey's "Visual Pleasure and Narrative Cinema," which introduced to the world the concept of the Male Gaze.

Let me jump ahead to 1980 and my final anthology, for Dutton again, *The American Animated Cartoon: A Critical Anthology*. This one was edited with my brother, Danny Peary. Interviews with Chuck Jones, John and Faith Hubley, Ralph Bakshi, my brother talking to Walter Lantz of Woody Woodpecker fame. E. M. Forster on Mickey and Minnie, Manny Farber attacking sacred *Bambi* [1942]. How could we get some lefty politics into a book on animation? An essay called "Strike at the Fleischer Factory" and a publication from government documents of Walt Disney's damning testimony before HUAC.

What I learned doing this book is that the people you bring into your project are not necessarily grateful for you doing so. For *The Animated Cartoon*, Danny and I went to a bunch of critics who specialized in writing about animation and commissioned articles from them. These they did grudgingly because they felt very territorial and that we, the Peary brothers, were interlopers in the animation field. Who were we to do this anthology? I can say that this experience left me with a bitter feeling that has never quite left. It's irrational, but since that book I've rarely wanted to look at animation. Sorry, Studio Ghibli.

And your dissertation?

I finally finished it in 1977 almost a decade after starting it: "The Rise of the American Gangster Film, 1906–1931." I was at last Dr. Gerald Peary, a title I have almost never used. As for the dissertation, a copy is somewhere lost in my basement. I did try to publish it when I completed it but to no avail. That was the time that film theory was taking over everywhere and my dissertation was an old-fashioned historic work. I will never forget one of the letters of rejection: "For me, this manuscript never fulfills the semiotic promise of page 73." No, it never did...

While at Livingston College, were you still contributing to film magazines?

I'm not sure if I wrote more for *The Velvet Light Trap* after moving away from Madison. My article, "*The Racket*, A Lost Gangster Classic," appeared in the Winter 1975 issue on "Forbidden, Forgotten, Neglected and Unlucky Films," and that could have been it. But because of my interest in politics, I had forged a relationship with the openly radical, quasi-Marxist *Jump Cut* magazine coming out of Chicago. I became friends with those putting it out and was appointed Book Editor. But things really fell apart. We at *Jump Cut* would pass freelance manuscripts back and forth and make judgments about whether to publish them. It turned out that my comments didn't always gel with what an inner cadre of the magazine, "the collective," believed was politically correct. Plus I often wrote humorous commentary which was considered insensitive and un-serious. I was shocked to be purged from *Jump Cut*. Fired from my non-paying job.

The protagonist of Milan Kundera's *The Joke* is a Czech individualist who writes "Trotsky Lives" on a postcard, which results in his being turned in to the Communist authorities by his friends. He is arrested and jailed. I thought often about *The Joke* in regard to the *Jump Cut* "collective." Would they have fingered me if we lived in a totalitarian society? Dear *Jump Cut*: I am unrepentant to this day, a card-carrying member of the Laughing Left.

In 1977, I drove to Montreal and went to the headquarters of *Take One*, another film magazine that I wrote for. As with *Jump Cut*, I was appointed Book Editor. But what a difference! The politics here were vaguely New Left but more just libertarian Canada. Anything interesting goes into the magazine. I loved working at *Take One*, and became lifetime friends with one of its brilliant writers, Will Aitken, openly gay forever and, like the magazine, blithely non-PC. Freed from the strictures of *Jump Cut*, I reviewed a frivolous feature about pro wrestling and did a major interview with Roberta Findlay, the first American woman to become a director of hardcore porn.

I also loved Montreal and secured a job teaching a film studies course in the summer of 1978 at Concordia University. What fun! On a tiny budget, I brought into the class some of Montreal's most important filmmakers, including the feminist director Mireille Dansereau and the great documentarian Donald Brittain.

By that time you were out of Livingston College?

My three-year contract expired in Spring 1978. What could I do next? Fortuitously, my old Madison film society partner, Patrick McGilligan, had moved to Cambridge, Massachusetts as a journalist and had been appointed the arts editor of the *Real Paper*, one of Boston's two alternative papers. He had commissioned me to write about the 1977 New York Film Festival for his publication. That went well, including interviewing with Michael Wilmington French filmmaker Éric Rohmer. And then I did this long and flashy New Journalism piece in which I covered the film pornography business in New York City, speaking with actors and directors and even being there for a live shooting of a porn feature. This piece was sensationalist enough that seemingly everyone at the *Real Paper* read it and appreciated it.

And here was my break: David Thomson of *The Biographical Dictionary of Film* fame was chief film critic for the *Real Paper* while teaching at Dartmouth College. But his incredibly weird judgments of films did not mix with the more mainstream taste of *Real Paper* readers. He was sending them to films which confounded them, like his four-star rave for the maligned *Bobby Deerfield* [1977]. Nobody had the nerve to fire Thomson but he was subtly nudged to the side.

He had fewer reviews to write, which I think was fine with him, with his full teaching load at Dartmouth. So who would become the chief film critic? And bring some normalcy back to the *Real Paper*? An offer was made to me. I accepted.

Can we blow a trumpet? You were a film critic!

A film critic is someone who is hired to be a film critic. Finally, at age 33, I was so hired. Was I right for this pretty major job? It was a leap of faith that I could do it. If I counted my reviews from all the publications, 1970–1978, I had written maybe 10–12 in all. Does that qualify me? Not quite. Luckily with Patrick McGilligan I had the right friend in the right place to lobby for me getting the job. I moved to Cambridge, Massachusetts in September 1978 to go to work. I still live in Cambridge 47 years later.

What was the film scene when you first moved there?

Cambridge had the legendary Brattle in Cambridge, site of Bogart festivals, which then and still now shows great double features every single day. And the Orson Welles Cinema, also in Cambridge, was the sexiest spot for seeing movies. In the days before multiplexes, it was an innovator with three screens. It was here that the wonderful *The Harder They Come* [1972] and the execrable *The King of Hearts* [1966] played for many months.

Coming in as the new gun in town was exciting but also intimidating. The *Real Paper* had a distinguished history of film critics. Before Thomson it had been the solid, highly intelligent David Ansen for some years and before that the colorfully opinionated Stuart Byron, who had arrived there from the *Village Voice*. But our rival alternative newspaper across town, the *Boston Phoenix*, had an even more glittery film critic history: David Denby was there before going to the *New Yorker*, Janet Maslin, also a music critic, wrote there before becoming chief film critic for the *New York Times*.

For ambitious young reviewers plotting for a future job of power and even money, and probably in New York, a stop in Boston was de rigueur. And best at the *Phoenix*. When Pauline Kael had an eye on some fledgling critic who she felt sufficiently talented and with whom she had a rapport, always male, she would call up the *Phoenix* and lobby that he be hired there. It became a definite farm team for "Paulettes." Denby had been an early one and while I was in Boston, the *Phoenix* had five of Kael's acolytes aboard. Stephen Schiff would become a staff writer for *The New Yorker*, Owen Gleiberman a film critic for *Entertainment Weekly*, David Edelstein a reviewer for *New York Magazine*. The Kael connection worked.

I arrived at the *Real Paper* as somewhat a Sarrisite, although Andrew Sarris never helped his followers to get prestige jobs like Kael methodically did. The *Real Paper* was certainly never a "Paulette" publication, but the only zealous Sarrisite in the past had been Stuart Byron.

Did you know Sarris and Kael?

Karyn Kay and I had friendly meetings with Molly Haskell, Sarris's wife, and we had bonded over our love of Dorothy Arzner. Haskell invited us to dinner with Andrew at their Upper East Side apartment. A cordial evening. Many years later, I did a Q&A with Sarris in Australia at the Sydney Film Festival. At dinner afterwards, the question came up of who was the sexiest woman in the history of cinema. Sarris voted for Kay Francis in 1930s melodramas, I went for Ann-Margret in *Kitten with a Whip* [1964]. Both Sarris and Haskell appear in my documentary about film critics. I do remember we broke the Sarris interview in two so that he could take a nap.

Before I speak about Kael, I should say that I was quite innocent of the Kael-Sarris intense feuding when I came to the *Real Paper*. My knowledge of the "Paulettes" came slowly, my realization — and irritation — that they fell in line with Kael's opinions and virtually wrote the same review all over America. So when Kael visited Boston for a book tour, I signed up for a talk in her hotel room. As a fan. This was April 1980 and she couldn't have been more pleasant and charming, and she inscribed my copy of *When the Lights Go Down*: "I hope you have as much fun writing about movies as I have had."

I met Kael once more at some New York event and she very nicely invited me to have a drink with some others afterward. Here I got a slightly different perspective. I observed one of the *Phoenix* "Paulettes" maneuver himself into a chair so he could sit next to Kael, who lorded over us at the head of the table. Somebody told me that Kael had disdain for this "Paulette" and complained that "he dressed like an agent." Anyway, *New York Times* critic Janet Maslin walked by and Kael somehow indicated to those at our table that we were not to make contact. And then Kael said these sentences which I will never forget. "Ah the *Times!*" she snorted. "One doesn't and the other can't!" Translation: Vincent Canby could write decent *NY Times* reviews but didn't bother to do it. Janet Maslin can't. Wow! An Algonquin Round Table level of cattiness!

What did Kael think of me as a writer? She never came to me offering to promote and mold my career as she did with so many others. Which meant that either she thought my criticism wasn't that special or that my sensibility showed that I could never be a "Paulette." Probably she thought both of these things.

Let's return to Boston and Cambridge in Fall 1978. Can you describe being on your new film critic job?

In 1978, Hollywood had not yet become the slave of high-priced genre films so I got to review some decent studio films while at the *Real Paper*. In 1979, for instance, I wrote favorably of *Manhattan*, *Wise Blood*, *The Wanderers*, *Over the Edge*, *The China Syndrome*, *Kramer vs. Kramer*, *Escape from Alcatraz* — not a bad bunch of pictures. Plus there were fascinating disappointments like *Hardcore* and *Apocalypse Now*.

With 23 universities, Boston was very much a film town in which, I believe, reviews counted. All over the city every Friday, people would hand over a dollar at a newsstand, or buy from a street hawker, a 50 cents copy of the *Phoenix* and 50 cents copy of the *Real Paper*. And they would read the film sections of both with great care. Over at the *Phoenix*, reviewers following their role model Kael at the *New Yorker* would do indulgent reviews, 2,000 words and more. At the *Real Paper*, I was happily restricted to a weekly 1,500-word column, which meant 1,000 words for the main review and 500 words divided between two other movies.

Having some Boston clout, I convinced the Coolidge Corner Cinema in Brookline to allow me to curate with a friend, Julie Levinson, the First and Second Boston Independent Film Festivals. We highlighted the local documentary scene and had the first public screening ever of a film by Ross McElwee, who later saw fame with *Sherman's March* [1985]. And because I was a slight Boston celeb, I was invited to appear regularly on an arts program on WBUR radio and interview movie personages passing through town.

Which is where we met, as I was employed on that program. We have known each other for 45 years.

An auspicious meeting for sure, and we will talk later about our current artistic relationship. But back to WBUR. I remember two programs distinctly. I interviewed Dudley Moore, who was starring in *10* [1979], and in real life Tuesday Weld had just dropped him. He was a glum guest, so I was the one who tried telling cheery jokes. Another day screenwriter Garson Kanin was at WBUR plugging a new novel. While I talked to him, his tiny wife Ruth Gordon sat silently by on a couch behind a huge pocketbook. When the interview concluded, Gordon boomed one word across the room: "MARVELOUS!!!!" Kanin and Gordon were so sweet, holding hands as they left the radio studio.

Your competition was the Boston Phoenix. *Were you antagonistic to the other paper?*

I got along fine with Stephen Schiff, their very bright lead film critic. We traveled the country on film junkets and hung out together, both having great disdain for other junketeers who were philistine star-worshippers and provided blurbs for the film companies, so-called "quote whores." But there was one grand competitive moment when the budget-conscious *Real Paper* flew me to New York to see *Manhattan* [1979] before its Boston release. I loved the Woody Allen film — would I now? — and provided my newspaper with a scoop cover story a week before Schiff could post his review in the *Phoenix*. A moment of journalistic triumph. I still remember watching a beautiful woman reading my *Manhattan* review on the subway. I was too shy to tap her on the shoulder and say, "I wrote that."

I believe you interviewed Fassbinder early on at the Real Paper.

It was the first day of the 1978 New York Film Festival and we talked about his adaptation of Nabokov's *Despair*. He was predictably snotty and it was a bit of a sparring match but also kind of fun. About an hour later, I sighted Fassbinder outside of Lincoln Center smoking a cigarette. When my photographer, Cory Braun, pushed forward to take his picture, Fassbinder got incredibly piqued. He walked to the curb, hailed a taxi, and disappeared completely from the New York Film Fest. He never returned! All reporters wanting to interview him in the next days were out of luck. It was a pretty devious way to accomplish it, but I got a scoop!

What were some of your other highlights working for the Real Paper?

Here are a few. Attending the surreal *Apocalypse Now* [1979] New York press conference, arguing publicly with Coppola about the muddled politics of the movie, being in the zany presence of Dennis Hopper, who probably hadn't bathed in weeks and seemed as drugged out as his character in the movie. Interviewing Martin Ritt about *Norma Rae* [1979]. A down-to-earth guy in a jump suit with a terrific movie, politically and aesthetically. A lunch with George Romero, another nice guy. Getting a phone call from film-maker James Bridges because he so liked my review of *September 30, 1955* [1977]. We became friendly and he gave me a tour of the Goldwyn Studio in LA. Being in Claude Chabrol's hotel suite at the New York Film Festival and watching him laughing his head off at Saturday morning cartoons. Interviewing Gérard Depardieu also at the New York Festival. He seemed to take to me, and I accompanied him to a liquor store so he could buy some Pernod. Speaking to Hal Ashby before the release of *Coming Home* [1978] and almost persuading him to change what I felt was the film's wrong ending.

Which side were you on, Coming Home *or* The Deer Hunter?

I was totally a *Coming Home* fan with its strong anti-war message. I thought *The Deer Hunter* was racist and xenophobic and, as a result, I did an action which was very peculiar for a film critic. I picketed *The Deer Hunter* at a theater in Boston and wrote an article about the reaction of those attending the movie to seeing me and my picket sign.

Probably the most thrilling *Real Paper* moment was attending the First Havana Film Festival in 1979. I drank in Cuba whatever Hemingway had drank, I had diarrhea under a tree after eating horse meat. Unlike many true believers in our American brigade, which was led by *Harlan County, USA* [1976] documentarian Barbara Kopple, I was wary of Fidel Castro and, among other horrors, his policy of imprisoning gay people. As there were neighborhood spies, the family that invited me into their apartment was enormously brave to do it. No, I told the boys in the family, I didn't know George Harrison. The festival showed us documen-

taries of Cuban soldiers in Ethiopia supporting the Marxist government against Eritrean independence. How did I feel about this?
Was I supposed to applaud? I was pleased to have a conversation
with Cuban filmmaker Tomás Gutiérrez Alea, world-acclaimed
for *Memories of Underdevelopment* [1968]. Like the estranged
intellectual protagonist of his movie, Alea chose to remain in Cuba
while others fled to the USA.

Didn't you also visit the Telluride Film Festival while at the Real
Paper?

I did twice, in 1980 and 1981, and that was a truly golden age
there. I saw the world premiere of Godfrey Reggio's *Koyaanisqatsi*
[1982] and ancient Abel Gance watched out of his hotel window an
outdoors screening of his *Napoleon* [1927]. I did two remarkable
interviews with Woody Strode and Joel McCrea, both so gentlemanly and gracious. I praised McCrea for saying to a feckless
young cowboy what might be the first ecological line in cinema
in *Ride the High Country* [1962]: "This river doesn't need your
trash." And I attended a nonpareil panel of Hollywood character
actors with John Carradine, Margaret Hamilton, and Elisha Cook,
Jr. I asked from the audience, "Who was Elisha Cook, Sr.?" I don't
recall Elisha's answer.

Did that whet your appetite for attending film shindigs?

Definitely. It's never stopped. Even when the *Real Paper* stopped.

So what brought about the downfall of the Real Paper?

In 1981, it became clear to everyone that we were in financial
trouble. The paper had shrunk in size and writers were asked to
double up and do a second column a week. I strongly contributed
to the demise of the *Real Paper* with a non-film news article about
a unionizing effort at a bookstore which was our second biggest
advertiser. My piece was not objective at all, highly sympathetic to
the complaints of those starting a union. The result: the bookstore
pulled all its advertising from the paper, a fatal financial drain.

One day I had lunch with my editor and we talked about
what films I'd be reviewing in the weeks to come. We returned to
the office to find that the *Real Paper* was being shut down on the
spot. The owner of the *Phoenix* had purchased our paper to silence

his opposition. What was my reaction? I tried to sneak my typewriter out of the building but was caught by security. Everyone was asked to exit with their belongings and a new lock was placed on the door.

For the record: my last review for the *Phoenix* in May 1981 was of *Raiders of the Lost Ark*. Usually a non-lover of action movies, I gave this Spielberg four stars. That review was a joy to write but I have a confession to make. After just 2 ½ years at the *Real Paper*, I was getting weary reviewing films all the time and especially reviewing what comes with the territory of being the first-string critic, the splashiest popular films. How long would I have remained in this position if the *Real Paper* had kept going? I know Renata Adler quit reviewing at the *New York Times* after one year. I can relate to that.

So I was out of work and even collecting unemployment. Luckily, I'd made a connection with the film magazine, *American Film*. I was a contributing writer doing regular columns about categories of film—Westerns, road movies, etc.—which had become available on video. Just as the *Real Paper* closed, I had my biggest *American Film* assignment. I was flown to Utah to write about the first incarnation of the Sundance Institute, pre-Sundance Film Festival. The key to the article was getting a sit-down with Robert Redford himself. I am still peeved remembering how, when our interview was scheduled, he kept me dangling for an hour or more for no reason and slowly licked an ice cream cone. The interview was a bit self-pitying. Redford complained to me how as a younger unknown he hitchhiked across America and now he couldn't be in public because of his fame. Poor Robert!

I returned to Boston to write up my Sundance article and without a clue about my next job. Tellingly, nobody at the *Phoenix* invited me to join their film staff. But one day I got a phone call from someone I didn't know inquiring if I had a Ph.D. I did, so virtually on the spot I was hired as a full-time instructor at Suffolk University in Boston. I was to teach journalism courses, and these later turned to film courses. I could never imagine when I said "Yes" to Suffolk that I would remain there for about 35 years. I will say almost nothing about my time there except that I enjoyed my students and the best occasions were "Great Directors" classes, which included courses dedicated to Ford, Buñuel, Cocteau, Richard Linklater, Clint Eastwood. I also liked co-teaching a "Women in Film" course with a very capable sociologist, Alexandra Todd, a dear friend.

What happened to your film critic career?

If I had grown tired of regularly reviewing films by 1981, I had not tired of the film critic life. l was hooked on going to film festivals. And I loved doing feature stories and interviewing those working in cinema. From 1981–1996, I was both teaching at Suffolk and a very active freelance film writer. I continued at *American Film*. I wrote at various times for the *Boston Globe* and the *Boston Herald*. Nationally, I provided articles to the *LA Times*, the *Chicago Tribune*, and other newspapers. I also did some pieces for *Sight & Sound* in England and *Positif* in France. Ideally, I would sell the same article to several places. I think my record was getting an interview with a French woman screenwriter into five newspapers.

You also traveled abroad to write about film?

The Berlin Film Festival was quite flush in those days, so for a few years my flights and hotel were paid for. There were so many excitements. It was the early days of gay liberation, and the Berlin Film Festival was the most gay-friendly festival on earth. I attended a then-daring feature by the pioneer gay German director Rosa von Praunheim, after which sobbing audience members stood up and confessed publicly their homosexuality. There was a tremendously moving evening when an aged group of queer survivors of Hitler's camps, those forced to wear pink ribbons, came out on stage at Berlin. What a standing ovation! Another thrilling event: bringing back to Berlin German-Jewish film personages who had fled into exile during the War. People like actress Dolly Haas. I got screenwriter Curt Siodmak to sign my copy of his horror novel, *Donovan's Brain*. He told me, "I'm a better scriptwriter than my brother but Robert was a better director."

I was so much younger then! I happily attended midnight screenings at Berlin, like the world premiere of Gus Van Sant's *Mala Noche* [1985]. And I made it all the way to the end of Norman Mailer's *The Executioner's Song* [1985], all 2 hours and 37 minutes of it. However, the pinnacle moment at Berlin was my being inside twentieth-century history. I was a festival guest in February 1990, a first-hand witness to the Berlin Wall coming down. That was the year an East German filmmaker walked over from East Berlin and showed at the Fest his newest film. Like many film critics, I spent hours away from the Fest joining the celebrants in the streets.

I actually stood on the Wall. A Canadian cinematographer took my photograph there. One of my regrets in life is that I don't have a copy of that photograph.

How were things back home in America?

Another place with government money for the arts was the province of Quebec in Canada. I managed to get myself invited to the Montreal World Film Festival, flights and hotel, and went there for more than twenty years. It was where I saw possibly the world premiere of *Blue Velvet* [1986]. Montreal had a massive budget to bring guests from as far away as Asia. That meant that I had a journalist meeting c.1980 with a delegation in Maoist garb from China, which felt like something comic from Billy Wilder's *One Two Three* [1961]. When I asked them what American films played in China, the delegation broke out in song, "Doe, a deer, a female deer, Re, a drop of golden sun…"

I had a rousing hotel room interview with Toshiro Mifune—who gets to talk with Mifune?—who called himself "a little boy" and bounced around the room like Jerry Lewis. He had once appeared in a film by Kenji Mizoguchi and, for my benefit, bent over and acted the part of the fastidious filmmaker checking out props for their authenticity. Honestly, I felt like a king, sitting there while Mifune did just for me his Mizoguchi imitation.

Most of Montreal's guests came from Europe. Fellini never showed up, but his actress wife Giulietta Masina was there one year, and I got her autograph. And I had a drink in a hotel lobby with a bubbly Anna Karina. She told us that the earliest issues of *Cahiers du Cinéma* sold out at the Paris newsstands because Godard secretly bought them up. Godard appeared at Montreal quite often, and I suspect he was paid well to be there. When he came to Canadian festivals in the fall, Godard mostly stayed in his hotel room watching tennis, the US Open.

After I'd been at Montreal a few years, I was approached by a couple of film critics from Toronto and told I should also come to the Festival of Festivals. It's quite new, they said, but we can arrange for your flights and hotel. I am unapologetically a festival slut, so I instantly said yes. That was about 1979, and I attended Toronto until about 2010. The first several years of the Fest were touching and amateur. "God Save the Queen" was sung before every screening and Ontario's censorship board checked out every film to be shown. I remember a projectionist coming into a theater and apologizing to the audience for his lousy projecting. But slowly Toronto caught on, and step by step it became a really major film festival, completely usurping Montreal by the mid 1980s.

I like to think I contributed to the tremendous jump in stature of Toronto. In 1981, the French filmmaker Jean-Jacques Beineix came there totally unknown with his first film, *Diva*. The screening was a smash and everyone was talking about it. American distributors had Toronto's first bidding war. I met with Beineix and he asked for my advice which distributor to choose. I highly recommended UA 16, and that's where he went. I gather UA 16 did a good job and *Diva* had fine reviews and excellent box office in the USA. In 1982, the next year after *Diva*, every distributor brought their whole office to Toronto to scout the movies projected there. Distributors no longer bothered to go to Montreal.

What about your writing? What opportunities were you getting?

This was fortuitous. One day in a movie line I met Jay Scott, the talented and very influential critic for the *Toronto Globe and Mail*, and we made a deal. I would recommend him to write for *American Film*, where I remained a Contributing Editor, and he would talk to his Arts Editor about me appearing in the *Globe and Mail*. It worked out magnificently. Through the 1980s, I wrote about 100 feature articles and interviews with such film luminaries as Julie Christie, Ginger Rogers, and Dorothy Malone for Toronto's best and most prestigious newspaper. It was a writers' paper with articles of 1,200–1,500 words and editors who appreciated and nourished first-rate journalism. I'm very proud of my contributions there. I was excited by the chance to expound at length about things in cinema I cared about. It could be argued that one's sharpest writing about cinema is in your late thirties and early forties, and that's when I freelanced for the *Globe and Mail*.

My reputation in Toronto spread. I was offered a monthly column on film for *Flare*, Canada's English-language fashion magazine. And I returned to reviewing films after a long hiatus now for *Maclean's*, Canada's version of *Time* or *Newsweek*. *Flare* managed in 1985 to get me a first-class plane ticket and a five-star hotel for the first Tokyo Film Festival. That's where a busload of international journalists was transported to a luxury hotel on Mt. Fuji to interview an imperious Akira Kurosawa about *Ran*.

So you were a film critic star in Toronto.

I actually was, so far from my home in Boston, where I was just a college teacher at a small university and now a film critic nobody. But my byline was known and respected in Toronto and Ontario. I should note that this was a great moment of an English-Canadian New Wave of feature filmmakers, with Atom Egoyan, Guy Maddin, Bruce McDonald, John Paisz, Patricia Rozema, Don McKellar, and others. I was writing about this world of filmmakers just as it was peaking. I guess I was what we now call "an influencer." English Canada had a great inferiority complex about its homegrown movies and local audiences stayed away from them, totally preferring Hollywood cinema. Whenever a Canadian critic wrote favorably about a Canadian film, nobody believed him/her, assuming it was just nationalist boosterism. But when I, an American, wrote in praise of a Canadian movie, people took notice. That film must be actually good!

Can I do some really unseemly bragging? I wrote in *Flare* an article in praise of John Paisz and his extraordinary comedy feature, *Crime Wave* [1985], then and now sinfully unknown. My payoff? Flings with two lovely women from Winnipeg who were grateful for me waxing so positively about their hometown director. Such things are supposed to happen to rock stars, not film critics.

Hmmm… So, considering all the romance and amusement, rare for film critics, why did you stop attending Canadian film festivals?

Before I answer, there's a third estimable festival we haven't mentioned: the Vancouver International Film Festival. Not only did I attend often but I worked as a scout for Vancouver recommending films to show. For a few years I was a programmer for retrospective screenings of Hollywood classics. I attended this festival faithfully until 2020, and it was where I was lucky to have yearly breakfasts with David Bordwell and Kristin Thompson. It's such a loss to the film world that David has died.

I stopped going to Montreal because the festival shut down in 2019. The director Serge Losique was such a divisive figure with many enemies and my guess is that the provisional government finally got tired of subsidizing the World Film Festival.

Toronto is a totally different story. I would hang out there every year with my great pal from Madison student days, Peter Brunette, who was a professor at Wake Forest University and author of wonderful books on Antonioni and Rossellini. In June 2010, my friend was attending an Italian film festival when he died instantly over breakfast from a brain aneurysm. I was too depressed to go to the Toronto Fest in 2010 or 2011 missing Peter being there. The years stretched out and somehow I never returned.

We should change topics. Let's discuss your Fulbright Fellowship.

I was offered a Fulbright to spend five months in Belgrade in the Spring of 1985 researching Yugoslavian film comedy. I had a glorious time. Honestly, one of the finest times of my life.

This was Yugoslavia before the dreadful war, when Serbs and Croatians and Bosnians mixed everywhere in the country. And though it was post-Tito Communist, it was a pretty free place. Of all Communist countries, this was the only one which looked West instead of East for cinema. The people were Hollywood-crazy. John Carpenter movies were especially admired and there was an ongoing John Ford series at the Kinoteca.

The filmmakers and critics I met were very familiar with Andrew Sarris and all preferred him to Pauline Kael! So I was a kind of minor celebrity, being a very rare American, and because I was a source of information about Hollywood movies. Specifically, I taught my friends how to pronounce Budd Boetticher and Frank Borzage. "Boetticher" was said correctly for the first time in a course at the university on the American Western. I also recall a long evening with a young woman cineaste in Zagreb offering her in minute detail the plots of Douglas Sirk movies she wasn't able to see in Croatia.

I made great friendships in Belgrade with two important filmmakers, Slobodan Šijan and Srdjan Karanović. Karanović offered to introduce me to whomever I wanted to meet. I would have dinner with Belgrade film actors and directors whom I admired, ideally in a scenic restaurant by the Danube. And I was invited into an elite monthly basketball game in which the participants were well-known Yugoslavian film actors.

Didn't you have to show something substantive to the Fulbright committee to justify your being in Yugoslavia? A book perhaps?

Fortunately not, because I only produced one essay about my time there, "Hollywood in Yugoslavia," for a 1990 book called *Before the Wall Came Down*, edited by Graham Petrie and Ruth Dwyer.

I did give a series of lectures to Yugoslavian audiences in Belgrade, Split, and other places. And I did my research as well as I could, going to several cinematheques to watch Yugoslavian film comedies in their vaults. Which were great, truly worthy of study.

I guess that's enough about me in Yugoslavia. I didn't add much to the world of scholarship, but I had one fine time.

Could you talk briefly about some of the film actors you interviewed in those years, at festivals and otherwise?

Julie Christie was sweet and so modest, just the nicest person to talk to. I'm sorry to say that Ginger Rogers had a touch of Norma Desmond prima donna, dramatically dolled up and painted up for the interview, very huffy about movies made today and revolted by sex scenes on screen. Jane Russell was down-to-earth, happy to reminisce about having to coax nervous Marilyn Monroe out of the dressing room for *Gentlemen Prefer Blondes* [1953]. Sterling Hayden began as a difficult interview. I met with him in Boston and he was clearly paranoid, smoking marijuana as we spoke, wanting to throw me out of his hotel room. His wife convinced Hayden that I was OK, and then it all settled down into a fabulous career interview. Hayden said something I quote all the time. I remarked that it must have been great appearing in *Johnny Guitar*. He answered, "It was the worst time of my life. I fought with Joan Crawford in the day and my wife at night." May I end with my unforgettable conversation with Catherine Deneuve, who also started out hating me but ended up asking my advice about what filmmakers I thought she should work with. You will never read that interview. I was so discombobulated when Deneuve barked at me that I hit the wrong button trying to start my tape recorder. Not one word was recorded.

Is there any other international film festival experience that you want to mention from this period?

I went twice to the Jerusalem Film Festival in, I believe, 1988 and 1990, when there was still a strong left and a strong Labor Party. Both supported this progressive festival in which many of the programmers were also regular protestors in the streets supporting Palestinian rights. It was here that I had one of my greatest coups as a journalist. For the first time under glasnost, the Soviet Union allowed a Russian Jewish filmmaker, Aleksandr Askoldov, to travel to Israel and to show his long-banned feature, *Commissar* [1967]. There was a meeting on a hill below the Jerusalem Cinematheque with folding chairs and a card table, and that's where Askoldov sat down with Israeli prime minister Shimon Peres. The third person at the table was me, reporting for the *LA Times*. I broke journalist rules by trying to intervene in world history. I nudged Peres to tell Askoldov to invite Gorbachev to come to Israel. That's exactly what he did. Whether Gorbachev was informed of Peres's invitation I'll never know.

My other excitement at Jerusalem was having breakfast with another festival guest, Chantal Akerman. She was shy but really nice. Several days after, I was walking through the city and wearing a t-shirt with the word "Hopeless" on it. Akerman saw me and asked with the greatest sympathy and enormous concern, "Are you really hopeless?" I assured her that I was not. When the sadly depressed Akerman committed suicide many years later, I got what "hopeless" meant to her.

What had happened to your life as a working film critic?

Though still writing for Canadian publications, I never considered moving to Toronto to be a full-time journalist there. Nobody in Canada ever offered me a staff position, and I'm not sure the government would have allowed the hiring of an American. But I was settled in Cambridge, Massachusetts, with a not-too-difficult teaching position and summers off, which allowed me ample time for freelance writing. But this is the really honest answer: I wasn't ambitious enough or driven enough to seriously pursue a film critic career. Unlike many other film critics, I did not use Boston as a stepping stone to go to New York. And let me confess more: I'm not sure I was talented enough to hold down some prestigious New York film critic position. I'm a good film critic, occasionally very good, but am I a great one? I don't think so.

I have to give credits to the "Paulettes." Like Pauline Kael herself, they really believe they are tremendous critics bringing something special to their lucky readers. They believe that being a film critic is a unique calling, almost holy, and they have no qualms about spending their whole adult lives writing movie reviews. I think of Owen Gleiberman, discovered by Kael when he was a college student, now still fifty years later writing with enthusiasm for *Variety*. And there's my good friend Peter Rainer, my best pal by far among "Paulettes." After splendid work at the *LA Herald* and the *LA Times*, Peter just never quits, as dedicated today to reviewing films as half a century ago, still writing beautifully for the *Christian Science Monitor*.

Let's get back to your being a film critic in Boston.

The folding of the *Real Paper* in 1981 left the *Boston Phoenix* as the only alternative newspaper around. It had a huge and flourishing film section. In the years after, four of the "Paulettes" on the paper moved to New York, one by one looking to further their careers. And for the first time a decided non-"Paulette," Peter Keough, my talented friend, became the *Phoenix*'s first-string critic. Around 1994 or 1995, the depleted *Phoenix* found itself in need of a second regular critic working behind Keough, and they looked to me. I accepted a position as a weekly freelancer and returned to reviewing films in Boston after a 13-year hiatus.

I was refreshed and ready to do reviews again, and this position as defined was ideal for me. I would never have to review the big movie coming out that week, nor most new Hollywood pictures. My 1,500-word column, called Film Culture, had as its beat independent features, foreign-language "art" films and documentaries. Just perfect! Plus interviews, film festival coverage, and weird items about the movie business. Basically, whatever I wanted to write about. I never had to suffer the fate of most film critics, interviewing film people whom I didn't care about. And I didn't have to see all those insufferable mainstream studio films. Not my beat!

The *Phoenix* was my longest gig. I wrote reviews up until the day the *Phoenix* folded in 2013, for approximately 18 years. Was my work there influential? Certainly my influence diminished as time went by, as print journalism in general meant less and less and was read less and less. But my employment for the *Phoenix* allowed for my election into the National Society of Film Critics. And being in the National Society qualified me to be on juries for FIPRESCI, the international critics association. This was the best! I can say I truly saw the world being on FIPRESCI juries, and usually appointed the president of these juries. Here's just some of the places I did jury duty at film festivals: Rotterdam, Hong Kong, Bangkok, Stockholm, Mannheim, Mara Del Plata in Argentina, Mexico City, San Sebastian, Moscow, Vienna, Venice.

I've probably done my last FIPRESCI juries. It was clear with two of my last three juries that the younger critics resented having an elder like me as the president. They didn't revolt, but the lack of respect was palpable. My jury at the Moscow Film Festival was particularly disdainful, including a wildly homophobic woman from Romania who told me she hoped all my homosexual friends would burn and die.

Did you ever go again to Cannes?

Twice in all, and I paid my way. That's not my favorite festival. It's prohibitively expensive. It's too much work, from early morning press screening to events deep into the night. It's also snobby and intimidating and perhaps the only fest in the world where critics seem to rank themselves in importance and only hang out with others at the same level. Here the *Phoenix* was a very minor journalism outlet and I felt myself a lowly and inconsequential critic. I was never invited on a yacht or for lunch at the Hotel du Cap.

So back in Boston you were teaching at Suffolk University and writing a weekly film column for the Phoenix. Anything else?

An L.A. film person named Mel Howard, whom you might remember for his acting in Yiddish in *Hester Street* [1975], was brought to Boston University to chair and wake up the Communication Department. He promptly hired me to instruct a film studies class each semester and I taught full-time there for one year, on leave from Suffolk. Perhaps my favorite course that I taught in my life was a BU class in the French New Wave. In Fall 1992, Quentin Tarantino came to town promoting *Reservoir Dogs* and I invited him to speak. This is how I introduced him: "Class, this is Quentin Tarantino. You don't know him now but he's going to be a famous filmmaker." With that, Tarantino came up front and offered a dazzling one-hour spontaneous lecture on Melville, Godard, *Cahiers du Cinéma*, the Nouvelle Vague. I am forever sorry that nobody thought to video his talk.

The BU teaching lasted only several years but something more important came out of that. Starting in 1995 and for 25 years I ran a Friday night series inviting filmmaking guests to show their work and speak with BU cinema students. My programming of the BU Cinematheque ended with Covid in 2020. Close to five hundred movie people came through, from Betty Comden and Adolph Green to Jerry Schatzberg to George Kuchar to Lena Dunham, and I pride myself with bringing to Boston University three guests responsible for three of the greatest screenplays of all time: Paul Schrader and *Taxi Driver* [1976], Robert Towne and *Chinatown* [1974], Budd Schulberg and *On the Waterfront* [1954].

You were also at the Harvard Film Archive?

I had one memorable year as the Guest Archivist, 1998–1999, programming the theater in the Corbusier-designed Carpenter Center and bringing filmmakers to speak. I'm extremely pleased with what I accomplished there, appearances by approximately 50 filmmakers and all done within budget. One highlight was a lengthy John Ford series, another of LGBTQ classic films like *Mädchen in Uniform* [1931]. A key guest was Stan Brakhage for an all-night affair I called "A Brakhage Be-In," with the great experimentalist speaking at various points into the early morning.

My position could have been permanent but I was not chosen from a group of candidates. My belief is that I was recognized as not a real Harvard type. There's nothing Ivy League about me at all: my lack of breeding is obvious. I gave it a real college try, delivering as part of the competition a terrific lecture on the "1940 Birth of Film Noir." I showed how Boris Ingster's *Stranger on the Third Floor* combined German Expression and new "noir" elements and how Raoul Walsh's *They Drive By Night* went from 1930s truck-driver social conscious medium shots to "noir" subjective closeups and murder and mayhem. Regretfully, I never turned this revisionist lecture on film history into a published article.

So that was my year at holy Harvard. In September 1999, I returned to teaching at humble Suffolk University. But one wonderful thing happened: that fall I met Amy Geller, a young film producer who had moved to Cambridge from New Hampshire. We became an item and eloped several years later. Amy would produce my first feature documentary and we would co-direct another documentary. As of this interview, we have been married for 21 years. We have two exceptional cats, Nick and Nora, named, of course, for *The Thin Man* [1934].

Had you any film production aspirations before meeting Amy Geller? You haven't mentioned any.

If critics Frank Nugent and Paul Schrader and Roger Ebert could write screenplays, why couldn't I? Many filmmakers will coax you to provide a screenplay for them on spec as there is nothing for them to lose. So three scripts were composed by me for Yugoslavian filmmakers whom I had befriended and who wanted to have something in English to show potential producers. One of these scripts, *Niagara Falls*, a forbiddingly expensive extravaganza of Raoul Walsh Americana, got me a $1,000 option. That's my total money for screenwriting! None of the scripts for Yugoslavians was produced. On my own, I did an ambitious adaptation of Nathaniel Hawthorne's novel, *The Blithedale Romance*, and some prestigious filmmakers considered it and decided there was no way to finance a period film.

Then there is my horror story: I was flown to L.A. and spent days and long nights doing a screenplay at the condo of a young and ambitious actress. Back in Boston, I got an insane telephone call from this actress telling me that she decided I didn't really co-write that script, that it was all her. WHAT? I decided to sue and she countersued, hiring a zillion-dollar lawyer who had counseled Spielberg. This Hollywood lawyer claimed that I had stayed at that actress' apartment wanting to have sexual relations with her! What could I do? After giving $5,000 to my Boston lawyer, I was out of funds. I was forced to sign an agreement that I was not the screenwriter.

Yes, this movie was made and it was beyond awful. I saw it an empty theater, listened to many of the lines I'd written being spoken badly by second-rate actors (the actress both starred and directed). I actually fell asleep at some point as the movie droned on. I'm listed in the final credits among the rolling titles, I forgot for doing what. I would say the title of the film but I'm scared to be sued again.

Did I learn my lesson? About eight years ago, I once again was seduced to write a screenplay on spec for an actor-director who had appeared in the TV series *Girls*. I modeled the comedy script to his specific talents. He read it and decided "No" to a movie because the main character was like what he'd done before, and with success. AAAGH! No more scripts, Gerald. No more scripts.

But what about work on actual productions?

I sometimes would be invited into the editing room of films being made by friends. I found I had an uncanny ability to see where edits should be made, how the order of scenes should be shuffled.

I often suggested subtle and valuable changes that nobody else had thought of. Two veteran documentarians hired me to work on their films, Errol Morris in Cambridge, Mass., and Ron Mann in Toronto. For a couple of months I went into Errol's office and sat down with his editors, including occasions when Errol wasn't even there. I wish I remembered the name of an Errol Morris TV episode that I was story editing. There's one showy cut in the final version that was totally my idea. Brilliant! Anyway, Errol came in once in a grumpy mood and fired me on the spot, just what he has done over the years with other employees. I still came around his office in the late 1990s because his editor, Karen Schmeer, was my girlfriend. She edited *Fast, Cheap & Out of Control* [1997] and Errol's Oscar winner, *The Fog of War* [2003].

Karen and I broke up in 1998. She moved to New York to pursue a career away from Errol, and she was killed in a tragic hit-and-run accident in 2010. There is a Karen Schmeer Editing Fellowship in her name. Karen, a kind and lovely person, was revered by her editing peers.

And Ron Mann?

I helped Ron with the structuring of his marijuana celebration, *Grass* [1999]. I believe I have a story editor credit. Earlier, he had flown me from Boston to advise him on the Toronto set of *Twist* [1992], which saw Chubby Checker, Joey Dee, and other Twisters reminiscing about the 1960s dance craze. Ron also brought a few of the original Philadelphia dancers from Dick Clark's *American Bandstand*. I gasped because there in Toronto and still living in Philadelphia was the amazing Linda, my *American Bandstand* crush when I was 15 and she was in high school. By the movie shoot, both Linda and I were deep in our 40s. She was long out of the spotlight so she was genuinely touched when I revealed that I'd been smitten by her. My wet dream: I actually danced with Linda on the *Twist* set. And she had a photograph taken of us together to bring back to Philadelphia! That was our moment, and I never saw Linda again. Or learned her last name.

It's time to talk for a bit about your 2009 documentary, For the Love of Movies: the Story of American Film Criticism. *Why did you make a film about film critics?*

I had no intention of making it. It happened because I'd helped Ron Mann behind the scenes on *Grass* and *Twist*. One day when we were having lunch in Toronto, he decided to reward me for my loyalty by asking, "Would you like to direct a film? I'll produce it." That sounded great. He then asked, "What would you like to make a movie about?" My suggestion had absolutely nothing to do with cinema. The documentary I wanted to direct was about barbecue! About barbecue masters going down into their pits early in the morning, and doing up their special sauces. I love barbecue, I love food, and that was my preferred project. And Ron said, "Gerry, I don't think so. But I do think you should make a film about what you really know best, which is film criticism." So that's how it started. I said "Yes" to the topic of film criticism because if someone offers to produce and finance your film, you grab the opportunity.

So how did you proceed?

As Ron was footing the bills, he brought on a Toronto line producer and he hired freelance cinematographers for wherever we'd go and we began to film. I don't know that we had any more plan than that we would interview American film critics about their profession. Our very first shoot turned out to be pretty eerie. We went to the New York Film Critics annual dinner in January 2001 at the World Trade Center. I was too spooked out to check but some of the waiters we filmed serving the food might not have survived 9/11.

We did have a small wish list of critics whom we absolutely wanted to get into the film. We went to Chicago and interviewed Roger Ebert on the set of his TV show with Gene Siskel. We also talked to the *Chicago Tribune* critic, Michael Wilmington, the guy who I had that fight with many years earlier when we were students in Madison. In 2002, we were friends. We filmed Michael lecturing about how in the 1950s the "cast of thousands" in DeMille's *The Ten Commandments* [1956] were real people versus now the unfortunate utilization of CGI. I so agree with him! Finally, we spoke with Jonathan Rosenbaum, then with the *Chicago Reader*.

Our freelance cameraman for at least one Chicago shoot was independent filmmaker Joe Swanberg. He did more shooting when we later did interviews at SXSW. We were lucky there to discover on a panel young Karina Longworth, many years before she became a podcast celebrity. I interviewed her as an example of the next generation of film critics. But we were there in Austin specifically to speak with Harry Knowles, then a major influencer as the fan boy behind *Ain't It Cool News*. If there's any kind of semi-villain in my documentary it's probably Harry. I call him out for his lazy-dude sloppy reviews, more for his being the little king of "quote whores," flown to Hollywood for advance screenings of movies so that he would supply a positive blurb for the ads.

Our big shoot was New York City: interviews with Jim Hoberman of the *Voice*, Stuart Klawans of *The Nation*, Jami Bernard of the *Daily News*, Owen Gleiberman and Lisa Schwarzbaum of *Entertainment Weekly*, and a fine meeting with Andrew Sarris and Molly Haskell in their home. Maybe my favorite conversation was with Stanley Kauffmann, the aged but very agile critic for the *New Republic*. He talked with excitement about the rise of cinema as being a "special moment in the development of human consciousness." That was one quote I knew would go into the film. Another was Hoberman saying with a grin, "We used to refer to Sarris's *The American Cinema* as 'the Bible.'" A third was from Sarris's description of his disillusioning first meeting with Pauline Kael: "She was no Katharine Hepburn. But then you don't stop to think what you look like. I was no Spencer Tracy either."

The film was starting to pick up momentum and I was discovering issues which I wanted discussed in every interview. I had today's critics commenting on earlier critics who influenced them and then offering their take on the Kael-Sarris debate. A friend gave me this fruitful suggestion: have critics speak dramatically about the film that most affected them—scared the shit out of them!—when they were young. Many of these colorful remembrances made the final cut: Gleiberman on creepy Ruth Gordon in *Rosemary's Baby* [1968], Haskell on the dead man rising in the tub in *Diabolique* [1955], Hoberman on the terrible circus train crash in *The Greatest Show on Earth* [1952], and Schwarzbaum on the very scene that also gave me months of nightmares: the kid waking up to an inexplicable and horrific change in his appearance in *The Boy With Green Hair* [1948].

Was there anyone whom you couldn't get to?

Manohla Dargis of the *New York Times* said "No" because she didn't want to be seen on camera. She was and is very comely so I still don't get her being coy. I believe that at least one woman

"Paulette" also balked at my offer to interview her, paranoid that I was going to make an overwhelmingly Sarris film.

Is her accusation correct?

For the Love of Movies may tip a bit toward Sarris, but I tried to be really fair to Kael in the film, including interviewing her daughter and getting very positive words about her from the then *New York Times* critic, Elvis Mitchell. Maybe I should have tried harder to get one more Paulette in the film, though I do doubt that the most devoted of her followers would have conversed with me. At the first public screening of the film at Telluride, rock critic Greil Marcus came out and whined, "You could have been nicer to Pauline." He was her good friend, meaning there were even Paulettes outside of film.

But did you make an honest try to get Kael into the movie? I mean, you feature Sarris.

Unfortunately, Kael was quite ill as we were shooting, and only her inner circle got in to see her in person. I wasn't in that circle. We managed to find some substantive interviews she'd done with others and made use of her best quotes. We also utilized a frothy conversation she had with Woody Allen.

Is there anyone else who turned you down?

Manny Farber. He answered my phone call sounding put off and pissed. I started a complimentary speech trying to rope him in for an interview. But he cut me off, saying "No" and hanging up. My thirty seconds with Farber! Again, I found a very good interview with Farber and used that, and also had other critics comment on his contributions. He might be the only critic whom seemingly everyone admires; Stuart Klawans and Jonathan Rosenbaum in my movie, both Sarris and Kael in real life. I might be the only critic who thinks Farber may be slightly overrated. Some of his judgments of films are disastrously wrong-headed and maybe he is too universally loved for his trick of jumping into the middle of the film for some daring observation. What about the rest of the movie, which he ignores? However, I do like that he moved easily from championing "B" movies to discussing avant-garde cinema. And I love his attacks on White Elephant movies and his celebration of "Termite" art.

So you continued going around interviewing film critics?

I got to Richard Schickel at the 2002 Montreal Film Festival, an important figure in my documentary. Less consequential, I interviewed there a married team of lightweights notorious for writing only positive reviews and getting lots of industry perks for that reason. In the middle of our on-camera talk, this couple caught on from my questions that I was kind of setting them up. I did feel a little guilty and I don't think I put them into the film.

I arrived at the 2002 Toronto Film Festival with a new strategy. Each day, I would arbitrarily interview any American critic who happened to walk by and who had time to talk for the camera. If somebody didn't walk by, or was at another theater than me, that person isn't in the movie. I have several film critic friends who remain resentful to this day for not appearing in *For the Love of Movies*. I say to them with honesty: if I'd run into you at Toronto, you'd be up there on the screen. I mean, Rex Reed, not the finest critic, is in the movie because he had a few minutes open at Toronto. I talked to Reed years later and he'd never seen my documentary and had no memory even of being filmed.

Beyond the interviews, something weird happened at Toronto that year. Ron Mann, my producer, was nowhere around the shoot, even though this was his hometown. What was up? Somehow, without an explanation to me, he'd lost his enthusiasm about my movie! I did know that he was having more difficulty than he'd expected financing it. One reason why was that I, an American, was directing the film in a country, Canada, which protects its own culture. Mann couldn't get government funding with me at the center. But was that the only reason he was stepping away? I was detecting a little jealousy maybe because so many people seemed excited about this film that I was directing and not him behind the camera. And this was the guy with whom I'd been tight pals for years, who had sent flowers and champagne to my hotel in New York on the day of our World Trade Center shoot.

There was a long period of inertia, nothing happening with the film. At some point, I was so frustrated that I bought from Ron the rights to the movie and all the footage for, I don't remember, $30,000? $40,000? And we stopped being friends to this day.

That happened probably in 2003. And suddenly there was this totally inexperienced filmmaker, me, with all this footage. The next several years are a blur. At some point my wife Amy Geller came aboard as the producer of the documentary. But she was reluctant about making this commitment. She had no interest at all in the subject of the movie, a history of American film criticism. Even worse, she had hesitations with me as the fledgling director. Although she was only in her mid-20s, Amy was already a seasoned producer who had worked with real professionals. It was not fun to be collaborating with a rank amateur who also happened to be her husband. An amateur who, Amy felt, had little knowledge of the rigorous process of filmmaking. Well, I *was* a bit lazy and lackadaisical about it all. I had said, somewhat smugly, "I don't understand why filmmaking takes so long to complete. What are people doing so long in the editing room?"

I would find out... It took us until 2009 to finish the film, more than eight years after the first shoot. Six years of struggle with Amy as producer to finance this work and edit it into a decent documentary. Along the way, there were many clashes between us, the closest we have ever come to getting divorced.

Did you do any more filming with Amy as producer?

At home, we filmed Wesley Morris, then a critic for the *Boston Globe*, in his apartment. And around 2005, Amy and I attended the Cannes Film Festival for what we insisted were our final interviews. We planned to hire a freelance cinematographer, but the first day there we ran into the French filmmaker Benoît Jacquot, with whom I was friendly. He advised us to do the filming ourselves. We nervously agreed, mostly to save us money, but what an unhappy shoot! Each morning we'd leave our faraway hotel with a heavy video camera we'd brought from Boston and walk through downtown Cannes. Poor Amy was stuck with the camera all day long as I was the one who could see movies with my press card. Meanwhile, Amy did "B" roll, things like Jim Jarmusch walking through a crowd, and then some excellently filmed hotel room interviews with critics A. O. Scott of the *New York Times* and Richard Corliss of *Time*. Amy was exhausted and irritated being the fill-in camera person, but Jacquot had been right. It all worked.

When you were finally editing your film, did some themes emerge?

These were the years when film critics started being fired right and left from newspapers everywhere. My documentary became a defense of film criticism as an important thing to do, and also an elegy to what was becoming before our eyes a dying profession.

There's one chapter called "When Film Criticism Mattered," and that was, for me, the 1970s and '80s, when people knew the bylines of many critics and cared what they had to say. Being a film critic actually had some sort of weight. But how things changed!

When I had filmed Michael Wilmington in 2002, he seemed entrenched at the *Chicago Tribune*. When we were editing, Michael lost his job to a younger film critic, so his dismissal became part of the movie. This was also the period when film criticism gravitated from print to the Internet. A young generation of critics popped up, mostly disapproved of by old-timers as having neither knowledge nor credentials, something that is discussed in the final chapters of *For the Love of Movies*: an upside-down universe in which "everyone is a film critic." The earlier chapters of the film are more traditional: a straightforward telling of the history of American film criticism literally from its beginnings. Nobody before had tried to accomplish this on film before.

Did you make some discoveries in your research?

I think few people knew that the screenwriter of *The Birth of a Nation* [1915], Frank Woods, began as a film critic before joining D. W. Griffith's company. I make a case for the cultural importance of the film criticism of Robert Sherwood before he became a successful playwright. Just two examples.

Can you talk about the voiceover for your film?

My first idea (not Amy's!) was that I would do my own voiceover. But I lost confidence when I tried to do an on-camera speech in front of the West Village home of James Agee and completely botched it. Who could replace me? When we interviewed Owen Gleiberman in New York, he had mentioned his friend "Patty." Patty who? Patricia Clarkson! Amy and I loved her! We asked Owen to intervene and we miraculously secured Clarkson for our film. For very little money, she came into a New York City studio for two long days and did the narration. She was lovely, totally cooperative, took my direction without argument. What a thrill to have Patricia Clarkson in our cast, and to hear her saying so beautifully words that I'd written!

What about the title of your film?

I can't remember how we decided on the *For the Love of Movies* part, deciding that's why film critics do their work. Clearly the whole thing is a bit bulky: *For the Love of Movies: The Story of American Film Criticism*. John Waters told me it was a terrible title because by the time he got to the end he couldn't remember the first part. Pretty funny!

There's also an excellent soundtrack. Who did that?

Amy and I attended a wedding of Amy's friend, a marriage that ended soon in divorce. But a good thing for us was that her friend had hired a band led by an extraordinary Massachusetts guitarist named Bobby Keyes. I was bowled over and approached him after his wedding set to do our music. He'd never done a score for a film and Amy had many challenges teaching him how to deliver what he wrote. But the score is wonderful original music composed by Keyes, from rockabilly to something akin to the Glenn Miller Orchestra. Plus over the final credits a powerful arrangement of Stephen Foster's "Hard Times," signaling what was happening by 2009 to film criticism.

What else helped kill film criticism besides the Internet?

The other thing would be shifting movie tastes. As many have noted, after Spielberg-Lucas the "B" movie became the "A" movie because audiences far preferred Hollywood genre flicks to serious-minded adult stories. And genre pictures are usually what we call "critic-proof," meaning that reviews hardly matter. Increasingly, serious movies didn't do much box office even with good reviews, but with bad reviews they were dead in the water.

Isn't the Gene Siskel-Roger Ebert phenomenon another element that helped kill substantive film criticism? They were both in print but became TV celebrities known for thumbs up/thumbs down and for quick, facile mini-reviews. And for showing high-octane, high-tech film clips which were really advertisements. To me, this explosion of technology and visuals also undercut the voice of film criticism.

I agree with everything you are saying. And we should note that the new group of film critics who appeared on the Internet were lovers of genre films above all else. And many of these younger critics, whom we call "fanboys," grew up not reading the *Village Voice* but watching with enthusiasm the Ebert-Siskel TV show. That adulation for Roger Ebert especially stretches from Harry Knowles to the current *Boston Globe* critic Odie Henderson.

You said you made your film as a kind of ode to film criticism. But aren't you, in truth, somewhat ambivalent about your profession?

I've gotten far more ambivalent as the years have gone by. I was first ambivalent when, as I've explained earlier, I reviewed first-string films for the *Real Paper*, and after two-and-half years realized I was getting bored and exhausted. But then I did make a leap of faith with a pro-criticism documentary when my veteran compatriots started losing their jobs and teen critics start taking over. However, when my film finally came out, I started to have grave second thoughts about the people in my profession. Hate them, hate myself?

How did critics respond to this film?

First I want to say that *For the Love of Movies* did extremely well for a self-distributed film, including play dates in Canada, Finland, Israel, Serbia, Argentina and Hong Kong. We had lots of screenings and Amy and I enjoyed going around talking with our film. The reviews were quite good except for a couple of young creeps who wrote, "I didn't learn a thing from watching this film." As if they already knew about Otis Ferguson and James Agee.

But what upset me were the festival occasions when we showed the film and then I was asked to join a panel of film critics. The same thing happened each time. The other critics would talk on and on without acknowledging the film that they just watched. They would never thank me for making a film in homage to their profession. There were no comments about what was on the screen, only thoughts about film criticism in general. It was like I wasn't there.

I found the same phenomenon on the two other documentaries I made, *Archie's Betty* (2015) and *The Rabbi Goes West* (2019), the latter co-directed by Amy. Never expect people in your film to be grateful that you made a film about them. Still, it was most disappointing when it was my fellow film critics. My conclusion: There's something weird about people who are film critics, including me, obviously, who would choose to spend their life in the dark. Maybe we're nice human beings, but we don't quite know how to act like gracious ones.

You would think that film critics, if they cared about what they did, would want to push your film, right? Would want to get the word out, right? Especially with film criticism being threatened.

That's what you would think.

Is there anything else you'd like to say about the documentary and its reception?

Well, it's had an amazing longevity. Sixteen years after, people still purchase the DVD. And TCM showed it several years ago. I don't like to ask young critics if they've seen it because the answer is always no, and I don't feel that they're thinking, "Wow, where can I see it?" But the world goes on. Anyway, I have a great affection for my film though my perfectionist producer wife Amy still wishes it was shot more professionally.

If I want to do the right thing, not the Siskel-Ebert way... What should a good film review contain for you?

Richard Linklater has a great few seconds on camera in the film in which... I love his term, he says, "you can smell" if a review is a worthwhile one. You can smell it! And he uses another key term: "context." It's about a critic being able to see a movie and place it in a genre, and among other films of the genre, other films by the film's director, also place it in a cultural context, to understand how this film fits or doesn't fit the zeitgeist of your country, your society.

For me, I think wit is good. To be funny in a review, that's nice. And good writing! Someone who actually uses the English language in an inventive way. That's a start for what I want to see in a review.

You don't use the word judgment. Isn't the critic there to judge a film as good or bad or mediocre or whatever? To take a position and then defend it?

Of course. A credible judgment. You are there to suggest to the reader whether it's worth seeing a movie and why.

What to you are the objectives of writing film criticism?

Ideally, it's to put in words what a filmmaker is trying to do on the screen. But the first objective for me is to persuade readers to attend movies which I believe are good movies. I want to put bodies into theater seats! But that influence really has broken down. Today, nobody seriously listens to critics, and certainly not to me.

The breakdown is systemic, right? The New York Times, The Washington Post, The New Republic, *all the little magazines that were publishing film reviews that actually could maybe make a difference, no longer have that clout.*

Right, no clout anywhere. Some days I wonder: why bother writing film criticism? I know, Bill, you disagree.

I think the value of criticism is the same it has always been, and that the judgments of critics are important. By rendering a judgment, you articulate the value of the art. The meaning of art. That responding to art is more than just being a consumer: "I see Jaws, Jaws *entertains me, I walk out." Think of Poe and Mencken, critics in the past who wanted to transform the culture. And they did that by articulating what they thought was good or bad or ugly, and persuaded other people.*

I'm not sure that it's the job of the film critic to persuade the person to look at a movie the same way as the critic, which is what Pauline Kael routinely did. She just assumed her view was right, and "you," she addressed the reader as "you," agreed with her reading of a film. Because she said so. If you're more humble, you accept that the audience doesn't necessarily share your point of view. Which is just fine. Let a thousand opinions bloom.

In one of her radio broadcasts, Kael described walking out of the theater after seeing Shoeshine, *believing it was great, overhearing a young woman saying, "What's so special about that film?" Kael expressed her alienation with that woman, writing "…if people cannot feel* Shoeshine, *what can they feel?" Kael is certain she's right about* Shoeshine *and the woman who disagreed with her is dead wrong.*

I don't care at all if someone ends up agreeing with my position about a film. But I do think it's valuable to shake up his/her position if it isn't thought out, if it's the conventional wisdom. I'm a contrarian. I love if my position is different from every other film critic writing. That's really fun.

What are some of the contrarian film reviews that you've written that come to mind?

My attacks on anything Wes Anderson made after *Rushmore* [1998]. My essay on the obscenity of *Life is Beautiful* [1997] and its "feel-good" Holocaust message. My two-star review of *The Shining* [1980]. My negative take on *12 Years a Slave* [2013], which to me is slavery porn, as manipulative as Mel Gibson dealing with the death of Jesus. *Birdman* [2013]—yuck! On the other hand, I loved the recent *Joker: Folie à Deux* [2024], a brilliant film despite its 31% critics approval on Rotten Tomatoes.

Eric Bentley said that the role of the critic is to say that the emperor is wearing no clothes, right?

That's my ideal, pulling the pants off of the emperor. Contrariness is my strength.

What are your other strengths and weaknesses as a film critic?

I've always been at ease writing from a personal vantage. I confidently have my own voice. My reviews rarely sound like the reviews of my peers. I'm good at writing about structure and theme. I know my film history and understand genre. I'm a pretty decent stylist, and I think I'm funny. My weaknesses are obvious to me. I'm terrible at following plots mostly because I'm not that interested in plots. But not knowing what is happening is not in the interest of writing reviews. My other weakness is that I've always been terrible describing acting. I usually stay away from it. I shouldn't be terrible because, unlike many film critics, I've acted myself. Pauline Kael is correctly lauded for her virtuoso descriptions of acting. Here let me applaud Kael also.

We haven't talked anywhere about film theory. Do you think its influence on film criticism has been positive or negative?

I think it has had almost no influence, and if it has any, it's been negative. I might sound here like a real anti-intellectual, but I think film
theory has been a detriment to the film world. It's especially insid-
ious taking over academia, pushing out courses which are about film
history or film directors or genres. Other academic departments
were traditionally suspicious of film courses for being too popular
and not part of the academic canon, and film theory emerged as a
way to demonstrate intellectual heft to the university community.
But my objection is that you don't need to be a film historian to be a
film theorist, you just have to have these theoretical tools and know
your Metz, your Derrida, your Lacan.

Here is my mantra: before you deconstruct a movie, you
should love a movie. Back to the title of my documentary! But film
theory begins with deconstruction, begins with a negative view of
mainstream narrative. Every film is colonialist, patriarchal, whatever. Every film is ideologically suspect. Has Trump yet banned
film theory? Maybe he will. (Joke.)

*Haven't some film theorists been very good critics? I think about
Robin Wood on Hitchcock.*

It needs to be decided if the auteurist theory which Wood applies
to Hitchcock is bona fide film theory. I think only in a loose way
is it theoretical. In fact, film theory is before all else a reaction
against auteurism as being romantic and impressionistic, elevating
the artist in a sentimental way. Film theory is supposedly a hard-
headed corrective to that.

You know, there's a kind of benign hypocrisy with certain
theorists, a split consciousness that I approve of. I talked earlier
about Peter Wollen, who wrote the intimidating *Signs and
Meaning in the Cinema* and talked of "the death of the author,"
meaning the auteur director. But when you hung out with him, he
screamed with excitement about Hitchcock and Douglas Sirk. He
made Ten Best lists! In contrast, a lot of theorists in universities
don't really love movies, or see a lot of them. They are too busy
trying to achieve academic power and get tenure.

But the real question is this: does film theory have any appli-
cation to being a film critic? The answer for me is absolutely not.
I've had a fine life, I've written some insightful reviews in the last
fifty years without theory. It's not that I don't deal with feminism,
colonialism, racism, ideological questions; I just do it in a non-theoretical way.

You come out of the more journalistic approach. You've written film criticism for a wider, broader readership, not for an academic niche.

My forty years in university consisted of courses taught by me that were all non-theoretical. I also chose to write about film in journalistic places and not for academic journals. I am writing journalism because that is my way of being in the world, being in the world non-theoretically. That's where I feel comfortable.

I talked about working for *The Velvet Light Trap* in Madison, which was a non-theoretical film journal with a respect for auteurism but which also saw film in a historical context, a political historical context. That's an approach I can endorse, though I don't practice it as much as I used to. In recent years, I don't have a pressing need in my criticism to push my politics, and I can get interested in things which stretch my politics, challenge them.

I don't race to movies which I agree with politically. I often will stay away from the earnest ones. I know where I stand, I'm a good leftist, I have good leftist beliefs, but I don't need to have that affirmed by movies.

So what do I think when writing today? You mentioned Ebert-Siskel supplying those really short reviews on TV, just kind of quick blurbs. Well, maybe I'm getting like Ebert-Siskel in a certain way, because my feeling the last years is that film reviews are just too damn long. I want to be rid of that tedious middle section of a review which has too many details that nobody wants to read and probably doesn't read.

I have put my current thoughts about criticism into practice. I have found a happy place to write very pithy, 200-word reviews of films. If this is an Ebert-Siskel equivalent, I don't know. But it's posts on Facebook. What do I offer on Facebook? A quick judgment on the film followed by a sentence or two about the movie plot-wise, and then three or four quick observations which I hope are sharp and thought-provoking. That's it—a little equivalent of a haiku. And a fruitful operation of my brain, like doing a crossword puzzle to be alert.

How am I doing after a decade on Facebook? I guess I'm an "influencer." I have a community of regular reader "friends" around the world who seem to appreciate my succinct reviews. Moreover, these "friends" often respond with their own provocative observations, sometimes agreeing with me, often not. They are extremely educated people with deep knowledge of the movies. I do not feel threatened if someone finds my review full of *merde* and has a totally different vantage. That's fun, having a counterargument.

I talked earlier about how as a teenager I admired Dwight Macdonald and found myself drawn to his elitist film criticism. I'm back to that writing for my erudite Facebook readers. It's terribly uncomfortable in daily life to be drawn into a conversation about the movies with "regular people," my well-intended neighbors for instance. We are just so far apart, and whatever I say sounds like snobbery. I have to bite my tongue. But my tongue is free to wag away when I write on Facebook, even if Facebook is run by Mark Zuckerberg and it's odious in so many ways.

I think Brecht talked about the world as awful, and you should strategize to find little pockets where you can kind of, you know, fight against the System and be free. That's me on Facebook with my 200 words of criticism. Though I'm incapable of understanding his theories, I always remember that Lacan as a psychiatrist started having 20-minute sessions. Maybe my 200 words are the equivalent of Lacan.

In 200 words can you really be a critic? May I challenge you on that? I don't know that you can accomplish much in that short a time. Your "haikus" on Facebook might be fun to read but they can't replace a substantial thought-out review.

I'm glad that you remain so valiantly committed to the worth of doing criticism.

Now let me say something that's quite heretical. At this point in my life, I am kind of weary of even reading film criticism, even though there are talented people out there. I'll read reviews just a bit to get a feel if this is a movie that I should bother going to in the theater. Should I venture out and pay the money to see the movie? Like most people right now, I have all these things available on my TV. I have MUBI and Turner Classic Movies, plus as a critic I get links sent to me all the time. But do I want to read someone's long judgment about a current movie? Usually not. Bad boy, bad boy.

You've essentially reduced film criticism to be nothing more than a consumer guide. Convince me it's worth twelve bucks, or whatever, to go to the movie.

That's exactly what I want of a review. Most times I'd rather read a book or go for a walk than spend too much time with film reviews.

That's me. I'm not saying that the critics are bad or that they have nothing valuable to contribute.

What kind of arguments have you had on Facebook?

Lots of back-and-forths with perfectly intelligent people who somehow fall for the twee works of Wes Anderson. Or quarrels with those who have fallen hard for *The Brutalist* [2024]. I wrote on Facebook that the *Brutalist* intermission was my favorite part. I've been attacked for announcing on several occasions that I've walked out of a movie after thirty minutes not caring what happened to its characters. Apparently it's blasphemous for some people to abandon a film without seeing it to the end. I say: a bad movie going nowhere? Leave it and get some air.

Curiously, I've had no fights with Paulettes on Facebook. But I've had some fairly heated exchanges with me the instigator badgering my fellow Sarrisites who I feel are frozen in time. They still love or hate the same directors whom Sarris championed or dismissed in 1968 in *The American Cinema*. For instance, they continue to abhor William Wyler and John Huston and ridicule Delbert Mann. I have found great pleasure in the films of all three of the directors. But my biggest Facebook argument is with some Sarrisites who I have labeled Extreme Auteurists (EA), who can't utter a bad word about any film by an auteur favorite; and they especially enshrine the late films of a sainted auteur. John Ford is my favorite director but I find *The Sun Shines Bright* to be a racist embarrassment with Stepin Fetchit still Uncle Tom-ing in 1953 and the protagonist Judge Priest being the very definition of a white savior. EA auteurists have pushed back on Facebook claiming *The Sun Shines Bright* as this momentous poetic work among Ford's greatest achievements, and almost beyond criticism. What can I say? Don't get me started on the politics of another EA revered Ford work, *Fort Apache* [1948].

Even with your quarrels, it does seem to me that your Facebook posts show that you remain interested in being part of a community and in having people respond to what you think.

I guess it's proper time in that context to bring up *The Arts Fuse*. It's an on-line cultural magazine in New England and the only place where I still write film reviews besides Facebook. My esteemed editor, Bill Marx, is the person I've asked to conduct this interview.

I've been writing for *The Arts Fuse* for 12 years now, since the *Boston Phoenix* closed. What's great about the *Fuse* is that Bill as editor prizes writing which is idiosyncratic and opinionated. Ideally, also progressive and political. Understandably, many talented print journalists now appear in the *Fuse* because it's a landing spot for smart and educated writing.

But to Bill's chagrin I've been contributing fewer and fewer film reviews for the *Fuse*. As we've established, I don't want to write long. But a deeper problem for me with the *Fuse* is that I can't determine reader response. There's a place below the articles which invites readers to speak up; but shy *Fuse* readers say practically nothing. For me, this is a very isolating, having no idea if anybody likes, dislikes, agrees with, disagrees with what I offer. And so, when it's deciding to write about a movie for the *Fuse* or Facebook, I usually pick Facebook, because what I write is going to have people responding. Yes, I do want a community, a community of those who know movies really well and are eager and forthcoming to talk about them.

I think we should end with the things you've done in the last decades outside of film criticism.

I've mentioned two other film documentaries that I made. And let me say that I became a far more professional filmmaker on these than when I began with *For the Love of Movies*. *Archie's Betty* was a search to find the real-life people behind the characters in Archie Comics, a favorite comic book when I was a boy. *The Rabbi Goes West*, co-directed by my wife, Amy Geller, is the portrait of a Hasidic rabbi from New York who brought his messianic Judaism to the state of Montana. Amy and I made this movie to see if we, non-religious liberal Jews, could find common ground with a mostly conservative true believer in our divided America.

I spent a bunch of years as the film editor at the University Press of Mississippi, charged with their ongoing series of interview books with film directors. I edited three of those books myself, *Quentin Tarantino: Interviews*, *John Ford: Interviews*, and *Samuel Fuller: Interviews*. University of Kentucky Press published my *Mavericks: Interviews with the World's Iconoclast Filmmakers*, a compilation of conversations I conducted over thirty years from the mid-1970s on. The book includes, among many directors, Ousmane Sembène, Marcel Ophuls, Martin Ritt, Hal Ashby, Liv Ullmann, Agnieszka Holland, Éric Rohmer, and R. W. Fassbinder.

With my wife Amy Geller as co-host, I did a 7-part history-based podcast called *The Rabbis Go South*, about a group of rabbis who joined Martin Luther King in protesting the segregationist policies of St. Augustine, Florida.

A highlight of my life was being cast in the 2015 independent feature, *Computer Chess*, directed by Andrew Bujalski. I was flown down to Austin, Texas for a week of shooting. I played an old-fashioned chess master who is challenged in a 1980s tournament by computer-run chess teams. The film played at Berlin and Sundance and my odd performance was praised by many, including a consideration by some film critics for Best Supporting Actor. What excitement! In my hubris I was hoping for some more movie roles. But they never came.

Still awaiting my second act as an actor, I continue on at *The Arts Fuse* and on Facebook. And I am performing, though not in movies. For the last year, I have been doing standup Open Mic comedy. The lowest of the low, but it keeps this film critic, 80, off the streets.

A final question. What would you say to a young person who wanted to become a film critic today? Any sage wisdom?

The only wisdom anybody has is "Get a day job." You can't pay your bills, you can't even buy a fancy dinner, being a film critic in 2025. Actually, I've been a freelance critic since 1981, always having a full-time teaching position up until my retirement. We talked earlier about my ambivalence being a film critic. I think it's been healthier that I've done so many other things. Some days I feel it's decadent spending your life only doing film reviews. A self-hating film critic? Perhaps.

INDEX

www.ingramcontent.com/pod-product-compliance
Lightning Source LLC
Chambersburg PA
CBHW060417130626
46555CB00005B/2100